ENNIS AND NANCY HAM LIBRARY
ROCHESTER COLLEGE
800 WEST AVON ROAD
ROCHESTER HILLS, MI 4830

MICHIGAN
CHRISTIAN
COLLEGE
LIBRARY
ROCHESTER, MICH.

Libraries
and
Young Adults

MICHIGAN
CHRISTIAN
COLLEGE
LIBRARY
ROCHESTER, MICH.

ENNIS AND NANCY HAM LIBRARY
ROCHESTER COLLEGE
800 WEST AVON ROAD
ROCHESTER HILLS, MI 48307

027.626
L697

Z
718.5
.L53
1979

Libraries and Young Adults

Media, Services, and Librarianship

Edited by
JoAnn V. Rogers

Libraries Unlimited, Inc.- Littleton, Colorado
1979

29186

Copyright ©1979 Libraries Unlimited, Inc.
All Rights Reserved
Printed in the United States of America

No part of this publication may be reproduced, stored in a retrieval
system, or transmitted, in any form or by any means, electronic,
mechanical, photocopying, recording, or otherwise, without the prior
written permission of the publisher.

LIBRARIES UNLIMITED, INC.
P.O. Box 263
Littleton, Colorado 80160

Library of Congress Cataloging in Publication Data

Main entry under title:

Libraries and young adults.

    Bibliography: p. 225
    1. Libraries, Young people's. I. Rogers, JoAnn
V., 1940-
Z718.5.L53   027.62'6   79-15
ISBN 0-87287-195-9

FOREWORD

Among the various types of library patrons and potential library users, young adults are perhaps the most easily and most often neglected in terms of collection development and the provision of services in many library settings. The types of libraries considered in this discussion and in the essays that follow include public libraries and libraries in both public and private institutions that include in their goals and objectives the collection of materials for and the delivery of service to the group of individuals whom we call young adults or adolescents. Part of the difficulty in trying to serve the young adult is that librarians and library or school board members who determine library policy do not share a common understanding of the characteristics and needs of young adults. They are not alone in their confusion and lack of understanding. In a recent report to the Ford Foundation presenting a review of research and programs concerning early adolescence, Joan Lipsitz concludes that, not only do researchers lack a theoretical framework on which to build knowledge of the adolescent but also "the society at large lacks a coherent concept of adolescence to inform its service agencies, which therefore all too often lack rational sets of purposes to guide policy making and service delivery."[1] Although the library is not included in this survey as one of the social institutions serving youth, many of the conditions that affect delivery of service in other institutions and social agencies also affect young adult services provided in the library.

The most simplistic way to define the young adult (YA) is by chronological age. An occasion for debate and a perennial thorn in the side of the Young Adult Services Division (YASD) of the American Library Association, the question of defining the YA in this manner was raised again as recently as the June 1978 annual meeting of the Association, when a petition signed by 37 personal members of YASD requested that the organization again discuss age level definitions of the young adult clientele.[2] Questions were raised about the age level that young adult librarians do serve, the age level that they should serve, and the possible need for an age level definition to be incorporated into the Division's statement of responsibility. The Division's current charge does not define the young adult by chronological age, and the feeling of the board, as it has been in the past, was that young adult specialists should provide services to all young people with no specific age limitations.

Those who feel a need to define the young adult in this way offer various age level and grade level categories, usually from grades 7 through 12; grades 7 through the second year of college; ages 13 through 18; ages 12 through 20; or more recently, ages 10 through 18, 20, or 22. The lowering of the age level designation seems to be a recognition on the part of practicing YA librarians that younger children are interested in topics and titles that are published for the YA market and found in YA library collections. Some professionals are uncomfortable with the overlapping of responsibility between the children's and the young adult collections and services. Many, however, have acknowledged that the overlap is unavoidable and perhaps even desirable, because various facets of an individual's character and personality develop at different times and at differing rates. Many of those who favor lines of demarcation argue that the onset of puberty, which usually occurs at approximately age twelve, marks the beginning of young adulthood; and the acceptance of personal economic and social responsibility marks the beginning of adulthood. This rationale for categorizing the twelve-year-old as a young adult and the working individual as an adult ignores psychological, intellectual, social, philosophical, and emotional aspects of individual development, however.

Wanting to define a client group to facilitate program planning is understandable, but perhaps it is counter-productive to the aims of a client-oriented institution such as the library, which should be able to meet the needs of an individual who may simultaneously demonstrate behavior characteristics of a child, a young adult, and an adult. Many children, for example, shoulder adult responsibilities within their family structure; many adults have not passed successfully through some of the developmental stages of childhood. In addition, many adults who lack reading skills that would enable them to deal with materials in the adult collection find materials of interest on an appropriate reading level in the young adult collection. Many libraries integrate the young adult and adult materials for this reason. Although categorizing people by age or grade level and trying to match materials similarly categorized is a popular approach to the challenge of providing the user with the right material at the right time, there is little research to indicate that this is a workable approach. As a guideline for use in administrative decision-making within an organization, defining the young adult population by chronological age may be of some use. The availability of materials and services to all current and potential users according to their individual needs should be the objective of the library's program of services, however. The blurring of the lines between and among user groups that we are tempted to categorize and label for easy handling should be seen as a desirable trend by librarians working with the public. A recent statement from the Services Statement Development Committee of the Young Adult Services Division expresses this point of view:

> The aspect of library service called work with young adults must be flexible enough to allow for [this] variation letting the developmental needs of individuals determine whether they will be best served as children, young adults, or adults.[3]

Perhaps we should go one step further and suggest that the librarian, who should be well acquainted with the paths of access to information and library services, has the responsibility to try to elicit enough information from users about their needs to be able to provide significant assistance. The young adult librarian should be serving the young adult client, not simply working in the young adult collection. Providing assistance in using all of the materials and services that the library provides is part of the responsibility of those who serve youth in the library.

Some aspects of the human condition seem to be of major importance during the adolescent years. These include a need to adjust to a rapid rate of physical growth and change, including sexual maturation; a need to develop techniques to acquire and deal with information; a need to identify and define the self more precisely and differently, both in isolation from and in relation to other individuals and groups; and an increasing awareness that one must learn to cope with change and live with the results of individual and group behavior. Those who work with young people in the library must be aware of these common themes and must possess the communication skills necessary to elicit enough information about the needs of individual young adults to ensure that the library's collection and program of services will address some of the needs of the individual. Young adult library work can conveniently be divided into three aspects: the collection of materials in print and multi-media formats; a program of services, some of which are provided in a young adult department and others of which are available to young adults in other areas of the library; and the personnel available in the library to build a collection and plan and carry out services to individuals, small groups, and large groups of young adults.

■　■　■

The pivotal point of reference in each of the articles in this collection is the young adult client in a library or media center. Many of the contributors have a public library orientation. Some have a school library background and reflect that experience in their papers. Most of the information presented and opinions expressed about young adults and libraries, however, relate to both school and public library settings and to many different types of individuals who happen to fall into the age categories or grade level designations that we use to identify the young adult population. Certainly school and public libraries share the responsibility for meeting both the curricular and extracurricular needs of young adults in their roles as students and private persons. These articles discuss the library's response to young adults' needs and view the young adult as a multi-faceted individual, not only as a student.

Each of the three sections of this collection of original essays explores one of the facets of concern to librarians and others interested in the part the library plays in the total program of community services for young people. The mixture is intended to provide an overview of some current issues concerning print and nonprint media, library services, and young adult librarianship. Although collection and services go hand in hand, some aspects of collection development and selection and the factors that affect them can be considered independently. A few of these issues are addressed in Part I. Two contributors representing the publishing world present an insider's view of choosing material and issuing a product for the young adult market. A young adult specialist who has served on the committee within the Young Adult Services Division responsible for the annual list of the best books for young adults comments on that list and its use for reading guidance. A factor particularly important in guiding the reading of young people is the level of reading difficulty of materials. A reading specialist discusses readability and techniques that can help the librarian to estimate more accurately the level of difficulty of materials. A survey of some selection tools used by librarians to choose materials for the young adult collection demonstrates that grade or age level designations for young adult materials need to be questioned by the librarian selecting materials of high interest and minimum reading difficulty. Intellectual freedom is a major concern of most librarians, but materials made available to young adults in libraries prove to be particularly vulnerable to censorship attempts. The final article in Part I focuses on legal considerations and comments on some of the issues most commonly associated with attempts to limit the access of young people to material found in libraries.

The issues of censorship and free access bring to mind the question of the existence of separate fiction and nonfiction collections for young adults in a library or media center also serving other patrons. Integration of young adult materials with the adult or children's collection has been tried, but most libraries do identify materials chosen for young adults and do provide a separate area for the collection. Many libraries, however, encourage the use of all materials in the collection by any patron. Not within the scope of this book's section dealing with media for young adults, but worthy of consideration, are selection criteria for those print and nonprint materials chosen for the YA collection; the relationship between literature as it is currently taught in our schools and the materials found in school and public libraries; the availability of nonfiction particularly suitable for young adults; and the influence of the paperback industry on the reading interests and habits of young adults. A survey of the current literature reveals much being written about the reading interests of young adults, and many useful articles that identify trends in materials published for this market are appearing in popular as well as professional periodicals. Also, guides to selection aids and bibliographic aids for selection and acquisition, although important, are not discussed because they are adequately covered elsewhere in the literature of librarianship.

Each of the authors in Part II views the library's program of services for young adults from a slightly different perspective. Each was chosen because of significant experience in providing young adults with library service. The first article identifies some social and economic trends that affect all services, including those provided for young adults. It also discusses from a historical point of view some of the issues that have been central to young adult work and points to categories of programs representative of current programming trends. The second article describes in some detail those programs that have been reported in the literature over the past ten years. The program descriptions and the evaluative comments of those reporting on the programs are useful both for libraries that already have an active program of YA services and for those librarians who are beginning YA services.

In an attempt to define and understand the adolescent, the librarian must look to other disciplines to provide a working definition. In order for the library to respond with appropriate materials and programs, the needs of the adolescent at different stages of development must be considered. Borrowing from the work of psychologists and sociologists, the third essay in this section looks at those developmental stages and suggests ways in which the library might plan to provide relevant services. Descriptions of some of the needs of young people resulting from crisis situations in their lives and the responses of the library follow in the next, personal commentary. The library's unfortunate lack of interface with other social service agencies and the constraints associated with a traditional definition of library service result in many roadblocks to providing referral or counseling service in the library.

Cooperation with other agencies and institutions that touch the lives of young people is desirable; cooperation between and among different libraries that serve them is becoming imperative. As independent study and investigation of topics in all areas of the school curriculum increasingly demand the use of library resources, the impracticality of the expectation that any one library, school or public, can provide all of the necessary resources becomes clearer. Designing independent learning experiences for students depends upon the availability of large numbers of different types of relevant materials. Cooperative planning (as outlined in the article on the topic) is the only answer. Coping with some of the difficulties associated with cooperative activities is important if librarians are committed to providing the best possible service to the young adult patron. With experience and understanding, some of the barriers to cooperative effort can be removed.

The unique way in which our society views youth and the different ways in which information useful to young people in different parts of the world is produced, disseminated, and collected by libraries are factors that complicate a discussion of delivery of library service to youth in other parts of the world. In the final article in Part II, an active participant in international librarianship gives us some insight into library activities that affect youth elsewhere. Although this part covers a great deal of ground and touches upon many topics associated with young adult library services, several important issues have not been addressed. One is the continuing need for librarians in all service areas, including young adult services, to search for ways to measure the impact of the services they provide. Defining service goals and objectives in such a way that the success and failure of programs of services can be studied by the application of appropriate quantifiable measures remains a challenge. Studies of patterns of use of different types of libraries (including public, school, academic, and special) by young adults for curriculum-related and recreational purposes can yield information helpful in planning cooperative efforts. A re-examination of what in the late 1950s and 1960s was called "the student problem" might help young adult specialists see how far we have come and provide incentive to increase our efforts to provide materials and services for student needs. An investigation of the ways in which adolescents view libraries and the librarians who serve them might yield some useful information about the differences between what we think we should be doing in the library and what young people need from the library.

The final part includes consideration of some topics relating to the practice of young adult librarianship. The difficulty in designing the content of a program of professional preparation for the young adult specialist results in part from what was referred to earlier in this foreword as a lack of universal understanding of adolescence, its meaning and its importance in differentiating the types of services which the library offers to the young adult and to other patrons. In the first article, which presents a survey of literature about the education of the young adult specialist and commentary about the topic, the need for special services and the personnel to provide those services is assumed. Accepting that point of reference, it is interesting to hear the recurring themes calling for course work to expand the students' awareness of adolescence, materials, and the functioning of libraries.

One recurring theme is the need for the library school student to develop some managerial skills. In large systems where there is a thriving young adult department, these skills are called for in the position of system coordinator for YA services. Although this is a staff rather than a line position, gaining an understanding of the library organization and how to make things happen within it are important. Although few examples of state coordinators of young adult services functioning through state library agencies can be found, the need for such a position is discussed in the next article. All of the states have an individual responsible for school library media programs, but again, few state departments of education have separate departments and staff positions solely for coordinators of middle school or secondary school programs.

Providing a necessary vehicle for communication and affiliation, the Young Adult Services Division of the American Library Association is an organization that encompasses all of those interested in serving young adults in libraries. Thus, the history of that organization and the way in which its current structure provides possibilities for action aimed at strengthening and enhancing the provision of YA service in libraries is the subject of an article. One of YASD's major undertakings in recent years has been the identification of research dealing with young adults and libraries, and an article discusses that project and other studies concerned with YA literature and services. Suggestions for areas of research that need to be explored are also identified. The final article in this section suggests that, in addition to participation in local, regional, and national organizations, professional awareness depends upon the librarian's ability to locate and read professional literature concerned with adolescents and with libraries.

A selected bibliography citing basic readings in each of the areas covered by the three parts—Media, Services, and Young Adult Librarianship—concludes the volume. In addition, a few titles that include information and opinion on more than one topic are included in a section designated General Titles. Because many lists of selection sources and review media are available elsewhere, these selection tools are not listed. The list does include references to some older works that continue to have impact on young adult resources and services as well as more recent items that reflect the current state of the art. References to short news items may be found in the bibliographies of individual articles, but these are not included in the selected bibliography.

For the information presented and invaluable insights shared by each knowledgeable colleague and contributor, the reader and I are indebted.

Notes

[1] Joan Lipsitz, *Growing Up Forgotten: A Review of Research and Programs Concerning Early Adolescence* (Lexington, MA: Lexington Books), p. xv.

[2] American Library Association, Young Adult Services Division, Board of Directors, Minutes of the 1978 Midwinter Meeting (Chicago), Exhibit XI.

[3] American Library Association, Young Adult Services Division, *Directions for Library Service to Young Adults* (Chicago: ALA), p. 2.

JoAnn V. Rogers
Lexington, Kentucky
1979

TABLE OF CONTENTS

PART I

MEDIA FOR YOUNG ADULTS

INTRODUCTION

Materials that libraries and media centers collect for young adult users—whether housed in a separate facility, in a separate area within the library, or integrated with the adult or children's collections—are the focus of this section. A philosophy of publishing and editorial decision making is presented by Dorothy Briley, currently editor-in-chief at Lothrop, Lee, and Shepard and formerly a senior editor for young adult materials at J. B. Lippincott. While at Lippincott, she was responsible for discovering and editing the work of several authors who currently enjoy outstanding reputations and great popularity with the teenage reading population. Her discussion adds a new dimension to our understanding of the term "young adult literature," material that publishers plan to market not initially to young adults themselves but to those institutions (and their selectors) that acquire materials that they as adults think appropriate for young adults. This is primarily the school and public library market. Briley's emphasis on recapturing the point of view of adolescent characters helps us to better understand why some YA titles are particularly popular over a number of years. Reminding us of the difference between literature that orchestrates themes to produce a satisfying whole experience and literature that attempts to present a thesis, usually in the hope of persuading the audience to accept certain points of view about controversial issues, compels us as buyers of YA materials to re-examine our criteria for including some titles by authors writing for young adults.

Long active in the Association of Media Producers and involved with marketing and special projects for Guidance Associates, which prepares multi-media productions for the YA market, Katherine Kish discusses the special appeal that non-print media has for the young adult. Special considerations such as currency of materials and avoiding pitfalls that would easily date an otherwise useful production are mentioned. A description of the step-by-step process of producing a multi-media item demonstrates some differences between publishing of print and nonprint media. Especially interesting is the large number of people performing different types of tasks, all of whom are involved with making decisions that affect the final product. The influence of marketing considerations is shown to be important early in the planning process for media productions. Based on the appeal of multi-media for young adults and the communication potential of various media formats, this author advocates the inclusion of a substantial number of multi-media materials in the young adult collection.

An annual book list that has a great influence on purchasing practices of libraries is the subject of the third article. The list "Best Books for Young Adults" selected yearly by a committee of the Young Adult Services Division of the American Library Association has been a concern of Eleanor Pourron, Coordinator of Young Adult Services in Arlington, Virginia, and twice chairperson of the Best Books Committee (1974 and 1975). The evolution of the selection criteria and the process of selection as it affects final choices and publication shed light on the mechanics of the list's publication. As one familiar with both the process and the product, the author offers some opinions about the value of the list and suggests ways in which it can be used. The wide distribution of the list (published in leaflet form by the American Library Association) and the inclusion of it in periodicals with high circulation figures insure its high visibility. A discussion and re-evaluation of past lists at the ALA conference in 1975 produced a cumulative list, "Still Alive in '75," to which were added several titles not included on previous lists but popular with young adults. One is tempted to conclude that the committee is becoming more responsive to the needs of the young adult reading audience in light of the fact that a greater number of titles published in years past were added to the revised cumulative list than were published in more recent years. However, as Dorothy Briley points out, because of the way in which young adult titles are initially marketed, it is difficult to assess a book's popularity and staying power until a number of years after its publication. It is also interesting to note that the procedures for selection of materials for the list parallel some general policy decisions of the organization to make ALA more responsive to all of its members. The open meetings of the selection committee are well attended by YASD members and others. The comparison of the YASD list with lists compiled by others interested in identifying good reading for teens points out some overlapping, but it illustrates the need for both the "Best Books" list and the others.

The need for communication and better understanding between librarians and reading teachers and specialists becomes apparent after considering the unfortunate distance between the two disciplines described in the report of Linda Evers, a reading specialist in Woods County, West Virginia. The categorizing of materials for children and young adults by subjective measures, often those of the publisher whose prime concern may be marketability and sales, suggests that there is a need for the application of more objective measures. Librarians need more reliable guidelines when considering purchase or when choosing materials appropriate for individual young people. Selection tools, periodicals that contain reviews of materials, and librarians all tend to categorize according to elementary, junior high, and high school levels, but more in terms of the appeal and treatment of the subject matter than in terms of the student's ability to read material of interest. As pointed out, readability formulas do not take into consideration subjective factors that may determine a young person's motivation to try to read difficult material, but they do provide some information that enables those who work with books and people to identify material appropriate for an individual in one important aspect.

The large number of meetings at professional conferences and the number of bibliographies compiled by librarians and others who have worked with reluctant readers to identify high interest-low reading ability materials attest to interest on the part of librarians in identifying these materials. In response to the requests of readers, one of the publications used in this survey (*Booklist*) has been attempting since October 1977, to identify these materials. The current *Booklist* editor for young adult materials, Barbara Joyce Duree, has explained that the young adult titles reviewed and recommended are titles appropriate for grades 9-12 or approximately ages 14-18. The new "high-low reading" section contains titles that first have been selected from among all of the books reviewed by children's, young adult, and adult reviewers as materials with a particularly high interest potential for the young adult. Then the Fry graph is applied to determine reading level. Certainly this attempt to alert librarians to those characteristics of the books listed is a step in the right direction.

Probably because the young adult is in transition between the child and the adult stages, questions about free access to materials and censorship often arise when controversial materials are available to young adults through public institutions, mainly the school and public libraries. Mary Woodworth, associate professor at the Library School of the University of Wisconsin—Madison, has done extensive research and writing about censorship issues and young adults, and here she brings into focus many of these issues. Problems caused by attempts to censor materials are usually motivated by the belief that young adults, like children, need to be protected from ideas and information because they do not have the maturity to understand and make adult decisions. Again, because of ambivalent feelings and the lack of a clear understanding of the meaning of adolescence on the part of the adult population, the position of the young adult in relation to his or her right of free access to information is not clearly defined either by custom or the law. A complicating factor is the stance of those who select materials for library collections. Many librarians think that age should be a factor in the modification of the explicit language of the First Amendment. Voicing support for the Library Bill of Rights, however, appears to be much easier for librarians than selecting materials that might be challenged.

PUBLISHING FOR THE
YOUNG ADULT MARKET

Dorothy Briley

It is a fact that people have babies and that, as a result, a market exists for various goods and services directly related to children and child rearing. In this age of specialization, we have divided childhood into stages of development, and industries that serve our progeny are geared to respond to the needs of the infant, the toddler, the kindergartner, the schoolchild, the preteenager, or the teenager. And now we have the young adult! Once upon a time there were fewer categories; there were just babes in arms and children, who quickly and far more quietly became young men and women who earned the title "adult" by going to work and/or getting married.

It is significant to understand in a discussion of publishing fiction for young men and women that the term "young adult" was invented to make it more convenient to market books to those who bring books and adolescent-age children together. This distinction is important, because if the market were the intended readers of young adult books instead of teachers, parents, and librarians, there would be no need to put "young adult" books into a labeled category. If publishers could sell directly to older children, life would be much simpler in many ways. We wouldn't have a category of books that the institutional market finds useful, yet bookstores don't know what to do with. Publishers would know much more quickly when a book is successful and when it isn't, and they would be able to gear their publishing accordingly. Far too many books published for this age group are successful initially with the adults who buy them, but then they are rejected roundly by the readers for whom they were bought. It can be two or three years before such success, or lack of it, can be detected.

When selecting books to publish, one must be careful not to put the market before the book. The decision to sell a book to a particular audience is properly made only after the book is written. This decision should be made on the basis of what the book *is*, not on the basis of what the editor, marketing department, educators, reviewers, et al., want it to be for their own professional or private reasons. A good book has an identity and life force of its own that is quite independent of any and all who have worked to create it—including the author. People, even

17

youthful ones, tend to be like that, too. One should keep in mind that just as individuals seldom fit the neat categories we busily make for them, the same applies to books. Creating a work to fit a category of people is guaranteed to produce the ultimate compromise—a book so innocuous that in trying to displease no one, it offends quite a few. In other words, writing a novel is not like knitting a sweater; if you're going to write a novel, it is counterproductive to measure the audience before you begin. The measure is within the writer.

The best writers put a great deal of themselves into their characters. They remember what life felt like when they were the age of their character, and they are able to transmit those feelings through their character's response to the things that happen in the story. Thus, what happens in a story is less important than how well the characters are developed. Nina Bawden, for instance, when she writes for children, seems to have a special memory of how she felt about herself, her parents, friends, and others when she was twelve. Her stories are alive with twelve-year-old insecurities, arrogance, charm, humor, and pathos. Vera and Bill Cleaver's characters tend to be a bit older—about age fourteen. Isabelle Holland's best "character-memory" is about age fifteen, though she is extremely good with nine- and ten-year-olds. Speaking as a young adult book editor, I firmly believe that the only significant difference in writing for children, young adults, or adults is the viewpoint from which the story is told, and the special feature I look for in a writer's work is the presence of character-memory.

Although a point of view true to the over-ten-year-old reader is the most important feature in the young adult novel, what the story is about almost equals it in importance. Robert Cormier faithfully reproduced the feelings of his teenage protagonist in *I Am the Cheese*, but the other ingredient that makes the book a successful adolescent novel is his imaginative use of endemic post-Watergate anxieties in his development of a tragic-victim theme. Any and all followers of spy thrillers and the six o'clock news can readily identify with the character and predicament in *I Am the Cheese*.

More than twenty years ago, Walter Kerr reminded us of the difference between thesis and theme in his critical analysis of the theatre, *How Not to Write a Play* (Simon and Schuster, 1955). Although the medium is different, those of us interested in the young adult novel would do well to remind ourselves that thesis and theme are not one and the same. When an author sets out to prove or present a particular "truth" and invents characters and action to support his thought, he has given us a thesis. This is very different from allowing characters to tell their story within the framework of a theme. I am afraid that much of our present-day "realistic" fiction falls into the thesis category, with all of the hindsight that middle age can provide sticking out like a sore thumb. Drug abuse, premarital sex, high school dropouts, runaways, abortion, etc., have been the focus of writers bent on well-meaning missions to direct young people's thinking on topical issues. We call it "realism," but in reality, it is propaganda. Of course, any of these subjects can be themes for a proper novel, and many of them are. It does seem from my vantage point as an editor that there is too much acceptance of books created in the hope that young people reading them will somehow be "saved from themselves." More than that, there seems to be a demand for this kind of book.

The major criticisms of Isabelle Holland's *The Man without a Face* were that it didn't go far enough in describing the homosexual act and that the death of McLeod at the end of the book was symbolic punishment for his wrongdoing. The critic was looking for a thesis when there was none and by so doing, completely misunderstood the theme of the book. Criticizing a novel for what it doesn't say is almost the same as suggesting that the author who dares to write on a controversial theme shall be conscience-bound to present "proper" thinking on the issue. *The Man without a Face* is not about homosexuality, but about loneliness, rejection, and personal awareness. The homosexual incident is but a part of the plot that develops young Charles's insight into who he is—nothing more.

We sell young people short when we ask for books that will do our parenting for us. Parenting is not a proper function for a novel. I do believe that honest novels can provide comfort, support, and some measure of insight into the human condition; and in that sense, I do not oppose the notion of bibliotherapy. However, manufacturing stories to perform a specific therapeutic task is not only counter to the process of serious writing, it is downright silly. Young readers are no less intelligent than adults. In many ways, their perceptions are actually keener than ours, because their minds are not as cluttered with the cares of everyday living. The thesis novel for young adults has even less chance of becoming popular than one for adults, because the reader is so frequently put off by characters and situations obviously invented to instruct him on how to think.

Recently I heard one of my colleagues declare that he was beginning to think that the young adult book is a paperback book. There is a large measure of truth in this, because only when a novel goes into paperback does the primary audience get the opportunity to respond without adult interference. The longer I work in adolescent fiction, the more negative I feel about the effect of having adults act as intermediaries. I do not feel the same way about having adults choose and judge children's books—adults have a responsibility to guide the reading experiences of young children. But at adolescence and beyond, adults have a responsibility to start letting go, to start letting the child learn how to become his or her own person. With the adult constantly between book and young adult reader, some books are only seeming successes early on, and some others never get the chance to prove themselves. All adults who stand between child and book—editor, teacher, librarian, and parent—constantly need to re-examine the criteria they use to judge books worthy or unworthy of adolescent readership.

There is medical evidence to show that the rites of puberty are enjoyed by children at an increasingly young age. It is apparently quite common these days for boys and girls aged ten or eleven to qualify physically for adolescent status. Certainly television and other communication media make it impossible to keep children innocent of what goes on in the world—whether good or evil. We clearly have a climate right for good adolescent fiction that does much more than merely serve as transition to adult fiction. Legitimate adolescent viewpoints on a myriad of subjects need expression through the talents of authors who remember the feelings of their own growing-up years and can apply them to situations familiar to today's youth.

Young adult fiction as a special category is about fifteen years old. We have published a good many brilliant books during this period and some that have not measured up. Now that our growing pains are on the wane and we have begun to have a real sense of what a young adult book should be, I would like to think that we can look forward to a body of criticism that understands these books as something other than precocious children's books or a transition to adult books. When we have accomplished that, we will have achieved a kind of publishing that deserves to be called Young Adult.

NONPRINT MEDIA AND THE
YA MARKET

Katherine M. Kish

According to Carl Sagan, in *The Dragons of Eden* (Random House, 1977) the left hemisphere of the brain is the one that picks up patterns, emotions, music, and intuitions. The right hemisphere does the heavy verbal and analytical work. Media zeroes in on the left hemisphere. A media experience can create an immediate understanding of an emotion, a complex idea, a contemporary issue, or a musical theme in very few frames or seconds, and the immediacy of experience seems to be particularly appealing for today's young adults. Media's power to create intuitive understanding is appropriate for young people, who are in a period of enormous emotional upheaval and constant change. Radio and record/tape music are the constant background in their lives. Television is their most frequent source of information and diversion. "Charlie's Angels," "Kojak," "Starsky and Hutch," "the Fonz," are all a part of the American vernacular because of teenagers. Also, Friday or Saturday night often means a film at the local theater or drive-in for teenagers.

Recently a college professor asked his students to do without all nonprint media for one week. No radio or television or anything else nonprint. At the end of the exercise, when he asked his students to write about their feelings, they reported a sense of great deprivation. Media is effective because teenagers are visually and aurally very sophisticated. As virtual "media babies," they are most comfortable when processing information, advertising, and entertainment from television and radio. Teenagers today like to get their information quickly—to get right to the point. Reading takes time, but media moves fast. Its impact is immediate. Its words and pictures must be clear and easy to understand, which is one of its strengths and one of its weaknesses. At its worst, it can be consumed like junk food, according to an ex-CBS executive. At its best, media holds attention, uses emotions, stimulates interest and involvement, leaves broad impressions, and stirs deep emotions.

Also, because of both the real and pseudo-sophistication of young adults, media materials planned for consumption by young adults must not talk down or seem phony to them. Media producers also must be very careful not to "date" a product; contemporary fashion, vernacular expressions, and inappropriate or out-dated music are things that "turn teenagers off." A good rule that producers and publishers follow is to "keep things honest and simple, and treat them like adults." The most successful media experiences in terms of numbers of teenagers who view or listen are based on today, tomorrow, self-identity, insecurity, achievement, sexuality, morality, love, justice, and hope. Media engages both the intellect and the emotions of those whom it reaches.

Nonprint materials can be sound filmstrips, 16mm films, slides, records, tapes, video cassettes, and many more formats. Their subjects are as varied as the world we live in. There is Kenneth Clark's "Civilization" on video tape or film, where magnificent photography and sound effects can bring to life the great architecture, painting, sculpture, and religion of the past. There are sound filmstrips on the important moral dilemmas involving young people today: how to deal with drugs and alcohol; how to answer important questions about sexuality; what to do when your best friend steals something and involves you; how to make career decisions while you are still in high school. Then a variety of nonprint materials is available on other topics that appeal to young people, such as oceanography, where the world of the sea can be made more exciting with films and direct tapes or records of underwater sounds. Other such topics might include solar energy, popular music, skateboarding, and stars. These topics and countless more can be uniquely and expertly presented in nonprint materials, where there is an immediacy that can add a dynamic dimension either visually or aurally to subjects that cannot be effectively handled with traditional print materials. Ideas as enormous as the dignity of humankind as seen through architectural abstractions or as straight-forward as the honesty of young people in various dilemmas can become real through media. Media makes it all part of a shared human experience.

Those not involved in media publication and production often wonder how an idea becomes a media production. Media production appears to be a glamorous activity where producers and directors are stars, and stars are media heroes. A lot of "hype" leads to a lot of copy. But often, people are not aware of the basic steps of putting together a media production. Publishing or producing nonprint media (e.g., 16mm films, sound filmstrips, slides, video) is a complicated but definable process. Some of the activities are similar to those associated with print publishing. However, sometimes nonprint media publishing has fewer steps and can be completed somewhat faster. A media production using only one nonprint for-mat usually takes seven to ten months to produce from conception to shelf. A multi-media production combining two or more formats can take as long as one and one-half years to two years. Writing and publishing textbooks takes much longer. Information in audio-visual formats can be current. If a subject or an event captures the great immediate interest of young adults, a television docu-mentary film or sound filmstrip can be produced faster than most print formats. (The newspaper, the magazine, and the instant paperback are the exceptions here.)

Whether done on a rush basis or on a normal schedule, the educational publishing process goes through a step-by-step procedure. First, a specific idea or concept comes to a publisher/producer. It can come from librarians, teachers, specialists in a subject, outside producers, or others not directly involved with media or education. The production staff focuses on the concept, using their expertise to create a first treatment, which must address several questions. It must tell for whom the production is intended and how can it be designed to present its ideas in a way most useful to the intended audience.

A refined second treatment then goes into a product planning session conducted by all who will be concerned with production and marketing. Satisfactory answers must be found for questions about the production. Such questions include: is there a need for the product? is the intended treatment the best way to convey the information? who would be the best available consultant in the subject area? what medium is best for the nature of the message? how long should the production be? how difficult will it be to produce? how many might be sold? what will it cost to produce, and for what price can it be sold? If the production idea survives that meeting, then it is on its way to implementation.

A media production team is then chosen. That team, led by the producer, includes the consultant and the writer, all of whom will shepherd the project through all stages of production. Other talent—including camera people, sound technicians, and editors—is assembled when needed. The script is developed, tested, and corrected. Then the storyboard, a cartoon-style drawing of camera set-ups and dialog, is created. Last minute changes must be made at this stage before the film is shot or other type of production is begun. The shooting involves all of the technicians and actors and requires much visual and sound footage, which then is roughly edited. A work print is screened, and final refinements in picture and sound quality take place. Finally, a master print is created, and copies are manufactured from it for distribution. This pattern is followed for all types of media productions that require both sound and visual elements. In television production, the same steps are followed for the program concept; but new video tape technology has changed some of the technical procedures.

All types of media are an integral part of young people's lives and basic education. In their homes and during their free time, they are surrounded by sight and sound. Most school districts use print and nonprint media to structure much of the school day, and nonprint media has been clearly acknowledged as an important teaching and learning tool. School systems usually house their 16mm film ıs in a district-wide distribution center, or they are a part of a county or regional cooperative. Often schools rent titles from a producer or film library, while other forms of media (frequently called "building level materials") are stored and used in individual schools. These building level materials include sound filmstrips, slides and silent filmstrips, slide-tape presentations, study prints, cassettes, and records.

In almost any junior or senior high school, you will find young people in the library/media center reading, viewing a filmstrip on individual rear screen projectors, or previewing slides for a research project. Down the hall, you will probably find a biology class watching a film on oceanography or a home economics class re-creating a recipe they have just seen demonstrated on a sound filmstrip. Further down the hall, a social studies class has turned off the "Carousel" projector and is breaking into small groups to discuss a series of slides on political cartoons.

Young adults expect media to be a part of all their activities. Local YWCAs or YMCAs give courses in first aid using sound filmstrips. At drug treatment centers, programs include film and filmstrip scenarios for teenagers to discuss. Inner-city church youth programs give career tips using video role-playing to simulate actual interviews. Teenagers now also expect the public library—the traditional community center—to provide not only book experiences but multi-media ones as well.

Libraries today are often very exciting places. Some are involving young people in genealogy by showing the film series *Roots*. Other libraries help teenagers to become interested in reading by introducing them to exciting fiction through film or filmstrips. Workshops sponsored by libraries teach teens how to plan and record their own videotape productions. There are even programs on skateboard safety using slides and film.

The use of media in a library setting often requires special facilities where television or slides or filmstrips can be effectively presented without disturbing other users of the library. Using media formats raises questions about handling the loan of equipment so that patrons can take media materials from the library for use in the home and elsewhere. Including media in a collection requires acquisition of additional bibliographic tools, professional reference materials, and catalogs. It also requires training of library staff. But, it is worth the effort of learning about new materials and dealing with sophisticated equipment to get young adults really involved in library programs.

Storage of materials as diverse as 16mm films, multi-media kits, and realia is a problem. Making media formats available for browsing is a challenge, and educating the patron to locate and use nonprint formats becomes necessary. Integrated shelving of materials or plastic bag displays make very good sense wherever practical. (It is so much more rewarding when you make it easy for young adult patrons to use *all* the information that your library contains.) Other pertinent considerations are: how do you accommodate the frequent need for discussion after group viewing of many materials? how do you clear schedules for rooms, equipment, and the film or other media? All of these potential difficulties can be worked through with good planning, careful scheduling, a little imagination, and lots of flexibility.

Media is not only right for young adults, it is right for libraries that serve young adults. It is easier than ever to select. Many publishers and jobbers offer media materials packaged with books. It is easier than ever to use. New automatic projectors and various video formats simplify operations and storage. It is more cost effective than ever for the numbers of young adults who can and do use it. Media brings up-to-date information, provides good program highlights, and creates the excitement that will make your library the important community center for young adults that you want it to be.

"BEST BOOKS FOR YOUNG ADULTS"
An Annual List

Eleanor K. Pourron

BACKGROUND OF THE LIST

The inspiration for *The Book of Lists*, according to its authors (David Wallechinsky and Irving and Amy Wallace), came out of their own fascination with lists. They tested the public appeal of lists with a small sample in *The People's Almanac*, and the response to this inundated them with ideas and . . . more lists. Lists, they found, have flesh and blood, "the stuff of life," even carry "the weight of authority," and "invite participation or controversy or both."[1] The annual list of "Best Books for Young Adults" as determined by the American Library Association's Young Adult Services Division certainly bears out these findings. It carries the weight of authority since it is compiled by a committee of librarians working with young adults and is published by ALA. It invites the participation of all librarians trying to promote books and reading with young people. It invokes controversy by the inclusion or the omission of titles on the list.

The list has a long and rather haphazard history. In fact, if there is one word that can characterize the history of the list, it is "confusion." There is confusion as to its purpose and the criteria for selection, resulting in further confusion among the committee members and those trying to use the list. Yet, in spite of these confusions, its use has grown and its reputation increased to the extent that it is now cited by publishers in their catalogs or on book jackets. It appears in library periodicals and *Today's Education* with combined circulation figures of more than one million, while more than 70,000 copies of the list are sold annually. Controversy over the list has increased perhaps not in the same proportion as its readership, but it has become more vocal through articles, letters to editors of library periodicals and educational journals, and in discussions within the Young Adult Services Division.

The closest thing to a complete history of the list appears in "An Analysis of the American Library Association's Annual List 'Best Books for Young Adults,' 1930 to 1967," a dissertation done by Michael Madden while a graduate student in the Graduate Library School at the University of Chicago. It is interesting to examine this history since it reveals much about the list today. The list has existed under several different names and sponsors since it first appeared in 1931. Appearing under the title "Thirty Books for Young People, 1930," the list was prepared under the auspices of the School Libraries Section of the American Library Association. The list was chosen by a committee from this section until 1936, when the sponsoring body became the ALA Board on Library Service to Children and Youth in Public Libraries and Schools. Until 1936, the committee members from schools predominated. Public libraries had been represented on the committees, but in 1937, the emphasis shifted to public libraries, and the list became a project of the Young Peoples' Reading Round Table. From 1945 through 1950, the list again became a joint venture of school and public librarians and was compiled by the Booklist Committee of the Division of Libraries for Children and Young People.

No criteria for including items on the list (from its beginnings) are to be found, but inferences from committee reports indicate that books selected were considered representative of good recreational reading for young people. The number of titles on the lists in the 1930s ranged from 30 to 50 titles and included juvenile titles. One committee member was always a children's librarian from an elementary school.

The decade of the 1940s saw dramatic changes in the list, with selection based on what public librarians found to be of interest to young people during the World War II years. In 1948, the name of the list was changed to "Adult Books for Young People," and it became a retrospective list of adult titles that had not appeared in the *Booklist* titles recommended for young people. Criteria for selection were assumed to be those in use by every good librarian, so there was no need to list them. However, the committee did express the belief in judging books with controversial ideas or language as whole works. Also of importance, they felt, was the need to determine if the book added in some measure to human insight or distorted it. The work's actual interest to young people was always a prime consideration.

The list was discontinued in 1950 when it was felt by some that the *Booklist* reviews were adequate. Others believed that the list should be continued as the best books of the year for young people. Thus from 1951 through 1957, the list became the responsibility of the Booklist Committee of the Association of Young People's Librarians. The name was changed three times: "1950 Books for Young People," "Some of the Best 1951 Books for Young People," and then "Interesting Adult Books of [year] for Young People." The titles were selected for those just beginning to read adult literature as well as for those more mature and discriminating readers. Too, a press release issued with the publication of the 1955 list mentioned that "general readability, integrity of presentation and literary quality as well as appeal to young people" were considered in the selection. The birth of the Young Adult Services Division in 1958 caused more changes, especially in the name of the committee charged to produce the list: "Book Selection Committee," "Committee for the Selection of Books and Other Materials," "Committee for the Selection of Significant Adult Books for Young People," and in 1967, "Best Books for Young Adults Committee."

By 1967, however, other problems inherent in the lists began to be addressed. Linda Lapides (in her article "Question of Relevance") voiced the concerns of many in regard to the selection of the annual list. Most glaring were the books omitted from the lists of 1960-1966. Lapides noted that a list purporting to include adult books of proven or potential appeal to teenagers neglected to include titles such as *Black Like Me* (Griffin), *Up the Down Staircase* (Kaufman), *We Have Always Lived in the Castle* (Jackson), and *I Never Promised You a Rose Garden* (Green).

With increasing pressures and rapid changes in the social climate of teenagers in regard to drugs, civil rights, crime, and sexual values, Lapides decried the omission of titles that, if not of high literary quality, are important because they are "readable, provocative and have something of value to say to the teenagers who have accepted them as their own."[2] She pleaded for the inclusion of important problematic books that possess positive values.

Speaking at a YASD Preconference some eight years later, and having the experience of being a member of the Best Books Committee, Lapides (quoting a committee chairperson of the period) characterized the lists of 1965-1969 as not being chosen on the basis of proven or potential appeal to young adults; the books were not "the most popular, nor the 'come-what-may young adults should read,' but rather books which were in our professional judgment the best."[3] She is aware of the discrepancy between "choosing the best books in a librarian's professional judgment and choosing interesting books on the basis of young adult appeal."[4] She points out that "those most appealing to youth are not necessarily the best and the best books are not necessarily those with the most appeal."[5]

The occasion of Lapides's remarks was the YASD Preconference, "Book You," held in San Francisco in 1975. One-hundred and fifty participants gathered to discuss and re-evaluate the titles chosen as "Best Books" between 1960-1974. The participants and the lists were divided into five-year blocks, and discussions centered on whether titles in each block were still being read by young adults. In addition, titles from those years not included on the lists but still being read by teens were discussed. The intensive discussions over the lists resulted in "Still Alive in '75," a list of books that reflected, in the judgment of the participants, the current reading of young adults. Of the 72 books included, 25 titles had not appeared on any of the Best Books lists.

Sixteen titles for the years 1960-1964 were chosen, nine of which had not appeared on "Best Books": *I Never Promised You a Rose Garden* (Green); *One Flew over the Cuckoo's Nest* (Kesey); *Stranger in a Strange Land* (Heinlein); *Catch 22* (Heller); *Separate Peace* (Knowles); *To Sir with Love* (Braithwaite); *We Have Always Lived in the Castle* (Jackson); *Black Like Me* (Griffin); and *One Day in the Life of Ivan Denisovich* (Solzhenitsyn). The seven titles that had appeared were: *To Kill a Mockingbird* (Lee); *When the Legends Die*

(Borland); *Born Free* (Adamson); *Incredible Journey* (Burnford); *Silent Spring* (Carson); *Von Ryan's Express* (Westheimer); and *April Morning* (Fast).

For the years 1965-1969, there were thirteen new and nine old titles. The new titles: *Flowers for Algernon* (Keyes); *Outsiders* (Hinton); *Mr. and Mrs. Bo Jo Jones* (Head); *Dune* (Herbert); *Pigman* (Zindel); *Manchild in the Promised Land* (Brown); *Autobiography of Malcolm X* (Malcolm X); *2001* (Clarke); *Trout Fishing in America* (Brautigan); *Slaughterhouse-Five* (Vonnegut); *Lisa, Bright and Dark* (Neufeld); *Reflections on a Gift of Watermelon Pickle* (Dunning); and *My Sweet Charlie* (Westheimer). The titles retained: *Tell Me That You Love Me, Junie Moon* (Kellogg); *House of Tomorrow* (Thompson); *Fantastic Voyage* (Asimov); *The Andromeda Strain* (Crichton); *The Ridiculously Expensive Mad* (Gaines); *The Peanuts Treasury* (Schultz); *Soul on Ice* (Cleaver); and *Coming of Age in Mississippi* (Moody).

The fewest additions were chosen for the years 1970-1974. Three in all of the 34 were new: *All Creatures Great and Small* (Herriot); *Our Bodies, Ourselves* (Boston Women's Health Collective); and *Foxfire I* (Wigginton). Among the 31 titles retained are the following: *Go Ask Alice* (anonymous); *Chocolate War* (Cormier); *Hatter Fox* (Harris); *Alive!* (Read); *A Hero Ain't Nothin' but a Sandwich* (Childress); *The Bell Jar* (Plath); *Gather Together in My Name* (Angelou); *To Race the Wind* (Krents); *Sticks and Stones* (Hall); *Watership Down* (Adams); and *The Friends* (Guy). The greater number of those retained from the later years is not necessarily due only to inspired foresight on the part of the committees that compiled the lists, but it may also be attributed to the fact that the titles were more current in terms of publication date and young adult interests. Too, the committees of these years had been choosing the books in a more open forum, with increased attempts to elicit active participation in the choice of titles from the YASD membership and the young adult readers themselves.

THE COMMITTEE AT WORK

The committee was composed for many years of nine voting members plus a non-voting consultant, the *Booklist* editor of the "Books for Young Adults" column. In 1976, the YASD Board gave permission to increase the committee by having non-voting participating library representation. By having participation from library systems with young adult services and large school systems, it was hoped that more regional discussion of books might take place before the selection of the final list, which would allow a broader cross section of opinion. What was most frustrating to the participating library members was their non-voting status, the knowledge that countless hours of reading and discussion had no voting voice on the committee. Thus the YASD Board changed the five participating libraries to individual voting members as of January 1978.

Procedures for the nomination and selection of titles for the list have also changed considerably over the years. The 1960 Committee followed a schedule whereby the chairperson asked each committee member, in October, for nominations of about twenty adult titles published since the previous January first. All of these titles were on the first ballot, and those titles that received two or more votes were placed on a second ballot. A special ballot of titles that received eight votes of the committee was then distributed to randomly selected librarians in public libraries and schools, who were asked to vote for twenty titles. Finally, a third ballot issued by the committee resulted in the selection of the books to appear on the list. The nationwide balloting from selected librarians was not considered binding on the committee, but it did have some impact on the content of the list.

A serious drawback to this timetable was that books published at the end of the year were overlooked entirely. This was somewhat alleviated in 1961 by changing the eligibility dates to books published between November 1 and October 31. A problem still exists, however, because books published prior to October 31 are not always readily available for the committee to read. Circulation of books among committee members, the executive secretary of YASD, and the *Booklist* consultant has helped but not completely solved the problem.

The process for the committee to nominate and consider books is now year-long, and committee members are expected to start reading and nominating titles for the next annual list almost before they have recovered from the marathon reading and discussion of the books chosen for the last list. In any case, by May, at least one list of suggestions has been published and distributed by the chairperson to the committee members. By the annual ALA Conference, there is yet another, longer list of nominated titles. During the meetings at the Annual Conference, all of these titles are discussed. Some titles are dropped while others are retained for more members to read. There is usually some consensus on a few books that are outstanding possibilities for the final list.

This list of nominations is carried over to the fall, when activity increases, especially in regard to the number of new titles suggested. The committee has in recent years attempted to increase the participation of public and school librarians in the process by asking for titles to be nominated. Several methods of "asking" have been tried with varying success. A few times, the list of nominations from the discussions at the Annual Conference have been published in the library press in the hope of eliciting comment and suggestions for additional titles that the committee may have missed. At other times, an announcement has been printed in *Library Journal, School Library Journal, American Libraries, Top of the News,* and *Young Adult Alternative Newsletter* asking for suggestions and ·providing the form in which they should be submitted.

Participation of this sort has been slowly growing. The biggest difficulties seem to be in responding to the form that committee members themselves must use in suggesting titles: author, title, publisher, date, price, and written annotation of the book (which gives some indication of why the book was nominated). Some of the more common problems are garbled bibliographic data, books not eligible for a current list (they may even have appeared on a previous list), and annotations taken directly from commercial reviews of the book. Nevertheless, the participation evidenced from these nominations is a healthy sign of the interest in and concern for young adult reading interests and the "Best Books" list.

As the publishing year begins to pick up in early fall, so does the reading activity of the committee. Several more lists of nominations are circulated among the committee members, and at times, these serve as voting lists for the committee. A majority of members might vote against including a title on the final ballot, and thus the title could be dropped from consideration. However, a title may be reconsidered and renominated (not necessarily by a committee member), so that it does eventually reach discussion at the Midwinter Conference.

The final ballot is the last mailed list of nominations that goes to committee members and 100 librarians around the United States who work with young adults either in schools or public libraries. Any librarian may also request a copy of the list from the chairperson or the executive secretary of YASD. The ballot must be returned to the chairperson before the discussions of the committee at Midwinter. The 100 librarians may have anywhere from four to six weeks to read some of the books on the list with which they are not familiar and to vote for, or against, 150 titles or more.

The most common and justified criticism of this final ballot is that there is no time for adequate consideration of all the titles, especially when many are not familiar to the voting librarians. The final ballot is intended as an indicator of value judgment on titles and of the interest the books may have raised in various parts of the country. It can indicate whether titles on the ballot have been in demand by teens, whether librarians have read and used titles successfully with teens, or whether certain titles have been passed over for any of a number of reasons.

Indications are that many of those who return the ballots have made an effort to read many of the books nominated in order to be able to vote intelligently on them. Librarians may have queried their young adult patrons and asked them to read some of the books, or they may have even joined with other colleagues in the area in their own "Best Books" discussions. Once the ballots are returned, the votes are tabulated and the results are available at the committee discussions. The number of ballots returned grows every year, but the actual return remains around 50 percent. The fact that a title may receive a large number of votes does not necessarily insure the book a place on the list. Conversely, a small number of votes does not exclude a title. It is in the discussion of each title that the committee members decide on the books for the list.

Indeed, such discussion frequently helps prompt more members of the committee to re-examine specific titles to bring them up for discussion again. Mention should be made at this point that would-be committee members should be aware of the hours spent in reading, not only before but also during the Midwinter Conference. Once the day's selection meeting is adjourned, the committee members go off with stacks of books to continue their reading for the next day's discussions. An attempt is made to have one copy of each book suggested, but this is not always possible.

The open meeting policy of ALA has been welcomed by recent Best Books committees. True, it has occasioned critical comments on the methods of selecting the list and the quality of the discussions. Sometimes heated debates between committee members and observers have occurred. Publishers' representatives have even been taken to task for wanting to influence the decisions. With each successive meeting, however, the committee has worked to better structure both their own discussions and the involvement of the observers.

Available at each of the committee meetings, in addition to the actual books and the nomination lists, are descriptive, brief fact sheets listing the committee members, describing the committee's function, and giving a few rules for observers. They are asked, for example, to limit their comments on a book to four minutes or less. Also available is an "Observer Evaluation Form," which allows further written comments on the selection meetings.

Still, personal feelings and opinions run high when some books are discussed: *Forever* (Blume); *Our Bodies, Ourselves* (Boston Women's Health Collective); and *Gramp* (Jury), to mention a few. Some books will always stir passions and feelings. The opportunity to give vent to these expressions and the willingness of librarians to do so in open discussion should be viewed as a common good for the profession as a whole. It is not so much an issue of who is right and who is wrong but a recognition of the differences that we all face in dealing with our own opinions and, more importantly, those of the teenage reader. During the 1977 Midwinter Conference, the Best Books Committee voted to reaffirm the practice of open meetings. In the memo to the YASD Board, Sue Tait wrote:

> Perhaps most important is the philosophical stance involved in the decision to have open or closed meetings. It indicates a willingness to be responsive to the membership, to criticism as well as praise, to a re-examination of our policy or practice if the occasion demands. The decision to have open meetings indicates a pride in the product of one's labors and a willingness to have others see the process leading to this product.

Once the seemingly marathon selection meetings are over and the final list selected, the work of the committee is still not complete. Annotations must be written for each of the titles, and every committee member participates. The closeness of the *Top of the News* deadline for the Spring Issue means that the bibliographic information and editing of the annotations must take place within a few days of the selection of the list. The chairperson is assisted by the executive secretary of YASD and the *Booklist* consultant to the committee. In the meantime, the chairperson has to write the press release announcing the titles for the list. This release is made available to those librarians and publishers attending Midwinter, who eagerly await its publication even though they may already know many of the titles on the list. Seeing the whole list in print has its own special aura.

The committee also chooses the cover design for the printed list. Making the list attractive to the young adults for whom it is intended has long been a project of the committee. The first attempt at soliciting student designs for the cover elicited only two entries, and those two only because a committee member had a good contact with a local Chicago high school, where two students were "inspired" to create a design for the cover of the list. Since that time, better publicity and more effort by committee members and other colleagues in the field have greatly increased the response; so the selection of the cover design is, in its own way, almost as hard as selecting the individual titles.

Another project of the committee has involved trying to make authors more aware of the list and its use. For several years, letters were sent to each author whose book appeared on the list, and in many cases, the authors were moved to respond. Responses ranged from a simple acknowledgment expressing a sense of merit recognized to a few moving lines in appreciation of the tribute paid to what the author had set out to accomplish with the book.

THE BEST BOOKS LIST
AND THE YOUNG ADULT READER

The only other nearly comparable nationally published list is one that appears every year in the January issue of *English Journal.* It is produced by the University of Iowa's Books for Young Adults program, under the direction of Dr. G. Robert Carlsen. It has a somewhat different emphasis, since the books on the list are totally selected from the recommendations of juniors and seniors in high schools near the university. For several years, the list was published under the title "Books for Young Adults, Honor Listing." A list of "books which reflect the feelings, concerns and problems of the older teenager."

With the publication of the 1975 list (January 1976), there was a name change. According to the authors (Dr. Carlsen, Tony Manna, and Jan Yoder) the name was changed to "Books for Young Adults Book Poll." This change was made "because these books have been chosen by popular appeal rather than primarily by literary quality. . . . "[6] From the books selected by the teenagers, there are several books chosen by the staff that "combine literary quality as well as subject matter pertinent to adolescent tastes;" these books are then designated as "honor books."[7]

In further explanation, the authors state, "the aim of honest reporting about what adolescents are reading is still primary. If some of these books appear questionable in terms of their topic, style or values, they nevertheless represent the viewpoint of the adolescent who has found them relevant."[8] A further caveat encourages teachers, librarians, and others to read the books before recommending them. The Best Books Committee adds no such caveat but assumes that those using the list will read or at least look at the books before buying or recommending them.

What is comparable about the lists is that they are directed to teens as readers. As has been pointed out, the books that are most appealing to this particular age group are not always the best, and the best are not always those with the most appeal. Both lists attempt to bring together books with appeal and quality. On the one hand, "Best Books" is chosen by librarians after some consultation with teens. For the other, choices are left to teens, while those items of particular quality are singled out by the research staff as "most appropriate for teaching."

It is interesting, for comparison, to see which books the high school students chose that were also chosen by the Best Books Committee. The "Books for Young Adults Book Poll" and "Best Books" do not cover the same time span, but over the past four years, the following titles have been included on both lists (not necessarily in the same year): *The Chocolate War* (Cormier); *All Things Bright and Beautiful* (Herriot); *Ellen: A Short Life Long Remembered* (Levit); *Alive!* (Read); *Trying Hard to Hear You* (Scoppetone); *May I Cross Your Golden River* (Dixon); *The Women and the Men* (Giovanni); *Of Love and Death and Other Journeys* (Holland); *Is That You Miss Blue?* (Kerr); *Eric* (Lund); *You Can't Get There from Here* (MacLaine); *Circus* (MacLean); *Headman* (Platt); *Do Black Patent Leather Shoes Really Reflect Up?* (Powers); *Feral* (Roueche); *If You Could See What I Hear* (Sullivan); *Life on the Run* (Bradley); *Why Am I So Miserable If These Are the Best Years of My Life?* (Eagen); *Distant Summer* (Patterson); *Are You in the House Alone?* (Peck); *Tunes for a Small Harmonica* (Wersba); *Hard Feelings* (Bredes); and *Zoo Vet* (Taylor).

Those books singled out as the "Honor Books" that were also on "Best Books" are: *If Beale Street Could Talk* (Baldwin); *A Cry of Angels* (Fields); *House of Stars* (Sleator); *The Lion's Paw* (Sherman); *Eden Express* (Vonnegut); *Massacre at Fall Creek* (West); and *Ordinary People* (Guest).

Revealing and sometimes surprising are some of the titles that the teenagers chose for the "Books for Young Adults Book Poll" and those which the librarians did not choose for "Best Books": *Loophole or How to Rob a Bank* (Pollock); *Theophilus North* (Wilder); *Jaws* (Benchley); *Marathon Man* (Goldman); *Caril* (Beaver); *Jack the Bear* (McCall); *Helter Skelter* (Bugliosi); *Fair Day and Another Step Begun* (Lyle); *Forever* (Blume); *After the Wedding* (Colman); *El Bronx Remembered* (Mohr); *Why Me?* (Dizenzo); *Spindrift* (Bartell); *Dog Days of Arthur Cane* (Bethencourt); *Plantain Season* (Hahn); *Raise the Titanic* (Cussler); *Magic* (Goldman); *Gramp* (Jury); *Gifford on Courage* (Gifford and Mangel); and *The Education of Little Tree* (Carter) to name only a few. Of the "Honor Books," these three did not appear on "Best Books": *In the Beginning* (Potok); *The Seeker* (Bales); and *The Shepherd* (Forsythe).

While both lists are chosen from different viewpoints and by people of different ages, there are, happily, enough instances of overlapping to lend credibility in the area of teen appeal to the "Best Books" list. To expect 100 percent duplication of titles is not suggested or desired. Each list retains its own unique focus and can be used in different ways. Where the two mesh is in the inherent intent of the compilers: that of fostering and promoting reading as an enjoyable process for young adults.

John Rouse, in his "In Defense of Trash" asks,

> How can we account for the curious fact that books which have
> delighted and instructed thousands are often regarded by teachers
> as bad, whereas books that have bored generations of school
> children and turned them against reading are thought of as good?
> Such views derive from an abstract literary standard that treats
> books as ends in themselves, quite apart from any immediate inter-
> est or usefulness these books may have for the reader.

It is impossible to *make* someone enjoy reading. Woody Allen thinks, "the
problem with reading now is that people approach it as a discipline, a chore;
and consequently they don't want to do it and I feel the same way about it
myself. If it's not joyful then I don't think it's worth doing."[9]

If as young adults people approach reading as a chore, where do they go
as adults but to more passive forms of entertainment such as television or films
rather than to books? In this day of low reading scores, and with renewed
emphasis on teaching reading skills, it seems incumbent upon us as librarians
to do as much as we can to foster the joy of reading. Thus, it seems proper to
base the selection of the "Best Books" list primarily on each book's proven or
potential appeal and worth to young adult readers. This does not mean that
quality of writing is sacrificed to appeal, nor does it suggest pandering to adolescent tastes and interests.

Ken Donelson, in "The Trouble with 'Read Only the Very Best,' " takes
issue with the dearly held belief in the promotion of the "classics" versus "inferior books." He believes:

> " . . . sympathetic and well-read teachers and librarians have much
> to offer kids. They can supply titles and authors and topics that
> just might give kids some impetus towards fresher and more percep-
> tive visions of the world. Those teachers and librarians I applaud,
> just as I abhor those who want to foist off great literature on young
> people in the mistaken belief that reading second-rate material is
> inherently bad."[10]

Donelson also believes that:

> " . . . sympathetic librarians and teachers who know kids and books
> can help many young people to enjoy reading. But the quality of
> the books gauged by whichever abstract literary standard is far less
> important than the fact of the reading and the enjoyment. . . . If
> someone doesn't enjoy reading, the very best literature may go
> eternally unread but then so will all other books. . . . Someone
> who enjoys reading at least one book, any book, no matter what
> its presumed literary value, has begun the process, and that is

worthwhile in and of itself. Perhaps there can be hope that wider and wider reading might lead to enjoying better and better literature."[11]

Donelson's hope is not an idle one. Many adults, librarians and teachers among them, "loved" the Hardy boys, Nancy Drew, or a myriad of other "inferior" books but still found their way to better literature. The "Best Books" list can help guide young readers in this direction. It can serve as a stepping stone on the way to better literature—not as a list of notable, literarily-above-reproach "classics" (or those expected to become such) but as a useful tool in the hands of a sensitive librarian. That is the librarian who reads, enjoys the process, and can communicate the pleasure to the young adult.

THE VALUE OF THE LIST

When something like a list of books chosen annually has managed to be rather regularly published over the last half century, it must be serving some needs and doing a few things right, in spite of its ambiguousness. During its history, it has been neither a list of all particularly "notable" books nor has it been totally a popularity poll. It lies between the two extremes. Even with the numbers of books published each year, the possibility of creating a list of thirty or more books with "notable" qualities and the amount of appeal necessary for teen interest becomes a difficult task. This is not to imply that the committee, or we as librarians serving teens, should ever give up or give in to the inevitable compromises. It makes the search for such books of quality and appeal more incumbent on us all, not just on members of the Best Books Committee.

Perhaps one of the biggest problems with the list has been the first word in its title, "Best." Best of what, for whom, by whose definition? Our perceptions of quality differ according to our own tastes and backgrounds. To suggest that this list of books "surpasses all others in quality" (*American Heritage Dictionary* definition of "best") is a misnomer. The thought of changing the title has occurred on more than one occasion to the committee and the YASD Board; but so far, all attempts to create a title that is more acceptable or descriptive of the list have been unsuccessful.

To choose a list of "Best Books" that would be suitable to every librarian in every public or school library is an impossible task. Also, the list can never be the perfect buying guide or reading list for every young adult across the country. What it can do is to suggest titles to entice a reader—a sophisticated reader, a young teenager, or an older one—to sample freely from the books. A colleague was approached at an annual gathering of librarians and was asked bluntly, "what's the first thing you think of when you think of 'The Best Books for Young Adults' list?" Pausing for a few eye blinks, she considered thoughtfully and then said, "I think it's the books kids will read." That's what it all comes down to in the end: "kids" and reading. Librarians may be interested in balancing lists and choosing the "best," but it's "kids" and reading that really count.

As long as the list continues it will have its critics and its champions. It will see changes perhaps in design, in selection, and even in content, as the fact of change is one thing that is certain. But let us be hopeful about the future of the list, of the young people for whom it is intended, and of our own roles in bringing "kids" and books together. That's the "best" of all possible worlds.

NOTES

[1] David Wallechinsky, Irving Wallace, and Amy Wallace, *The Book of Lists* (West Caldwell, New Jersey: Morrow, 1977), p. xix.

[2] Linda F. Lapides, "Question of Relevance," *Top of the News* 23 (1967): 57.

[3] Linda F. Lapides, "Choosing with Courage: The Young Adult Best Books, 1965-69," *Top of the News* 32 (1976): 359.

[4] Ibid., p. 360.

[5] Ibid.

[6] G. Robert Carlsen, Tony Manna, and Jan Yoder, "1975 Books for Young Adults Book Poll," *English Journal* 65 (1976): 95.

[7] Ibid.

[8] Ibid.

[9] Harold Mantell, "The Words and Ways of Woody Allen: An Interview," *Media and Methods* 14 (1977): 44.

[10] Ken Donelson, "The Trouble with 'Read Only the Very Best,' " *Media and Methods* 14 (1978): 33.

[11] Ibid., p. 70.

BIBLIOGRAPHY

Burgess, Eileen E. "The Book Is Alive and Well . . . " *Top of the News* 30 (1974): 267-69.

Carlsen, G. Robert, Tony Manna, and Jan Yoder. "1975 Books for Young Adults Book Poll." *English Journal* 65 (1976): 95.

Donelson, Ken. "The Trouble with 'Read Only the Very Best.' " *Media and Methods* 14 (1978): 32-33, 68, 70.

Fader, Daniel. *The New Hooked on Books.* New York: Putnam, 1977.

Lapides, Linda F. "Choosing with Courage: The Young Adult Best Books, 1965-69." *Top of the News* 32 (1976): 359-64.

Lapides, Linda F. "Question of Relevance." *Top of the News* 23 (1967): 55-61.

Losinski, Julia. "A Closer Look: The Young Adult Best Books, 1960-1964." *Top of the News* 32 (1976): 353-57.

McCue, Michael, and Evie Wilson. "Book You—Book Now: A Survival Preconference." *Top of the News* 31 (1975): 30-35.

Madden, Michael. "An Analysis of the American Library Association's Annual List 'Best Books for Young Adults' 1930-1967." Master's thesis, University of Chicago Graduate Library School, March 1964.

Mantell, Harold. "The Words and Ways of Woody Allen: An Interview." *Media and Methods* 14 (1977): 44-46, 48, 50-51, 67.

Rouse, John. "In Defense of Trash." In *Literature for Adolescents: Selection and Use.* Richard A. Meade and Robert D. Small, Jr., eds. Columbia, OH: Charles E. Merrill Pub. Co., 1973. pp. 90-94.

Wallechinsky, David, Irving Wallace, and Amy Wallace. *The Book of Lists.* West Caldwell, NJ: Morrow, 1977.

READABILITY AND
SELECTION OF MATERIALS

Linda M. Evers

Much has been written on the selection of materials for young adult library collections. A large body of literature also has been written on the subject of readability. Many librarians and reading specialists, however, are unaware of the other professionals' resources and points of view. Perhaps brief definitions of the concepts "selection of materials" and "readability" will help to bridge the terminology gap.

To librarians, the phrase "selection of materials" usually refers to the careful evaluation and choosing of print and nonprint items in order to serve a particular clientele as well as to fulfill qualitative criteria and meet collection developmental needs. To locate materials, the librarian typically relies on such resources as *Junior High School Library Catalog*,[1] periodical reviews, lists of "best" or "favorite" books, and personal experience. *Media Programs: District and School* offers a more formal description of the resources available to help in the selection process:

> The district media program supports the selection process by providing examination collections of materials and equipment . . . and conducting an active evaluation program involving media personnel, teachers, other staff, and students. Published evaluations, including those in reviews, recommended lists, and standard bibliographic tools are used in selection.[2]

"Readability," the other key term in this discussion, denotes some estimate of a passage's level of reading difficulty. Klare lists several methods for measuring this complex variable.[3] Among these methods are judgments of students, teachers, and other experts; comprehension test scores; cloze procedure scores; and readability formulas. Readability studies have their foundation in vocabulary lists and, according to Bormuth, have their future in manipulation of language to control difficulty, not merely to predict it.[4]   The ability to estimate reading difficulty has proved unique in such diverse areas as rewriting technical manuals for poor readers and teaching English as a second language.

In the past, standard selection aids have assisted the library professional in meeting the interests and needs of young adult patrons. Perhaps the word "average" should be inserted in the preceding statement, because use of these resources has enabled the librarian to meet the interests and needs of young adults reading at their approximate grade-placement level. For example, a majority of fourteen-year-old ninth-graders are able to read and understand materials written at about a ninth-grade level of difficulty. However, with the increasing emphasis on individualization of educational programs, the young adult librarian is faced with the fact that an alarming number of students cannot read and understand materials written at or near their grade-placement level. Such students have compensated by relying heavily upon pictorial or aural information, thereby enabling them to pass from one grade to the next but without being able to read at grade-placement level. The other side of the readability coin finds gifted students in need of books and other print materials written well above their grade-placement level. It remains for the librarian to guide young adult readers through a myriad of reading possibilities to the most appropriate selections for each particular individual.

The consequences of either over-estimating or under-estimating a book's difficulty or a student's ability to read the selection can prove disastrous. A gifted student's interest in independent study might wane considerably without sufficiently challenging materials, while the remedial reader's enthusiasm for a topic would be effectively squelched by being handed a book that yields more frustration than accessible information.

In conjunction with the trend toward individualization, librarians and teachers are increasingly using non-traditional print materials in their work with young adults. As is the case with traditional print materials, not all of the teen magazines, pamphlets, or other ephemeral material are listed in commonly used selection aids. The challenge is in finding ways in which librarians and teachers can effectively assist the young adult reader in selecting both traditional and non-traditional print materials containing suitable subject matter written on an appropriate level of reading difficulty.

If the selection aids for educational and non-curriculum oriented materials for children and young adults included valid and reliable grade level indications, selection would be simplified. Publishers' lists and publicity often indicate reading level, but while this grade-level assessment is usually easy to locate, it may not provide reliable information. As Ellen Rosen and other researchers have noted, there is often quite a discrepancy between publishers' suggested reading levels and those calculated by readability formulas.[5] A survey of publishers conducted by Mills and Richardson revealed that a majority of the respondents relied upon the author or an educational consultant for a readability estimate.[6] Of several common selection aids examined by this writer, very few stated the specific criteria upon which grade level assignments were based; instead, the rather hazy suggestion of "for high school" or "seventh grade and up" was provided without rationale or qualification. When criteria for determining readability were given, the publisher had relied upon the collective opinion of a committee of unidentified "experts" in the field.

Too often, the prospective buyer bases selection decisions on the grade level information listed by selection tools only to receive a box of books painfully beyond or ridiculously below the reading abilities of a significant number of the young adults for whom the material was intended. In addition to knowing upon what criteria grade level assignments are based, one should know whether or not grade levels are equivalent from one selection tool to the next and whether or not a particular tool uses the same criteria consistently throughout. For instance, do selection aid compilers consider maturity of subject matter more important as a criterion for determining appropriate grade level at the senior high level than when evaluating materials at the junior high level? It seems in the consumer's best interests, be it purchaser or reader, to know upon what criteria suggested grade levels are based rather than assuming that the publisher knows best. Caveat emptor!

It is evident that the discerning librarian or teacher needs an additional tool in deciding which book for which reader. Greater precision in determining levels of reading difficulty is readily available to the professional through use of one or more readability formulas. Thus, a working knowledge of these formulas automatically frees the professional from total reliance upon published selection aids, personal experience, or even hearsay for readability information. Ideally, of course, several sources of information would be considered (e.g., opinions of students, teachers, and other qualified persons; first-hand perusal of the material; etc.) before determining grade level. When other information sources are limited or unavailable, however, readability formulas may be effectively employed. A common-sense analysis of the readability methods earlier suggested by Klare reveals the following: subjective judgments often fluctuate from one reading to the next, comprehension tests are time-consuming in the school and impractical in the public library, and the cloze procedure, while accurate, also requires administration of a pencil and paper test.[7] After winnowing through the list of available methods, readability formulas remain a viable, convenient means for estimating the reading difficulty level of a written passage.

A readability formula as defined by Klare is "a method of measurement intended as a predictive device that will provide quantitative, objective estimates of the style difficulty of writing."[8] Presumably, "style difficulty of writing" is an indication of difficulty in reading with comprehension. Several formulas have been devised since the turn of the century to estimate readability, and researchers have examined such factors as average number of words per sentence, number of syllables per hundred words, number of difficult words, and number of personal reference words. Values for these factors (or for many others found to be significantly related to readability) are inserted into regression equations to predict the relative degree of difficulty. Readability formulas have many advantages. They also have limitations, including an inability to reflect conceptual complexities or organizational patterns, and they are applicable only to the type of material upon which they were initially calculated. Some of the more complicated ones are quite time-consuming to calculate. However, readability formulas still provide the most objective, accurate estimates of passage difficulty.

Four of the most popular readability formulas have been devised by Lorge,[9] Flesch,[10] Dale-Chall,[11] and Fry.[12] The Dale-Chall and Flesch formulas are appropriate for grade levels three to eight; the Lorge formula extends its range of measurement from third through twelfth grades, while Fry's is applicable to grades one through college. All four utilize average sentence length as a reflector of style difficulty. Dale-Chall and Lorge require reference to Dale's word lists for number of difficult words, while Flesch and Fry calculate the average number of syllables per sample as an indication of vocabulary "load." Lorge also includes a count of prepositional phrases as a linguistic element of importance. The *McCall-Crabbs Standard Test Lessons in Reading*[13] passages were used as grade-level criterion by Dale and Chall, Flesch, and Lorge. Fry, however, determined grade level designations by "simply plotting lots of books which publishers said were third grade readers, fifth grade readers, etc."[14] Fry judges his formula to be accurate "probably within a grade level."[15] The other three popular formulas incorporate more elements than Fry and thereby produce somewhat more accurate results. In terms of ease of calculation and application, the Fry and Flesch formulas require less counting than Dale-Chall or Lorge and, consequently, they require less time to determine readability level.

To illustrate some of the difficulties inherent in the traditional selection process (that is, one done without benefit of the additional, objective information provided by one or more readability formulas), the following study was conducted. The study was divided into two parts: Part I examined grade level scope, specificity, and criteria of a number of standard selection tools; Part II compared readability levels as estimated by the selection tools examined in Part I and by the four formulas.

In Part I, the initial source of secondary level selection tools to be examined was *Aids to Media Selection for Students and Teachers.*[16] The authors of this government document included "only reviewing tools published since 1970, except for those lists which have not been revised or replaced are considered essential in developing a well-rounded media collection."[17] Twelve titles in this publication were chosen for the study of selection tools for secondary level materials.[18] Examination of selection tools sought to answer five questions: 1) what is the scope of grades or ages covered by the tool? 2) is the suggested grade estimate for a given book fairly specific (i.e., a span of three years or fewer)? 3) does the publisher state what criteria were used in determining grade level estimates? 4) of those publishers stating criteria, which relied upon committee consensus? 5) of those stating criteria, which incorporated readability formula results in determining those grade level estimates?

For Part II, the comparison of readability estimates, five popular young adult titles were examined.[19] Every fifth book of the 25 most popular listed in the *New York Times Report on Teenage Reading Tastes and Habits*[20] was chosen. Only those titles selected both by school librarians and bookstore employees were included in this study to ensure obtaining titles popular on all fronts. Of the tools examined in Part I, only those stating grade levels and listing at least one of the five selected titles were considered in Part II. Readability formulas were calculated according to their respective published guidelines.

Results of the study are presented in Tables 1, 2, and 3 (beginning on page 42). Table 1 indicates that few selection tools specialize in secondary level materials. Six tools supplied grade level estimates specific to within three years; the other six did not. All except two of the tools cited grade level criteria; of these ten, all but one relied on committee consensus rather than a readability formula. Only one selection tool made use of a readability formula (Spache's *Good Reading . . .* ; he also devised the Spache readability formula).

Table 2 shows a fairly wide range of opinion among the six tools stating grade levels for the five popular titles. It is precisely this wide range of opinion that points out the need for objective readability formula results. For example, while *Booklist* recommends *Tuned Out* for ninth through twelfth graders, the other tools recommend it for seventh graders and up. The selection tools' suggestions average about mid-eighth grade. The results of application of readability formulas to the same five titles are found in Table 3. The readability formulas estimate *Tuned Out* to range from low- to mid-fourth grade (Fry and Lorge) to sixth grade difficulty (Flesch), with Dale-Chall predicting a fifth or sixth grade level of difficulty. Keep in mind that formulas cannot consider subject matter as a quantifiable entity. In *Tuned Out*, the term "LSD" was used several times, yet the Fry and Flesch formulas would count it only as a simple, one-syllable word. Dale-Chall and Lorge would give it added weight as an unfamiliar word, but there is a very controversial issue behind that unfamiliar acronym. In terms of quantifiable linguistic elements, the formulary predictions average fifth grade for *Tuned Out.*

Strictly speaking, none of these estimates of reading difficulty can be considered as equivalent measures. Nonetheless, practicality dictates that users of selection tools and readability formulas consider both types of grade level estimates in order to make the best decision about selection. One should neither condemn standard selection tools nor consecrate readability formulas. Selection aids have proved useful with traditional materials and average reading abilities, and they will probably continue to do so. Readability formulas, however, can be an important objective source of information, especially when used in conjunction with other pertinent data.

As is demonstrated by this study, no one source of information on reading difficulty is sufficient. Each source draws on different aspects of communication through the written word. Considering only objective variables such as the average number of sentences and the unfamiliarity of vocabulary may produce results not in agreement with personal opinions. The converse holds true as well. Subjective judgments are usually biased and should be tempered by objective information. Publishers of selection tools may eventually consider objective readability information in their grade level suggestions, but at present, readability formulas seem to be a do-it-yourself job.

Table 1

Characteristics of Selection Tools

Selection Tools	Grade Scope	Specific Grade Estimate	Stated Criteria	Assessment by Committee	Application of Formula
Adventuring with Books: 2400 Titles for Pre-K through Grade 8	Preschool-8th	*	yes	yes	-
Best Books for Young Adults, 1974	7-12th	-	yes	yes	-
Books for the Teen Age, 1973	7-12th	-	yes	yes	-
Books for You: A Reading List for Senior High School Students	10-12th	yes	yes	yes	-
Children's Books in Print, 1973	Preschool-12th	yes	-	-	-
High Interest Easy Reading for Junior and Senior High School Students	7-12th	-	yes	yes	-
I Read . . . I See . . . I Hear . . . I Learn	Preschool-9th	yes	yes	yes	-
Junior High School Library Catalog	7-9th	yes	yes	yes	-
Library Journal/School Library Journal	1-12th	-	-	-	-
Senior High School Library Catalog	10-12th	yes	yes	yes	-
Good Reading for Poor Readers	Preschool-12th	yes	yes	yes	yes
The Booklist	Preschool-12th	-	yes	yes	-

A dash (-) indicates that either no information was available or a lack of sufficient information was provided.

Table 2
Grade Level Estimates Found in Selection Tools

Selection Tools	Catcher in the Rye	Go Ask Alice	Lord of the Flies	Mr. and Mrs. Bo Jo Jones	Tuned Out
Children's Books in Print, 1973	7th & up	-	9th & up	9th & up	7th & up
I Read . . . I See . . . I Hear . . . . I Learn	-	-	7th-9th	7th-9th	-
Junior High School Library Catalog	-	-	-	-	7th-9th
Library Journal/School Library Journal	Adult	8th & up	-	Young Adult	7th-10th
Senior High School Library Catalog	10th-12th	10th-12th	10th-12th	10th-12th	-
The Booklist	-	9th-12th	-	"Mature Girls"	9th-12th
Average Estimate	10.0	9.6	9.9	8.6	8.4

Table 3

Grade Level Estimates Using Readability Formulas

Selection Tools	Catcher in the Rye	Go Ask Alice	Lord of the Flies	Mr. and Mrs. Bo Jo Jones	Tuned Out
Lorge	4.5	5.3	5.2	4.5	4.6
Flesch	6th	7th	6th	7th	6th
Dale-Chall	5th-6th	5th-6th	7th-8th	5th-6th	5th-6th
Fry (1968)	low 5th	mid 7th	low 6th	low 7th	low 4th
Average Grade Estimate	5.25	6.3	6	6	5

How can the readability formula novice begin to incorporate this new source of information into the daily scheme of things? The first step is to gain access to a relatively simple readability formula. Fry's formula is among the easiest to calculate and has been published as an even more convenient slide rule-type scale.[21] The first version of the graph appeared in 1968[22]; an extended version appeared in the *Journal of Reading* (December 1977) and is reproduced below.

GRAPH FOR ESTIMATING READABILITY —EXTENDED

by Edward Fry, Rutgers University Reading Center, New Brunswick, N.J. 08904

Average number of syllables per 100 words

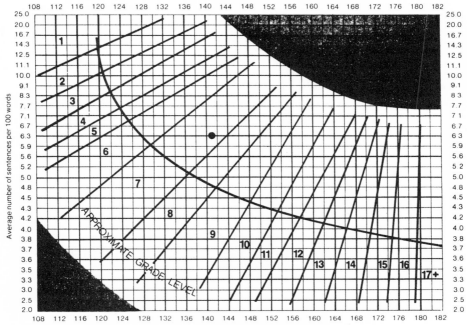

DIRECTIONS: Randomly select 3 one hundred word passages from a book or an article. Plot average number of syllables and average number of sentences per 100 words on graph to determine the grade level of the material. Choose more passages per book if great variability is observed and conclude that the book has uneven readability. Few books will fall in gray area but when they do grade level scores are invalid.

Count proper nouns, numerals and initializations as words. Count a syllable for each symbol. For example, "1945" is 1 word and 4 syllables and "IRA" is 1 word and 3 syllables.

EXAMPLE:	SYLLABLES	SENTENCES
1st Hundred Words	124	6.6
2nd Hundred Words	141	5.5
3rd Hundred Words	158	6.8
AVERAGE	141	6.3

READABILITY 7th GRADE (see dot plotted on graph)

Armed with freshly calculated readability estimates, the librarian then must decide how to make use of them in developing a collection and in advising young readers.

In this article, we have briefly examined two complex topics—readability estimates and selection of materials. It was noted that standard tools are helpful in the selection process, but they are limited to evaluating traditional materials for average readers. Some other indication of reading difficulty is needed to resolve discrepancies among selection tool suggestions, to help evaluate non-traditional materials, and to obtain greater precision in estimating grade levels for remedial and gifted readers. Fortunately, readability formulas are able to meet all three needs. It remains for librarians, teachers, and selection tool publishers to use them to both the reader's and the librarian's advantage.

NOTES

[1] Estelle A. Fidell and Gary L. Bogart, eds., *Junior High School Library Catalog*, 2nd ed. (New York: H. W. Wilson, 1970).

[2] American Association of School Librarians and Association for Educational Communications and Technology, *Media Programs: District and School* (Chicago: American Library Association, 1975), p. 65.

[3] George R. Klare, *The Measurement of Readability* (Ames: Iowa State University Press, 1963), p. 29.

[4] John R. Bormuth, "Measurement of Readability," in *The Encyclopedia of Education*, Lee C. Deighton, ed. (New York: Cromwell-Collier, 1971), p. 366.

[5] Ellen Rosen, "Readability Analysis of SRA Power Builders," *Journal of Reading* 19 (1976): 551.

[6] Robert E. Mills and Jean R. Richardson, "What Do Publishers Mean by Grade Level?" *The Reading Teacher* 16 (1963): 359-62.

[7] Klare, p. 29.

[8] Ibid., p. 3.

[9] Irving Lorge, *The Lorge Formula for Estimating Difficulty of Reading Materials* (New York: Teachers College, Columbia University, 1959).

[10] Rudolf Flesch, *The Art of Readable Writing* (New York: Harper and Row, 1974).

[11] Edgar Dale and Jeanne S. Chall, "A Formula for Predicting Readability: Instructions," *Education Research Bulletin* 27 (1948): 37-54.

[12] Edward Fry, "A Readability Formula That Saves Time," *Journal of Reading* 11 (1968): 513-16, 575-77.

[13] William Anderson McCall and Lelah Mae Crabbs, *Standard Test Lessons in Reading* (New York: Teachers College Press, 1925).

[14] Fry, p. 515.

[15] Ibid., p. 514.

[16] Kathlyn J. Moses and Lois B. Watt, *Aids to Media Selection for Students and Teachers* (Washington: U.S. Government Printing Office, 1976).

[17] Ibid., p. iii.

[18] For citations for selection sources used, see the "Bibliography of Selection Sources" at the end of this article.

[19] Titles include:

> Anonymous. *Go Ask Alice.* New York: Avon, 1972.
>
> Golding, William. *Lord of the Flies.* New York: Capricorn Books, 1959.
>
> Head, Ann. *Mr. and Mrs. Bo Jo Jones.* New York: Signet Books, 1967.
>
> Salinger, J. D. *The Catcher in the Rye.* Boston: Little, Brown, 1951.
>
> Wojciechowska, Maia. *Tuned Out.* New York: Dell, 1968.

[20] Rema Freiberger, *New York Times Report on Teenage Reading Tastes and Habits* (New York: New York Times, 1974), p. 12.

[21] Edward Fry, *Fry Readability Scale* (Providence, RI: Jamestown, 1976).

[22] Fry, "A Readability Formula That Saves Time," p. 577.

BIBLIOGRAPHY

Bormuth, John R. "Measurement of Readability." In *The Encyclopedia of Education.* Lee C. Deighton, ed. New York: Cromwell-Collier, 1971. pp. 361-68.

Carlsen, G. Robert. *Books and the Teen-Age Reader.* New York: Bantam, 1971.

Dale, Edgar, and Jeanne S. Chall. "A Formula for Predicting Readability: Instructions." *Education Research Bulletin* 27 (1948): 37-54.

Flesch, Rudolf. *The Art of Readable Writing.* New York: Harper and Row, 1974.

Freiberger, Rema. *New York Times Report on Teenage Reading Tastes and Habits.* New York: New York Times, 1974.

Fry, Edward. *Fry Readability Scale.* Providence, RI: Jamestown Publications, 1976.

Fry, Edward. "A Readability Formula That Saves Time." *Journal of Reading* 11 (1968): 513-16, 575-77.

Klare, George R. *The Measurement of Readability.* Ames: Iowa State University Press, 1963.

Lorge, Irving. *The Lorge Formula for Estimating Difficulty of Reading Materials.* New York: Teachers College, Columbia University, 1959.

McCall, William Anderson, and Lelah Mae Crabbs. *Standard Test Lessons in Reading.* New York: Teachers College, Columbia University, 1925.

Media Programs: District and School. American Association of School Librarians, and Association for Educational Communications and Technology. Chicago: American Library Association, 1975.

Mills, Robert E., and Jean R. Richardson. "What Do Publishers Mean by Grade Level?" *The Reading Teacher* 16 (1963): 359-62.

Moses, Kathlyn J., and Lois B. Watt. *Aids to Media Selection for Students and Teachers.* Washington: U.S. Government Printing Office, 1976.

Rosen, Ellen. "Readability Analysis of SRA Power Builders." *Journal of Reading* 19 (1976): 548-51.

Seels, Barbara, and Edgar Dale. *Readability and Reading.* Newark, DE: International Reading Association, 1971.

Wynar, Christine L. *Guide to Reference Books for School Media Centers.* Littleton, CO: Libraries Unlimited, 1973.

Wynar, Christine L. *1974-75 Supplement; Guide to Reference Books for School Media Centers.* Littleton, CO: Libraries Unlimited, 1976.

BIBLIOGRAPHY OF SELECTION SOURCES CONSULTED

Children's Books in Print, 1973. 5th ed. New York: Bowker, 1973.

Children's Services Division. American Library Association. *I Read . . . I See . . . I Hear . . . I Learn . . .* Chicago: ALA, 1971.

Committee on Books for Young Adults. *Books for the Teen Age, 1973.* New York: New York Public Library, 1973.

Fidell, Estelle A., and Toby M. Berger, eds. *Senior High School Library Catalog.* 10th ed. New York: H. W. Wilson, 1972.

Fidell, Estelle A., and Gary L. Bogart, eds. *Junior High School Library Catalog.* 2nd ed. New York: H. W. Wilson, 1970.

Library Journal. John N. Berry, III, ed. New York: R. R. Bowker, 1876- .

National Council of Teachers of English. *Books for You: A Reading List for Senior High School Students.* New York: Washington Square Press, 1971.

Root, Shelton L., Jr., and a Committee of the National Council of Teachers of English. *Adventuring with Books: 2,400 Titles for Pre-K—Grade 8.* 2nd ed. New York: Citation Press, 1973.

School Library Journal. Lillian N. Gerhardt, ed. New York: R. R. Bowker, 1954- .

Spache, George D. *Good Reading for Poor Readers.* 7th ed. Champaign, IL: Garrard, 1972.

The Booklist. Chicago: American Library Association, 1905- .

White, Marion E., ed. chair. *High Interest-Easy Reading for Junior and Senior High School Students.* 2nd ed. New York: Citation Press, 1972.

Young Adult Services Division. American Library Association. *Best Books for Young Adults, 1974.* Chicago: ALA, 1975.

INTELLECTUAL FREEDOM
AND THE YOUNG ADULT

Mary L. Woodworth

To speak of intellectual freedom and the young adult is to raise questions and breed controversy. Opinions differ sharply here; little research, definitive or tentative, is available; and few court cases exist that enlighten us. Until fairly recently, the question probably would have been moot, as the rights of youngsters seemingly were those allowed by the parent. Even the state hesitated to interfere with parental rights. The one right that the young adult had was protection against physical abuse. But, today we see conflict over the schools' teaching sex education or evolution, and the library's having materials depicting sexual acts or using language that to some adults may be profane or indecent. And, these controversies run the gamut from the quiet phone call or letter of complaint to a community uproar, sparking strikes, school closings, and even bombings.

Nor are librarians immune from the dilemma. Some librarians who subscribe to intellectual freedom sometimes also will set up or accept restrictive lists of questioned books and films, or establish coded patrons' cards or labeled books. The purpose here is to implement parental restrictions; the result is that the librarian becomes the agent and enforcer of censorship. The 1977 issuance of the film, "The Speaker," by the American Library Association Office for Intellectual Freedom produced extended argument. Designed to show the events in a high school when a student committee invites a speaker who believes in and advocates the racial superiority of whites, the film generated disagreement within the profession as to whether the film is a true representation of First Amendment principles or primarily racist. Some viewers also purport to see an anti-youth bias in the film, which essentially questions the right of any committee of high schoolers to choose all-school program speakers.

In our society, the position of adults seems relatively unhampered—they are free in reading, listening to, and viewing non-obscene materials. The child, on the other hand, is generally protected by parents, librarians, teachers, and other adults from materials that adults perceive as being too advanced, too concerned with sex, too questioning of adult authority, and too controversial in general. The young adult age group (ranging roughly from the junior high student to the college sophomore) is wedged between the pressures on the child and the latitude allowed the adult. This indeterminate status may be one reason that the tide of intellectual freedom ebbs and flows. Young adults have no defined position in custom or in law and seem forever to struggle against both individual and group adult restraints in their attempts to define themselves and to make their places.

The rights of young adults in relation to public libraries and school libraries are also not well established. Within a school, young adults can protest, if they do not disturb the school. They are partially protected from searches of their persons and possessions. They and their parents have access to their school records. School officials may not interfere capriciously with the school newspaper's freedom of the press. Nor may students be dismissed or suspended in disciplinary action without due process. In their position outside of school, young adults find changing boundaries. A minor may have the right to deposit and withdraw in a bank savings account, but in some states, a minor may not allow the adoption of her child unless she first has the permission of her parents. A youngster may enlist in the armed services and find his or her enlistment legally binding, when at the same time, if she or he signs a lease, it may well not be enforceable.

But, at the present time, when it comes to having access to information of all kinds, the opinions and rights of parents seem paramount. Parents are able to restrict the reading, viewing, and listening experiences of their own children. Parents generally, it is believed, are knowledgeable about their children's degree(s) of maturity and their capacity to cope with controversial materials. Thus, the parental responsibility for nurturing the minor can include definite restrictions on reading or information gathering by a young adult (except, in some states, information on contraception and venereal disease). The restrictions are begun, outlined, and enforced by parents who, for the most part, believe that they are protecting their children. Surrogates who can match solicitous parental understanding of the young adult are few, and persons acting in the place of parents need ever to be cognizant of their own limitations.

On the other hand, librarians are confronted daily with questions from young adults without a caring, intact family structure. Or the home situation may well be a hostile one, actively antagonistic toward the young adult, purposely ill-disposed, physically threatening, or entirely indifferent. Librarians are asked by these youngsters for information on, and referrals to, abortion clinics and centers for drug control, among other things. In many states, librarians may not give that information, contrary to the parents' expressed desires. Librarians may find that discussions held with the young adult are not legally a "confidential" interview and that the library's circulation records are public records. In places where no laws or legal precedents exist guaranteeing certain young adult rights, or where the individual situation of a young adult makes help imperative, the librarian must reach a professional decision whether to provide the materials available. Making that decision necessitates weighing the needs of the young adult, respecting the desires of the parents, and delineating the role of the youth-serving librarian. The most important aspect is the well-being of the young adult.

The Young Adult Services Division of the American Library Association in its 1978 Midwinter Meeting endorsed this statement: "Young adults have the right to free access to all information in all formats. Librarians have the responsibility to insure this access." Laying down guidelines to implement the statement may well be very difficult, given the nature of libraries and schools, and the snarled roles of parent, librarian, and young adult. But the intent seems very clear: to promote as far as possible the free and easy access of any young adult to search for answers to any questions. This, of course, is an extension of the Library Bill of Rights' statement: "the rights of an individual to the use of a library should not be denied or abridged because of his age. . . ."[1]

The legal aspect needs to be considered here. Censorship efforts quite often concern problems of religious thought, social and political views, and questions of obscenity. Today issues in religion center principally on Darwinian evolution. However, many parents also find the literature of such religious groups as the followers of Reverend Moon, the "Moonies," to be threatening. And, the general atmosphere of public school was deemed contaminating to Amish youngsters, who were removed from these schools by their parents, despite compulsory attendance laws. The removal was upheld by the Supreme Court in *Wisconsin v. Yoder,* 1972. Social and political views from the far right and far left tend not to be represented in libraries nor fought for very strenuously by librarians. Few libraries have materials from the American Nazi Party; some have them from the Communist Party. Some librarians still hesitate to purchase, for example, materials that threaten adult authority or that advocate governmental take-over of the steel and coal industries or of the utilities.

A problem of another sort arises when materials are said to portray groups in our society in a stereotypic way. These tend to be in older books, but certainly such problems can appear in the most recent. Librarians must surely be sensitive to the image of the Chicano, American Indian, woman, black, Asian-American, and others as they are portrayed in our collections. Challenges on the inclusion of books that may be stereotypic must be forthrightly faced. Taken as a whole, does the book, despite a supposed stereotype, make a contribution to the knowledge or understanding or perception of young adults? If so, the book remains in the library despite the fact that it may appear on lists that label it "anti-human" or that indicate that a revisionist ought to change and, thus, "improve" it. When parents requested the removal of *Oliver Twist* and *The Merchant of Venice* because of their seeming anti-Semitism, the courts rejected it and replied, "if evaluation of any literary work is permitted to be based upon a requirement that each book be free from deorgatory reference to any religion, race, country, nation, or personality, endless litigation respecting many books would probably ensue. . . "[2] (*Rosenberg v. Board of Education of City of New York,* 1949). As long as school officials acted in good faith in using the books, the courts refused to interfere.

But the leading problem that recurs is obscenity, and a major difficulty is in the attempts to define it. Art Buchwald reports,

I have an aunt who lives in Boston and she thinks *Vogue* magazine is obscene because it has printed photographs of topless models. One of my best Catholic friends believes *Ms.* magazine is obscene because it publishes stories advocating abortion. A liberal friend of mine has told me he considers Bill Buckley's *National Review* obscene, and a columist colleague . . . keeps telling me my humor appeals to people's prurient interests. So everyone in this country and many in the same towns and cities have their own definition of what obscenity is.[3]

Prior to 1973, definitions of obscenity had been devised through a series of legal cases, which then allowed judgment on ofttimes slippery grounds. Challenged materials, examined as a whole (i.e., not in isolated, out-of-context sentences, paragraphs, or scenes) and for their effect on an average person, needed to have been "utterly without redeeming social importance." The dominant theme must have appealed to "prurient interests," and have been "patently offensive" as judged by contemporary national standards. These criteria (founded chiefly on the *Ulysses,* Roth, Alberts, and Jacobellis cases) then obtained, with some modifications. It was, of course, the responsibility of the prosecutors to prove the books, films, and magazines obscene.

A turnabout came with the 1973 case of *Miller v. California.* Here the Supreme Court laid down new rules for determining obscenity by questioning whether a whole work has "serious literary, artistic, political, or scientific value."[4] This appears to shift the burden of proof from the accusor to the accused, and also redefines community to mean local, not national, communities. *Miller v. California* was greeted with consternation by many librarians and library-related organizations, who pointed out the possible threat to movie theaters, book stores, and libraries, all now vulnerable to the eager police chief, ambitious prosecutor, or insatiable local censor. Court rulings since 1973 have modified slightly the *Miller v. California* guidelines, but have, essentially, left intact the obscenity definition, determined by local standards. Localities have found themselves deeply divided. Madison, Berkeley, and Charlottesville exhibit some of the divisiveness. Should community standards in these places be those of the relatively liberal university group or reflect the views of the surrounding countryside, relatively conservative? And how are the rights of an individual protected in such a situation?

Rights of the individual young adult to read, view, or listen are interpreted differently from those of the adult. In 1965, the owner of a Long Island luncheonette, Sam Ginsberg, sold two "girlie" magazines that contained photographs of female nudes to a sixteen-year-old boy, who had been induced by his mother to go to the luncheonette and purchase the magazines. Ginsberg was arrested and convicted of selling obscene materials to a minor. This case, *Ginsberg v. New York* (1968), was appealed to the U.S. Supreme Court. Several points were considered. In questioning a conflict between the minor's constitutionally guaranteed right of free expression and those of the state and parents to protect the minor, the court stated, "it was constitutionally permissible for the state to so accord minors under 17 a more restricted right than that assured to adults to judge or see."[5]   Delivered in the context of the right of the state to protect the well-being of its children, the decision supports parental direction of the rearing of children and the state's interest to safeguard the child from abuses and to assist the parent in the child's care. The issue of whether or not the material was harmful was defined by New York state law, and accepted by the Court: "The pictures were 'harmful to minors' in that they had . . . that quality of representation . . . of nudity . . . [that] (i) predominantly appeals to the prurient, shameful or morbid interests of minors, and (ii) is patently offensive to prevailing standards in the adult community as a whole with respect to what is suitable material for minors, and (iii) is utterly without social importance for minors."[6]   Thus, the concept of "variable obscenity" was upheld.

In a related case (Bookcase), the U.S. Court of Appeals declared, "material which is protected for distribution to adults is not necessarily constitutionally protected from restriction upon its dissemination to children. In other words, the concept of obscenity or of unprotected material may vary according to the group to whom the questionable material is directed or from whom it is guaranteed."[7]   The Ginsberg decision was hailed as a solution to the difficult problem of obscenity and the minor, and it surely led to the many state statutes dealing with selling and sometimes lending materials to minors, all such laws being firmly based on "variable obscenity."

Justice Fortas, in a dissenting opinion in *Ginsberg v. New York*, commented

> the Court certainly cannot mean that the States and cities and counties and villages have unlimited power to withhold anything and everything that is written or pictorial from younger people. But it here justifies the conviction of Sam Ginsberg because the impact of the Constitution, it says, is variable, and what is not obscene for an adult may be obscene for a child . . . It begs the question to present this undefined, unlimited censorship as an aid to parents in the rearing of their children. This decision does not merely protect children from activities which all sensible parents would condemn. Rather, its undefined and unlimited approval of state censorship in this area denies to children free access to books and works of art to which many parents may wish their children to have uninhibited access. For denial of access to these magazines, without any standard or definition of their allegedly distinguishing characteristics, is also denial of access to great works of art and literature.[8]

What is the extent of censorship—that denial of access—in libraries? We don't know; we have few studies we can turn to here. The classic 1959 investigation by Fiske explored the relationship of book selection and censorship in public and school libraries in California. The Fiske study found that many librarians had been so careful in selection practices that controversial materials typically did not appear in their libraries. Some librarians also did not purchase books that might *become* controversial,[9] and an overwhelming number (82 percent) put some restrictions on circulating disputed materials.[10] Librarians in the Fiske study tended to resist pressures from outside the library or school and to submit to those from within.

Both the 1974 study by Pope and Busha's 1972 investigation tend to corroborate and confirm the Fiske inquiry. Busha surveyed public librarians in five midwestern states and attempted to determine their attitudes on intellectual freedom. "When it comes to the concept of intellectual freedom, almost all midwestern public librarians were for it."[11] But, "a marked disparity between the attitudes of many librarians toward intellectual freedom as a concept and their attitudes toward censorship as an activity" was shown, as some 14 percent were sympathetic in attitude toward censorship, with 22 percent strongly opposed to practices of restriction.[12] Busha found significant relationships between attitudes toward censorship and the librarians' age (the older librarians tended more toward censorship), their sex (the female appears more often as pro-censorship than the male), the size of the community (the larger cities' librarians seemed to be more pro-intellectual freedom), and their level of education (the more education the librarians had, the less likely they were to tolerate censorship).[13]

Opinions on "unresolved issues" were also solicited by Busha using a Likert-type, five-category scale, which forces a response from "strongly agree" to "strongly disagree." These opinions were perhaps more directly related to minors and library usage. Some 75 percent of the librarians agreed or strongly agreed that "what a child reads should be more the responsibility of parents than book-sellers and librarians." And, although a majority disagreed or strongly disagreed, 28 percent were undecided on the statement that "there is a direct causal relationship between reading and juvenile delinquency."[14]

Additionally, in a section on attitudes toward authority, Busha found 39 percent of the librarians agreeing or strongly agreeing that "obedience and respect for authority are the most important virtues children should learn," and 44 percent that "young people sometimes get rebellious ideas, but as they grow up they ought to get over them and settle down."[15] This research by Busha may give us an indication of the censorship problems faced by the young adult in public libraries.

What about school libraries and censorship? When Wisconsin high school principals, librarians, and teachers of English, social studies, and science were asked in a 1976 state-wide survey whether or not there had been any objections to school library materials or to textbooks in the past three to four years, about 58 percent said yes. Most of the affirmatives reported one to three incidents (84 percent); some 10 percent recorded four or five; and a minority (about 5 percent) noted six to ten or more. One beleaguered school person reported 24 incidents. Most of the objections (84 percent) came from outside the school.[16]

A steady stream of censorship cases as related to young adults is being reported in the news media and library literature. Recent issues of the *Newsletter on Intellectual Freedom* report questions on the book, *Our Bodies, Ourselves*, in Prince George's County, Maryland, and Ludlow, Massachusetts. In Maryland, after the library got an authoritative legal opinion that *Our Bodies, Ourselves* was not obscene, parent groups attacked the "suitability" of the book. *Dinky Hocker Shoots Smack* fell to the charge of "vulgarity" and "defamation," in Kent, Washington. Both Minnesota and Texas have had difficulties with *The Inner City Mother Goose.*

We find other reports on films, such as *The Lottery* and its supposed depiction of a vengeful god;[17] the abuse of prisoners in Nazi concentration camps and the bulldozing of bodies in *Night and Fog*; and the picture of the medical treatment of wounded Japanese civilians of *Hiroshima-Nagasaki.* Philadelphia had problems with a branch film festival of Hitchcock's *The Thirty-Nine Steps, The Birds,* and *Suspicion.* The *Life* magazine special issue on American women was banned from an Oregon school because of a picture of a nude woman.

Some of these confrontations develop into major cases with national publicity, such as Chelsea and Island Trees. Others seemingly are buried from public view, surfacing occasionally to surprise even those still flinching from a former encounter. Within the space of one week in February 1978, I found 1) my friendly local druggest informing me of how carefully he picked out children's and young adult books he would sell in his store and how discreetly he weeded out the profane and violent; 2) a book jobber who inserts in some of his books a bookmark stating that some of his customers had objected to the " . . . content or vocabulary of this book [as being] . . . inappropriate for young readers," and suggesting that the librarians examine the book,[18] and; 3) an accusation by a local newspaper that advocating "cultural diversity" in library materials means that

> children must be taught to respect and hold hands with perverts, bigamists, etc., and be willing to learn about and respect their "lifestyles." The American social controllers . . . moved the classics and the masterpieces out of the school libraries long ago. They brought in as much garbage as they could as rapidly as they dared. Now the parents who want their children to be exposed only to the better literature are accused of burning books when they are only asking that smelly garbage be removed.[19]

The above diatribe came in response to the publication of *Suggestions for Dealing with Censorship of Media Center Materials in Schools* by the Wisconsin Department of Public Instruction.

Objections to young adult books and films seem to cluster around certain themes, and even certain titles. Biographies and novels dealing with social commentary (*Autobiography of Malcolm X, If Beale Street Could Talk*), or with life styles that differ from the majority (*Manchild in the Promised Land, Hatter Fox, Sidewalk Indian*) are questioned. Crucial topics of concern today, such as war, draw criticism of titles such as *If I Die in a Combat Zone, Box Me Up and Ship Me Home* or *Friendly Fire* or *Born on the Fourth of July.* Or different worlds are represented by *Catch-22, Brave New World, Lord of the Flies, One Flew Over the Cuckoo's Nest,* and *Slaughter-House Five.*[20]

But major objections seem to concentrate on language which is too realistic and on the depiction of sexual acts. In the 1976 study of school censorship in Wisconsin, the five titles most often objected to were (in order): 1) Salinger's *Catcher in the Rye*; 2) *Go Ask Alice*; 3) Steinbeck's *Of Mice and Men*; 4) Raucher's *Summer of 42*; and 5) Steinbeck's *The Grapes of Wrath*.[21] The two most popular with the young adult here are *Summer of 42* (a tale of summer, the war, and a young man's foray into sex) and *Go Ask Alice* (a modern morality play on the degradations associated with using drugs). Steinbeck certainly is one of the modern greats, who wrote of things as they were—not glossed over, not prettied up, but described in accurate, realistic language. And *Catcher*, of course, is considered by many to be the modern classic in young adult reading. Holden gets thrown out of school; he swears; he loves and protects his sister; he contacts a prostitute in a hotel room. From the outcry that has accompanied this book since its publication in 1951, you might begin to nominate this as young adult literature's *Fanny Hill*. But, Holden might be better characterized as ingenuous and innocent. Librarians and teachers should take note that while parents and other adults quarrel over *Catcher*, young adults are beginning to view it as an interesting historical relic.

The surveyor was puzzled with some of the titles that appeared, and wondered why the top five were such old books? Some date back to the '40s and '50s. Where were the "best sellers" *Love Story* and *The Godfather*? Or social commentary like *Soul on Ice* and *1984*? These are old, old books, particularly if you look at them from the perspective of the young adult. Where are such titles as *The Chocolate War, Trying Hard to Hear You,* or *The Man without a Face*? Where are the other books in the forefront of current young adult literature? Is it possible that such books never appeared because parents and teachers didn't know about them, and they were protected by the young adult from adult scrutiny? These things do happen. Or is it possible that these books have not yet appeared in libraries? Is it possible that they will not appear in some youth-serving libraries? Or that they, along with *Catcher*, will have to wait an indecent period of time before they can be listed in standard catalogs and other "respectable" bibliographies, and made admissible to libraries? Or will they and their earlier counterparts fall victim to the charge of obscenity?

A major, key figure in censorship fights is the librarian. What, then, is the role of the youth-serving librarian in the young adults' quest for intellectual freedom? Librarians first need to put their own house in order. They need to identify and clarify what intellectual freedom is and what its role is in a democratic society. Some librarians state that intellectual freedom depends on the client (meaning age and, sometimes, social or community position). Some do not attempt a definition. But, almost all librarians assert their belief in the concept of intellectual freedom. What they practice may indeed be something else.

We know from our investigations going back to the California study by Fiske that librarians tend to resist attempts at censorship on the part of the public—of those people outside our institutions of the public library and the public school. We also know that librarians are apt to agree with internal censors—with teachers, library administrators, principals, and fellow librarians.

So, if a librarian objects to a library book, chances are that he or she will not select it for purchase, will restrict access to it, or will remove it after a problem has presented itself. The librarian is the most effective censor in our society. The librarian, at times, does and does not recognize conflicts between the ideas incorporated into the phrase "intellectual freedom" and the challenges hurled against them every day. The professional may or may not resist, and may or may not give ground in a controversy. Some are prepared for a dispute, while to others, it comes as a shock. But when a librarian is the force behind the campaign, the librarian's methods of imposing and administering censorship are myriad. To recount them is almost a how-to-do-it course in restricting access to materials. Some of these tactics include: 1) restricting the inspection of reviewing periodicals to *Booklist* or *School Library Journal* or *Council on Interracial Books for Children Bulletin*; 2) refusing to buy materials that a teacher or librarian has not vouched for; 3) allowing deletions from a materials order by a business manager or other lay person; 4) purchasing books, but not cataloging them, or cataloging them and not filing the cards; 5) housing a questioned book behind the loan desk, in the librarian's office, in the teachers' collection, in the teachers' lounge, on a reserve shelf, or on permanent loan to a nurse, counselor, or principal; 6) placing the book in a locked case so that a young adult patron must ask a library staff person, at a public information desk, to unlock the case and get the book for him or her; and 7) removing sections of a book, or drawing diapers or fig leaves on nudes, or snipping out sections of a film, or tearing out magazine illustrations and covers. And, there are others.

Often differences appear between upholding the ideas of intellectual freedom and allowing or disallowing access to materials. The crux of the problem of intellectual freedom and the young adult lies in our need to examine our concept of, and commitment to, intellectual freedom, and to reaffirm our obligation of service to the young adult.

NOTES

[1] American Library Association. Office for Intellectual Freedom, *Intellectual Freedom Manual* (Chicago: ALA, 1974), p. 11.

[2] *Rosenberg v. Board of Education of City of New York*, 92 N.Y.S. 2d 344 (1949).

[3] Art Buchwald, "A Buchwald Civil Liberties Sampler," *Civil Liberties Review* 4 (1978): 44-45.

[4] *Miller v. California*, 413 U.S. 15 (1973).

[5] *Ginsberg v. New York*, 88 S.Ct. 1274 (1968).

[6] Ibid.

[7] Ibid.

[8] Ibid.

[9] Marjorie Fiske, *Book Selection and Censorship* (Berkeley: University of California Press, 1959), p. 64.

[10] Ibid., p. 69.

[11] Charles H. Busha, *Freedom Versus Suppression and Censorship* (Littleton, CO: Libraries Unlimited, 1972), p. 144.

[12] Ibid., p. 147.

[13] Ibid., pp. 143-47.

[14] Ibid., p. 208.

[15] Ibid., p. 209.

[16] Mary L. Woodworth, *Intellectual Freedom, the Young Adult, and Schools*, rev. ed. (Madison: University of Wisconsin Extension, 1976).

[17] K. Jamieson and V. S. Freimuth, "The Banning of 'The Lottery': Implications for Censorship in the Schools," *Sightlines* 11 (1977): 14.

[18] Bookmark of the Follett Library Book Company.

[19] Wisconsin Department of Public Instruction, *Suggestions for Dealing with Censorship of Media Center Materials in Schools* (Madison: Wisconsin Department of Public Instruction, 19 Jan. 1978).

[20] Woodworth, *Intellectual Freedom, the Young Adult, and Schools*, p. 57.

[21] Ibid., p. 56.

BIBLIOGRAPHY

American Library Association. Office for Intellectual Freedom. *Intellectual Freedom Manual.* Chicago: American Library Association, 1974.

Buchwald, Art. "A Buchwald Civil Liberties Sampler." *Civil Liberties Review* 4 (1978): 38-45.

Busha, Charles H. *Freedom Versus Suppression and Censorship.* Littleton, CO: Libraries Unlimited, 1972.

Busha, Charles H., ed. *An Intellectual Freedom Primer.* Littleton, CO: Libraries Unlimited, 1977.

Fiske, Marjorie. *Book Selection and Censorship.* Berkeley: University of California Press, 1959.

Jamieson, K., and V. S. Freimuth. "The Banning of 'The Lottery': Implications for Censorship in the Schools." *Sightlines* 11 (1977): 14-17.

Konopka, Gisela. "The Needs, Rights, and Responsibilities of Youth." *Child Welfare* 55 (1976): 173-82.

Levine, Alan. *The Rights of Students: The Basic ACLU Guide to a Student's Rights.* New York: Dutton, 1973.

"Librarians' Group Divided by Conflict over a Rights Film." *New York Times* (Feb. 9, 1978).

National Education Association. *Kanawha County, West Virginia, A Textbook Study in Cultural Conflict.* Washington: National Education Association, 1975.

Parker, Franklin. *The Battle of the Books: Kanawha County.* Bloomington, IN: Phi Delta Kappa, 1975.

Pope, Michael. *Sex and the Undecided Librarian.* Metuchen, NJ: Scarecrow, 1974.

Schimmel, David, and Louis Fischer. *The Rights of Parents in the Education of Their Children.* Columbia, MD: National Committee for Citizens in Education, 1977.

Sussman, Alan. *The Rights of Young People: The Basic ACLU Guide to a Young Person's Rights.* New York: Avon, 1977.

U.S. Commission on Obscenity and Pornography. *Report.* Des Plaines, IL: Bantam, 1970.

Wisconsin Department of Public Instruction. *Suggestions for Dealing with Censorship of Media Center Materials in Schools.* Madison: The Wisconsin Department of Public Instruction, 1978.

Woodworth, Mary L. *Intellectual Freedom, the Young Adult, and Schools: A Wisconsin Study.* Rev. ed. Madison: University of Wisconsin Extension, 1976.

Woodworth, Mary L., ed. *The Young Adult and Intellectual Freedom: Proceedings of an Institute.* Madison: University of Wisconsin Library School, 1977.

PART II

LIBRARY SERVICES FOR
YOUNG ADULTS

INTRODUCTION

Various factors that affect the provision of services for young adults in the library provide the focus for the first article written by the editor. Current economic realities, the need for increased broad-based support, the need to move forward in cooperative planning between and among all public institutions including libraries, and the realization that the library is going to be held account-able for its performance are issues that should concern those serving young adults. As with other types of library service, there seems to be a movement toward a client-centered approach rather than to an approach that emphasizes collection development and warehousing of information and knowledge. Changes in facilities to make possible new types of programming are common. Buying materials about controversial topics and sponsoring innovative programs explor-ing issues and problems relevant to young people today take place in many libraries. There is a challenge, however, to find ways to measure the impact of young adult services, especially in light of the relatively recent recognition of the importance of YA services and in light of the shrinking library budgets with which the profession must live.

An inventory of programs and services reported in the literature of librarianship is the subject of the article by Carolyn Hammond, a media special-ist in Boyle County, Kentucky. Perhaps representative of the types of services currently being offered, this report provides concrete examples of ideas that have been tried, some successfully and some not successfully.

There seems to emerge no universal understanding of what really consti-tutes programming in a library. The term is used to describe a single event, a series of events inside the library or held elsewhere under library sponsorship, or the total package of services available to the young person through all of the service points in the library (reference services, information and referral services, audiovisual services, and others). In planning to serve all of the varied needs of young adults, it seems to be more productive to identify their needs and ask what materials and which services within the organization can meet their needs most effectively. Most of the reports in the literature, however, do not begin with ascertaining the clients' individual needs but describe some type of group activity planned to respond to common needs of groups of young people. Some individual case studies of young people and their use of the library or media center might yield useful information from a different point of view.

There is also an unfortunate common denominator found in the reports of programs or library programming for young adults. Most of the articles are descriptive only, and seldom are goals, objectives, or the criteria by which programs might be measured included. There is a great need to develop ways to measure the success or failure of the services that we think are answering the needs of young people. Several factors that are emphasized by those librarians writing about programs in their libraries include an emphasis on the importance of publicity, an attempt to provide less formal and inhibiting environments for teens, the use of media formats as form and content of programs, and attempts to reach outside of the small circle of regular users to attract the unserved. Several projects discussed also were begun with seed money from federal, state, or local governments. There needs to be some evaluation of the results of these expenditures to determine whether the types of projects attempted were successful and to learn ways to continue innovative programs after the initial support has stopped.

Looking at the major challenges that the young person faces in the transition from childhood to becoming an adult, Marilyn Greenberg, coordinator of the Library Services Credential Program at the School of Education at California State University, begins with a working definition of developmental tasks. For each of these broad categories that require adjustment on the part of the young person, she then outlines implications for library service to help the young person adjust successfully. Her suggestions address some questions about the types of materials appropriate for young adult collections and allude to types of programs that will meet the needs of adolescents (as described by leading psychologists who study adolescent behavior). The themes include those related to physiological changes, identity development, development of individuality with the ability to relate to peers and others in a social context, and preparation for work.

The next author, Rosemarie Falanga, currently information systems consultant for Pyramid, a resource sharing network for drug abuse prevention, shares personal insights and information about providing help for young adults caught in a crisis situation. Having worked with young people in libraries and in other agencies, she is not optimistic about the possibility of the library's overcoming the difficulties inherent in providing meaningful help for those young adults with acute and serious problems. The library as an institution is in itself a barrier. The attitudes of staff toward young people, the expectations that young people have of the services they will receive in the traditional library setting, and the difficulty that librarians have with interpersonal relationships with young adult clients all make the goal of relating to young adults in a helpful way a difficult one to achieve. In exploring the rationale behind the belief that the library is the proper setting for community information and referral services, Falanga comments upon the image of the library in the community, the types of materials and information that the library possesses to provide this type of service, the interest and skills that library professionals must have in order to perform adequately in this role, as well as the financial and political barriers that make in-depth information and referral service a challenge to deliver.

As pointed out by Peggy Sullivan, assistant commissioner for extension services of the Chicago Public Library, library cooperation is an idea that has the support of most library professionals. Putting the idea into practice, however, demands creative determination and perseverance. Making a commitment to develop channels of communication for joint decision-making concerning cooperative efforts, with the best interest of the patrons of all participating libraries kept as a focus, is a formidable undertaking. To be most effective, discussions about cooperative effort should involve staff at every level, because all functions are necessarily affected by interagency activity. The advisability of experimenting with a unified library program intended to serve drastically different types of clients is questioned on the basis of past observation of these types of efforts. Also, cooperation with other types of agencies and communicating directly with young adults themselves to identify their real needs in library services and resources (within the realm of fiscal responsibility) may re-direct some programming efforts, either with cooperating institutions or within one library. Overcoming barriers to the development of cooperative efforts is a challenge that those serving youth should welcome if the best possible service is to be made available with the least public expense. The examples of cooperative activities and comments about them are drawn from Sullivan's extensive background in work with young people in both public and school libraries, and they demonstrate the depth of understanding of this library historian and administrator.

As president of and delegate to the International Association of School Librarianship, delegate to the International Federation of Library Associates, and member of ALA committees concerned with international librarianship for youth, Jean Lowrie, director of Western Michigan School of Librarianship, has had a unique opportunity to observe library service to young people in other countries. Dealing with a topic of enormous scope and great variety, she initially points out that many of our basic assumptions about literacy, the publishing industry, universal education, and economic and political systems (which to some extent determine availability of education and library service) must be discarded. The discussion is divided into two parts, the first of which looks at programs in developed countries, with emphasis on European countries and Australia. Delivery of service to young adults in the United States and Canada is excluded from this survey. Illustrating general points with descriptions of specific library settings or with information from primary sources about libraries in other countries, the paper covers active programs in Great Britain, Hungary, West Germany, and Australia. Descriptions of efforts in countries with less well-developed programs for delivery of library service include coverage of a conference with representatives of thirteen Asian countries, descriptions of programs in several African countries, and descriptions of some programs in the Caribbean and Latin America. Concluding that few countries can claim programs equal to those found in the United States, Canada, and several other

Western European countries, the reader is left with an understanding of some very basic needs, which in many cases must precede development of any delivery system for library service. Because many of our basic assumptions do not apply to other cultures and countries, the reader also begins to see that, as well-intended as it might be, our desire to aid others by superimposing our patterns of delivering library service on their diverse environments is inappropriate.

TRENDS AND ISSUES IN
YOUNG ADULT SERVICES

JoAnn V. Rogers

In the absence of a much-needed national survey of public and school library services for young adults, identifying meaningful trends in library services for this age group is a difficult task. Identification of trends or directions maintained in spite of some wandering must rely on news items in the literature of librarianship, descriptions of programs, and statements from professional associations on the local, regional, and national levels. This information can be augmented with several reports of state surveys, observation, and information and opinion gathered from persons active in young adult librarianship. Reports about successes and failures of innovative and traditional library services aimed at meeting the needs of young adults in the library can be helpful in planning for YA service. Librarians who specialize in work with young adults need to know what library programming is having positive impact in other communities. Library administrators and library boards can learn which approaches to YA service have proven workable by seeing examples of services tried in other library settings. Library science students can use information about trends in YA services both for career planning and for input in program planning in libraries where they will work. Also, individuals working with teenagers through other service agencies, including the school, need to know what libraries are doing and hope to do to help meet the needs of young adults. The most effective type of program planning for young adult library services views the library as one of many public and private institutions that share responsibilities for meeting the needs of this segment of our population.

All of the factors affecting the library as an institution must necessarily affect the young adult services provided by that institution. In the past ten years, several changes or shifts in emphasis have been made in the goals and objectives of libraries, which then have had impact on YA programming. Also, changes in the economy have affected the provision of library service. Three themes that recur with some regularity include the need for the library to broaden its base of support by responding to the needs of all segments of the population, the increasing need for multi-type library cooperation and cooperative planning with other types of organizations, and the increasing awareness that the library must become more accountable in light of shrinking budgets and increasing demands from the library's actual and potential public.

Librarians have been interested in the young adult patron for a number of years. As early as 1929, this interest was reflected in the formation of the Young People's Reading Round Table, which was a part of the Children's Library Association of the American Library Association. By 1941, the Round Table had become a part of the Division of Libraries for Children and Young People, which also included the School Libraries Section and the Section for Library Work with Children. In 1949, the Round Table became a section and adopted the title the Association of Young People's Librarians, which, in 1957, became a separate division and changed its name to the Young Adult Services Division. YASD is interested in the improvement and extension of services to young people in all types of libraries.

Momentum for the development of specialized YA services began to increase at the end of the 1940s. The American Library Association Committee on Post-war Planning published a set of guidelines for YA service entitled "The Public Library Plans for the Teen Age" as a supplement to *A National Plan for Public Library Service.* Perhaps the most noticeable event marking the beginning of the modern era of young adult librarianship was a conference sponsored by the Graduate Library School of the University of Chicago. The conference and publication of papers presented there, entitled *Youth, Communication and Libraries,* were to have a great and lasting effect on YA library services. Ideas explored then provide the underpinnings for a philosophy of service. Many library activities today are manifestations and extensions of the ideas taking shape then. The conference also helped to redefine the role of the YA specialist. Emphasis began to shift from providing reading prescriptions for young adult patrons to focusing on the young adult as a unique person who has informational, recreational, and curricular needs that the library can help to meet.

There are several ways in which changes in the goals and objectives of library service have been reflected in the program of services intended for young adults. Looking at the past ten years (1968 to the present), activities new to the library setting and an emphasis on different types of service have given YA services some new directions. Probably the most obvious change has been in the nature of the facilities that libraries provide for young adults. More libraries are providing space designed to attract young adults both to the traditional library setting and to alternate facilities outside the library.

In many cases, facilities have been designed or changed to accommodate new types of activities while also making the young adult more comfortable in the library setting. Collecting nonprint formats and programming with multimedia materials are often initiated by the YA librarian. Many facilities have been changed to accommodate individual, small group, and large group listening and viewing areas for YA and other patrons. Also reflected in the design and decoration of YA facilities is the idea that the library should promote its services by providing surroundings not only utilitarian, but also attractive, in the hope of retaining the interest of the regular patron and attracting the non-user as well. Reflecting changes in the philosophy of service, the library environment is less formal, more creatively decorated, and more promotionally oriented.

Not limited to the YA services, but reflected in the content of recent YA programs, is the recognition that the library, if it is to survive in the competition for tax dollars, must become more broad-based in its appeal and subsequent public support. One way that this can be done is to hold the attention of the patron through the teen years, when many users have traditionally become library drop-outs.

When new target groups are identified and new programs and services are suggested by YA staff, changes do not immediately or necessarily occur, however. Library policy makers, public library boards, and school boards continue to be heavily representative of the most conservative elements in our society. Change is slow and difficult. Many services that might help to meet the needs of young adults do not become a part of the library's program because they are not considered to be legitimate types of activities by board members.

At one time, many libraries were reluctant to sponsor recreational programs lacking mitigating educational objectives. The idea that the library's mission is to uplift and educate is still evident in collection development and services, but programming for entertainment now is generally accepted in the YA area. Concerts, theatrical productions, and "happenings" of the late 1960s (presented live or preserved on tape or film) have become the medium and the message of much YA programming. Popular culture has become more significant in the shaping of recreational program content. YA specialists are expected to be in tune with what is happening with teenagers in order to be able to collect relevant materials and provide popular programming.

Libraries are accepting some responsibility for responding to the recreational needs of adolescents and are attempting to determine other of their needs to which the library might or should respond. Evident in the choice of program materials and content over the past ten years is the belief that program content must be based on the planner's understanding of the adolescent's many different types of needs. In many cases, young adults have been included as advisors in the planning process. Rather than an evolutionary change from the earlier reviewers' groups and literary clubs, this is a revolutionary change welcoming input from the served, the underserved, and in some cases, the unserved. Increasingly, those people who choose young adult library work are client-oriented in addition to being materials-oriented. Administrators are looking for people who can communicate with youth in order to determine their needs.

The content of many facets of the library's program of services in the last ten years has focused on the young adult as an information seeker. In addition to finding in it information needed to complete school assignments, the young adult uses the library when it can supply pertinent, appropriate information about topics of individual interest not associated with school subjects. Young adults use services that provide information that can help them in their search for personal identity in the world of their peers and in the adult world. Although common educational practice prolongs the dependent years, young adults want information that will help them to function independently. Many libraries have found information, materials, and programs dealing with job possibilities, career information, and counseling information and referral to be particularly popular in recent years. A program package that includes making available crisis information for the young adult who is having difficulty coping with the transitional role from child to adult is found in some libraries. The legitimacy of this type of service is questioned by some library policy makers, however. Also, the traditional posture of the institution precludes the expectation of young adults, their parents, or youth workers that help can be found in the library. Librarians who feel that the library could and should respond to needs of the young adult in a crisis situation are beginning to say that in most libraries, YAs won't ever be able to find the information, direction, and help that they need.

When thinking about young adults and libraries over the past ten years, single programs or a series of programs sponsored by the library are often viewed as its YA program. In talking about services, however, the entire program of services available to the young adult under the aegis of the institution should be considered part of the package. Any materials, information, staff help, and facilities available to children and adults should be available to young adults, with due consideration being given to legal realities and parental prerogatives. In some unfortunate cases, limited YA collections and services have been instituted in order to siphon off demands from YAs that can't or won't be handled by those serving adults. This has been particularly true in the delivery of traditional reference service. Although some libraries do not afford the young adult equal opportunity to use all of their resources, the lines between young adult and first class citizenship are becoming blurred in the more service-oriented institutions.

The more visible, pre-packaged program is an important facet of YA service, but the importance of the less obvious one-to-one services of the librarian with a young person is being recognized increasingly. The traditional role of readers' advisor is being expanded to include responsibilities for helping the user to develop information-seeking skills and coping skills. Helping the young person to communicate needs to a library professional is a current focus of young adult work.

Small group programs with emphasis on attracting patrons as individuals with specialized interests rather than on broad-spectrum and large-group programming is becoming more popular. This is particularly true when the library administration and the YA specialist agree that the number of people attending a program is only one measure of its success and impact. Many group programs, both small and large, also emphasize participation rather than passive listening or viewing. Activities like traditional film viewing have evolved into workshops, where program participants make films or tapes and view the works of other young filmmakers. In some instances, the library has become the focal point for community action programs organized by young adults. The lecture presentation by an authority figure is now a program format of the past in YA library programming.

In terms of collection development and the implementation of services intended to spark young adult interest, changes in content of materials, changes in types of services, and changes in the format of materials are evident in many libraries. Subjects receiving new or increased interest include individual rights, survival in a natural and man-made environment, crafts, women's lib, men's lib, contemporary music, drug and alcohol use, living inside and outside of the family unit, love, sex, and the occult. Innovative services include clinics, hotlines, reference and referral, live entertainment, training courses, workshops for media production, art fairs, and craft workshops. Emphasis is on the active participation of young adults.

Libraries are collecting materials in traditional formats with a new slant as to content and also those in many types of newer formats. The contemporary YA novel, which reflects the reality of today's teenage environment, can be found in most collections. Novels in paperback and also non-fiction in paperback make up the majority of volumes in many YA collections. Comic books, posters and other types of print material are being collected and made available. Films continue to be popular. Films that primarily entertain and films that inform as well as entertain are found in most libraries serving young adults. Other multi-media productions, including slide-tape presentations and videotape presentations produced specifically for this age group, are finding their way in increasing numbers into YA collections and programs.

Unfortunately, institutional support for YA services in public and school libraries has not kept pace with interest on the part of YA specialists in making YA services a more dynamic part of the total library program. In the late 1960s, most school libraries were riding the crest of increased financial support and recognized importance buoyed by federal involvement. Now as federal dollars and local monies become more difficult to channel into the library, interest in supporting excellence in school media programs is ebbing. Many programs, however, have become well enough established within their school organization to have a power base to help insure continuation of adequate support. The late 1960s also saw increased interest in young adult services in public libraries supported, in many instances, by increased budgets for personnel and new programs. Unfortunately, many of the innovative services were viewed as add-ons, which in times of fiscal crisis are the first to be eliminated. A number of programs described as "outreach" efforts fall into this category. Some services *initially* characterized as outreach, however, have become permanent parts of the library's program of services. It is interesting to note that many of the suggestions made by the YASD Committee on Outreach Programs (published in the booklet, *Look, Listen, Explain: Developing Community Services for Young Adults*) are applicable to types of programming commonly found in libraries today. In the most recent statement about YA programming from YASD, *Directions for Library Service to Young Adults*, the term outreach is applied to types of service aimed at a special and relatively small portion of the YA population who experience barriers to service imposed by institutionalization, handicaps, or extreme social and cultural differences.

Although not officially sanctioned as a statement of standards for YA service in public libraries, these guidelines emanating from a committee in YASD were based on the work of the Task Force on Young Adult Services of the Public Library Association, a group constituted to help PLA arrive at goals and determine guidelines for new standards. Two members of the PLA Task Force also served on the YASD Services Statement Development Committee responsible for the new statement. *Directions for Library Service to Young Adults* can be viewed as a set of guidelines for the continuation of current trends in young adult services. The discussion is divided into three sections: services, materials, and administration. Aspects of service include reference, referral, reader's advisory, programs, outreach, and publicity. The discussion of materials focuses on selection criteria and formats. Concerns of administration include facilities, collection, budget, and staffing. Rather basic in its approach, the document is intended for experienced and new young adult specialists and for libraries beginning or expanding YA services. Much of what is discussed reflects current practice in systems committed to YA work.

The emphasis on the needs of the age group and on the library's program of services designed to meet those needs is evident in the statement of directions. The service orientation is underlined by the fact that the chapter on services comes before the chapter dealing with materials. Different facets of a program of services for young adults are covered in some detail. The concept of YA reference is expanded to include not only reference needs dictated by the classroom assignment but also the information needs of young people that stem from a need to know about things not included or emphasized in most school curricula. Personal information needs and the possession of skills in using materials in a library collection are considered in the reference service section in the guidelines. Related to reference needs are needs for referral to not only books and library materials, but also to community agencies and individuals who might be able to provide information and assistance to young adults.

Perhaps not universally agreed upon are the suggestions that YA librarians in connection with young adult referral work become more activist in their approach to the provision of non-traditional types of library service. The suggestion is made that librarians should stimulate action by the library and other community groups to meet the needs of young adults. The librarian is urged to become an advocate for youth. The definition of readers' advisory service, however, remains the rather traditional one of guiding the young adult to those materials that would be most enjoyable and appropriate for the reader's ability and interest. Programs as defined by the guidelines are those formal and informal happenings, sometimes but not always pre-planned, usually for a group of people either in or outside of the library and under library sponsorship. There is some overlap between programming and other service aspects, but programs are by definition group events. Active involvement and participation of the young person in activities suited to the interests of the young adult age group are said to be basic to meaningful library programs. Outreach is a term used here to denote an attitude toward all types of service rather than particular types of services. The *outreach attitude* includes determining which young adults are not able or willing to use the library and attempting to provide some types of services relevant to their needs and in a way that will capture their interest.

Just as the unique characteristics of young adult literature and young adult librarianship are being recognized by the library profession, the special aspects of serving youth in the library are being given more consideration by library planners and administrators. A great number of varied library responses to the needs of young adults are detailed in state-of-the-art papers in the literature describing young adult services. The expanded coverage of young adult issues in library literature reflects both more recognition of the importance of young adult work and more emphasis on YA services in libraries, as measured by the numbers and types of programs described.

Assessment of the impact of young adult services poses the same problems as does the measurement of any type of library service. Perhaps now that young adult services have become recognized as a legitimate and necessary facet of the library's program package, evaluation of different types of programs and services developed during the last decade will reveal which of the many services are the most effective in different library settings. Proof of impact is the key to the survival of any type of service in a public institution, and perhaps it is time for those who believe in the importance of young adult services to determine which evaluation techniques could be used to provide information about the value of young adult services. Certainly young adults comprise a large segment of our population, and one to which the library should be accountable. If young adult specialists and other library administrators can point to success with a large proportion of the young adults in a community, some of the traditional and newer types of services that are being tried and reported in the literature will have a good chance of surviving and growing.

BIBLIOGRAPHY

American Library Association. Young Adult Services Division, Committee on Outreach Programs for Young Adults. *Look, Listen, Explain: Developing Community Services for Young Adults.* Chicago: ALA, 1975.

American Library Association. Young Adult Services Division, Services Statement Development Committee. *Directions for Library Service to Young Adults.* Chicago: ALA, 1978.

Henne, Frances, Alice Brooks, and Ruth Ersted, eds. *Youth Communication and Libraries: Papers Presented before the Library Institute at the University of Chicago, 1947.* Chicago: American Library Association, 1949.

Post-War Standards for Public Libraries. Chicago: American Library Association, 1943.

A DECADE OF
PUBLIC LIBRARY PROGRAMMING

Carolyn G. Hammond

In *Fair Garden and the Swarm of Beasts*, by Margaret Edwards, there is a section entitled "YA–the Library Bastard." This is most indicative of the neglect that young adult services have suffered in past decades. Edwards expounds the philosophy that "we should attempt through books to take each individual, whatever his reading level, and develop him to his full potential as a reader, widening his interests and deepening his understanding. . . ."[1] This goal could not be reached by shelving books but would have to be accomplished through direct contact with young people. Edwards's ideas concerning the library's approach to young people were adopted by several libraries, and programs with the purpose of attracting young adults to books were developed. Realizing that books are not the only source of information and enjoyment today, young people have been inclined to underestimate the library's potential. To attract young adults, libraries have had to change their images, as youth were no longer going to conform to the staid, quiet world of the public library. Thus, libraries began to venture into a new era of programming for young adults.

One of the innovative programming attempts that was unique for its time was a project of the Oxon Hill Branch of Prince George's County Memorial Library (Maryland). Librarians there responded to an ad in the *Washington Free Press* to rent a group of hippies for a program at the library. The hippies agreed to assist and even to donate their time. Local papers, school papers, and flyers were used to advertise the program. The auditorium was filled to its 250-seat capacity with a jeering crowd when the hippies arrived. Obviously angry with the hippies, the young adults threw eggs, pennies, and a stink bomb. When some order was finally restored, the questions asked generally centered on the Vietnam War, family relationships, use of drugs, and the neo-American church to which these hippies belonged. In reviewing the program, the librarians noted that one goal had been met: young adults who had not previously been to the library attended, and some returned later.[2]

Oxon Hill's "Rent a Hippie" program exemplifies the efforts in the 1960s to design one-shot programs. Others became more involved and dealt not only with programs but with physical facilities as well. Young Adult Project (YAP) was one such program. Officially named the Federal Young Adult Library Services Project, the program was a result of the cooperative efforts of several libraries to determine what was happening with young adults in their communities. The participating libraries—Mountain View Public, San Jose Public, Santa Clara County, and Sunnyvale Public—received a grant from the California State Libraries under Title II of the Library Services and Construction Act. The two-year demonstration grant provided for work with young adults who were "disadvantaged, disaffected and generally non-responsive to public libraries."[3] The projects centered on satellites, YAPs, and a YAPmobile. Begun in the summer of 1968, the first efforts were to put paperbacks on spinner-style racks in common young adult hangouts such as Youth Opportunity Centers, Economic Opportunity Centers, and parks. From that initial effort, locations for YAPs were sought. Some, such as one in Santa Clara, were enthusiastically received by the young people but were met with opposition from adults in the community who did not understand the goals of the project.[4]

YAPs collections were as varied as the clientele which they served. An effort was made to treat all groups alike—Mexican-Americans, hippies, straights, Anglos, and blacks. The young people adopted their own rules, the Six Commandments of YAP, and the centers were run accordingly. Far from the traditional setting of the library, YAPs were decorated with psychedelic posters, and music was played none too quietly. The floors usually were covered with rugs, and furniture was from Goodwill stores. Aside from film programs showing movies such as *Caine Mutiny, The Mouse That Roared,* and *Fail-Safe,* programs were mostly impromptu group discussions, rap sessions, and jam sessions.

The YAPs purchased almost 32,000 books, mostly paperbacks, covering some 2,000 titles, but the biggest attraction for non-readers was the collection of 2,300 record albums. These could be checked out, as could portable typewriters, tools, posters, and 8mm film loops.[5]

Models such as YAP led to the development of still more programs and facilities for young adults in the 1970s. "Levels," named by its users at Great Neck, New York, was a facility for young adults that was developed in a 3,500-square foot area of the lower level of the Great Neck Library. "Levels" was staffed by youth workers and functioned as a semi-independent department funded through the library budget.

There was a community need for a facility open in the evenings for young adult use. Because the area was designed with youth in mind, there were spaces for study and reading, workshops, and discussion groups, and larger areas for dances and performances. Brightly colored walls and ceilings were sound-proofed. A central sound system, paperbacks, periodicals, cassette players, headphones, piano, vending machines, art supplies, and board games were available for the young adults' use. A separate entrance allowed flexible hours apart from those of the main library. Saturday night featured live music with musical groups donating their services. Theatrical groups developed as well.[6]

In an effort to attract young adults, the Oak Park Branch Library in Sacramento, California, converted an office into a "Rap Room" to be used for studying, talking, or small group meetings. A small area in one corner of the library had posters in fluorescent colors with black lights. Materials of interest to young adults, including records, tapes, and games were made available.[7]

The Mount Vernon (New York) Public Library opened a multi-media room for youth. "The Room" was developed primarily for use by junior and senior high students, but it was open to anyone. The purpose was to attract new young adult patrons and to help them make better use of their time by having a place of their own in the library. An advisory group of twenty young people was established to decide policy regarding equipment, materials, and decorations and to assist in paperback and periodical selection. Available for use were a record player with headphones, cassette player, and stereo cassette. Local distributors donated films for programs.[8]

A most unique facility was established in Terre Haute, Indiana, where a center for young adults was placed in a railroad car that had been donated. The Vigo County Public Library wanted to provide more service to the youth of the Hyte Community. The Young People's Advisory Committee was formed to help in decision-making, and Neighborhood Youth Corps enrolees monitored the facility in place of librarians.[9]

Because young people enjoy talking so much, discussion groups are a natural format for young adult programs. The Canton (Ohio) Public Library had a group called Black Pow-Wow, which discussed problems of interest with members of the community. The Free Library of Philadelphia sponsored "The Heavy Weights," a film discussion series on such topics as war, poverty, premarital sex, and drugs.[10] Bridgeport's (Connecticut) library held rap sessions. The Tulsa (Oklahoma) City-County Library promoted spontaneous group discussions that centered on pertinent teenage topics. The public library in Amarillo, Texas, supported discussion groups for high school and college students using current issues and "intercultural selection" as source materials.[11]

The High Point Public Library (North Carolina) had "Young in Touch," a series of monthly programs with the purpose of providing young adults a means of reaching the world through films, books, recordings, and group search. The latest multi-media approaches to problem solving were used in the sharing sessions, which were led and summed up by an adult. One program focusing on man as creator used as a basis for discussion such books as *Introduction to the Art of Movies* by Lewis Jacobs, *The Liveliest Art* by Arthur Knight, and *The Medium Is the Message* by Marshall McLuhan and Quentin Fiore. Examples of records used were *Rubber Soul* by the Beatles and *Steppenwolf* by Steppenwolf. The academy award winning film *Why Man Creates* examined man's motivation, life style, and need for creative expression.[12]

The Ferguson Library of Stanford, Connecticut, presented "Wo/Human: Her Story, Her Options," a program including the film *Anything You Want to Be* and a panel of community women who discussed the topic with young adults.[13] In

Riverside, California, a group at the public library produced a stimulating session by inviting Rita Norling of Los Angeles to speak. Mrs. Norling, who claims to be a real witch, spoke on witchcraft as a religion. Also on the program was Dr. Elizabeth Green, a doctor of metaphysics who discussed astrology.[14]

Don Roberts, writing in *Library Journal*, contends that youth today communicate through music. Their message, their literature, their poetry is transmitted through radio and stereo listening. He claims that librarians too often discard this obvious medium, music, in the belief that young people can be once again returned to the printed form of communication.[15] Being aware of this all-consuming interest in music, many librarians have seized this medium as a basis for programming for young adults.

Grove Hall Branch of the Boston Public Library presented a "soul sound" evening, inviting teenagers to "come hear your sisters sing the music of today."[16] The Forsyth County Library (Winston-Salem, North Carolina) turned its library into a discoteque with strobe lights. The event was broadcast live by radio station WTVB. John W. Jones, spokesman for the library stated that "most YA programming is a failure because it fails to attract youngsters, but we packed them in."[17]

At the Withers Memorial Public Library in Nicholasville, Kentucky, a pilot program for young adults was introduced by a library science class from the University of Kentucky. The topic, "What Makes the Top Twenty?," was supported by Al Snyder, a local disc jockey, who gave a 20-minute presentation. A "Name That Tune" contest was held, with prizes donated by a local music company, and the film *Discovering Jazz* was shown.[18] At Riverside, California, a group of teens gathered each Monday evening in the auditorium of the library for soul sessions. One member of the group acted as disc jockey for each session.[19]

Film programs have long been an area of successful programming for young adults. The Kansas City (Missouri) Public Library sponsored Saturday "reel breaks," which featured films of current interest.[20] The Greensburgh Public Library (Elmsford, New York) worked with two other community agencies to present a film and discussion series concerned with helping youngsters to learn about sex and to protect themselves from child molesters and rapists.[21]

The Boston Public Library's programs for young adults have relied heavily upon the library's film collection. Films are linked with and used to support such topics as sports, comedy, horror, or teen problems.[22] The New York Public Library has had film programs too numerous to mention. In Columbia, Missouri, 200 young adults were welcomed to their new headquarters at the library with "Mini Movies at Midnight," which showed continuous movies, some of which were University of Missouri football game films borrowed from the M.U. Athletic Department.[23]

Young adults are interested not only in watching films but in doing their own filming. A videotape workshop for teenagers was begun by the Film Library and the Office of Young Adult Service of the New York Public Library. Funded through a special grant from the New York State Council on the Arts, the workshop included videotape instruction, special interviews, and location tapes. The equipment came from the Media Equipment Resource Center (MERC), a film, videotape, and sound equipment loan service sponsored by the Council and the Young Filmmakers Foundation. The purpose of the program was to prepare tapes for cable TV. Some items filmed were the Harlem Children's Art Carnival, the South Street Seaport historic area, and a peace march.[24] Young Adult Services of the Los Angeles Public Library sponsored film festivals at the Venice Branch Public Library and the Westchester Branch. Films made and submitted by young people were shown, and prizes were awarded.[25]

A group of black teens in Boston's Roxbury branches created a slide-tape presentation called "Black Is Beautiful." These young people were motivated to do their own money raising for costs of film and processing. In another part of Boston, Andrea Brooks directed to completion a fifteen-minute 16mm film entitled *God Helps Those Who Help Themselves*, which was produced from a script written by twenty young adults. The film is about the emerging criminal adventures of a fourteen-year-old boy and includes a death scene filmed in a casket at a local funeral home.[26]

The Connecticut Young Filmmakers (Children and Young Adults) was formed in August 1971 by Faith Hektoen to encourage young people's skills and enthusiasm in filmmaking throughout the state. Festivals held at public libraries were designed to promote the interchange of films among young people and interested adults. Young people would also be given an opportunity to share their problems, interests, and talents in filmmaking.[27]

As a part of the New York Public Library's young adult program, a group of teens developed a presentation, "Mars Flight," on man's first trip to another planet. The New York Public Library also sponsored video workshops and an on-going radio program, "Teen Book Talk."[28]

"On Your Own" was a 30-minute multi-media assembly program created by young adults at the Free Library of Philadelphia. The presentation featured films, slides, tapes of music and narration, and librarians who gave one-minute book spots. Focusing on the theme of being on your own after school, the main sections were on movies, sports, problems, arts and crafts, the occult, love, and sex. The program was introduced by "Ashes of Doom," an anti-smoking commercial featuring Dracula, and concluded with *Vicious Cycles*, a satiric movie on a cycle gang minus motorcycles.[29]

A group of teens at the Brighton Branch of the Boston Public Library created a media talk based on Paul Zindel's *My Darling, My Hamburger*, using tapes synchronized with a series of pictures for opaque projection.[30] In an effort to get young adults to sell paperbacks to each other, the Maple Heights Regional Library in Cleveland, Ohio, had area high school students develop slide-tape presentations of book talks to be given at local libraries, schools, and other youth organizations. Some titles used were *Forever* by Judy Blume; *Summer of Fear* by Lois Duncan; *We Almost Lost Detroit* by John G. Fuller; *Two from Galilee* by Marjorie Holmes; and *The Late Great Me* by Sandra Scoppetone.[31]

Several branches of the New York Public Library showed films made by young adults in what was probably the city's smallest theater, the Movie Box.

Viewers could see the twenty-minute continuous-loop cartridges on request. Designed and executed by the Young Filmmakers Foundation in cooperation with the Office of Young Adult Services of the New York Public Library, the Movie Box was a three-sided frame, 7'x7' by 4' deep. The Box could be used in a library without disturbing others and could be moved from one branch to another. Life-sized photos of young adults working to produce the films were mounted on the Box to create a mood for the continuous rear-screen projection. The projector was contributed by Fairchild Industrial Products, and the exhibit was made possible through funds of the Film Program of the New York State Council on the Arts. An example of the films used is *Flash* by Jose Colm, a science fiction story about a boy from another planet who saved the earth from an outer space menace. *The Museum Hero*, by Alphonse Sanchez, was a guided tour through the Metropolitan Museum presented as a cops-and-robbers nightmare in a dream.[32]

At the Baker Street Branch Library of the Kern County Library System in Bakersfield, California, fifty seventh grade students joined the library's Video Club, which had been organized as a summer program. These students met in small groups and developed video projects. Programs included interviewing patrons of a nearby car wash to get their views on the gas shortage, working on a young people's talk show, and preparing a series of interviews with a "vampire family of today." The library staff assisted by checking equipment, and one or two adults volunteered to supervise equipment usage. The Video Club provided a means of communication for the young adults as well as an opportunity to learn to use the video equipment as a mode of expression.[33]

Young people are creative and always searching for ways to express themselves. A number of successful programs centered on creative expression in writing, music, theater, and art have been used. The East Los Angeles Library presented "Teatro Popular de la Vida y Muerte," a Chicano theater group from Long Beach State College.[34] The Los Angeles Public Library sponsored a creative art series at its Baldwin Hills Library with an emphasis on original writing and drama. The Riverside (California) Public Library had an "act-in" for teens, and the Queens Borough (New York) Public Library had a four-day festival, "Maytime Maxi," for creative activities.[35] The New York Public Library had a theater workshop for young adults, led by Andora Hodgin, Total Theater, Inc., that resulted in the formation of the New York Youth Theater Alliance, which gave performances at the branches.[36]

Opportunities for criticism and review without the restraints of excessive adult editing and censure have been popular. Published examples of this type of effort are: Enoch Pratt Free Library's *You're the Critic*; Nassau Library System's *Scrutinize*; Prince George's County's (Maryland) *Bookworms*; Dallas's *Whangdoodle*; Boston's *In Books in Boston*;[37] and Queens Borough's (New York) *Verdict*.[38]

The Lincoln Heights Branch of the Los Angeles Public Library published *The Inner Eye*, a creative writing magazine. Through this publication, "culturally deprived" young people were reached and given the opportunity to do away with that misleading label. The magazine provided an outlet for pent-up emotions among Chicanos of the area. The first issues contained poetry and prose that dealt with such topics as war, peace, love, school, and prejudice. There was difficulty in getting participants until the young adults realized that they really could say anything on any subject within the bounds of decency.[39]

Boston Public Library invited answers to the question "What Is a City?"; the response was so great that the library published a book of the verses, essays, and art. Enoch Pratt Free Public Library, with poet Sam Cornish on its staff, involved youth to participate in creative poetry and drama.[40] Orlando Public Library published *The Padded Cell*, a teen magazine of review, art, and opinion. The staff has decided that much can be learned about thought and opinion through a graffiti board and by having school literary magazines and papers available in the library.[41]

The Central Library's Young Adult Department of the Boston Public Library sponsored a summer writing program for teenagers and asked local authors to participate. The librarians also wrote authors across the nation and asked them to contribute. Among those participating were Frank Bonham, Susan Beth Pfeffer (tapes), John Neufeld and Barbara Wersba (letters). Participants were given a packet of materials related to writing. Tapes were played, and the film *Story of a Writer*, in which Ray Bradbury discusses his craft, was shown. Guests were Elvajean Hall, contributor to Lippincott's Portrait of the Nation series; Adrienne Richard, author of *Pistol and the Accomplice*; Laura Shapiro, feature columnist of *The Real Paper* (one of Boston's alternative newspapers); and three local poets, Louis Sasso, Joel Sloman, and Joan Michaelson. As a follow up, three of the young adults were on a local television program to discuss the series and read selections from their own works.[42] Also given at the Boston Public Library was a program on communication by Paul Williams, author and founder of *Crawdaddy* magazine; Williams began his creative work in the Boston Public Library. An on-going program at Boston's Grove Hall Branch has drawn interested young adults to a literary workshop.[43]

A branch of Sacramento City-County Public Library planned a painting class with supplies donated, and paintings were later displayed at the Library.[44] In Orlando, Florida, the library had exhibits of junior and senior high school art works that changed every two weeks. During the summer months, one-man shows by local teen artists were given.[45]

Queens Borough (New York) Public Library had a ballad writing competition, with the only requirement being that the ballads relate in some way to the library. Tampa (Florida) Public Library worked with Youth of Tampa Association to support activities in folk singing, rock concerts, art films, and dancing.[46]

Rather than attempting to draw young people to the library, programs often involve taking the materials to popular teen centers. Part of a federally funded project for Latin Americans in Oakland planned to use a small bookmobile to serve young adults. New York State's Mid-York Library System had a van for its outreach programs to underpriviledged in Utica. The van, called a "Whatz It," provided multi-media service and was equipped with a 16mm projector and a rear-view daylight screen for sidewalk shows. Its public address system could play the latest in soul or rock music, and paperbacks were plentiful. The Tulsa (Oklahoma) City-County Library has a bookmobile that carries not only books but also materials for such activities as basketball games, parties, or drawing classes.[47]

In the summer of 1970, the Rochester (New York) Public Library's Charlotte Branch took its service to the Charlotte Beach. Dick Gervichas, librarian, parked a station wagon at the gate, put books on the tailgate and hood, and posted signs, "Roast and Read" and "Borrow a Book."[48] Buffalo and Erie County's (New York) "Ram Van" had a canopy and a wide assortment of media. Babysitter training courses, storytelling workshops, and a variety of film festivals were offered.[49]

Libraries also provide practical services for young adults in the areas of job counseling, job hunting, and tutoring. The Oakland (California) Public Library had a Job Information Day, with counseling on how to apply for a job, how to act in an interview, and how to hold a job. They also had college clinics for the college-bound.[50] In addition, they had a tutorial program using 65 tutors for some 100 students in subjects ranging from math to chemistry.[51]

The Mesa (Arizona) Public Library conducted special training classes to help high school drop-outs obtain education and training.[52] New York's Babylon Public Library used an Odd Job Bureau with the purpose of helping young people locate part-time jobs. Job hunters registered with the library noting the type of job that they would like. The only requirement for the job hunter was a library card.[53] The Carnegie Library in Pittsburgh, Pennsylvania, sponsored "Careers without College Day" to call attention to local training and apprentice programs. Individuals consultations were available.[54]

The St. Louis County Library had cyclo-teacher machines, programmed self-instruction devices, available for use by young adults. Students could try some 276 study cycles in such areas as reference skills, English and spelling, math, social studies, science, and family activity.[55] As a part of the Enoch Pratt Community Action Program, a group of teenagers was given an opportunity to work under the direction of supervisors in a variety of situations. Some places to which the students were sent included children's departments of libraries, a Catholic women's college, the State Library for the Physically Handicapped in recording for the blind, the mental hospital library, and the audio-visual department of the Health Library.[56]

In an effort to attract and please young adults, libraries have attempted to develop collections specially geared to their interests. In Warwick, Rhode Island, the library had the "Bike Rack," a paperback section stocked with fiction and non-fiction of young adult concern. No signs labeled the collection as young adult; the only mark was an old-fashioned, high-wheeled bike stamped on the back of each book to aid in shelving—thus the title "Bike Rack."[57]

In Merrill, Wisconsin, a Youth Advisory Committee helped to build a collection of paperbacks and cassettes (music and documentary). Through a grant under the Right to Read Program under Title I of the Library Service and Construction Act, the library began its collection. It also obtained three cassette players for circulation and racks to hold the books and cassettes.[58]

In Orlando, Florida, the library staff decided to concentrate on a collection of materials and services rather than on a series of programs to attract young adults. The emphasis was on paperbacks, although they did continue to have some hardbacks in both fiction and non-fiction. They also subscribed to some thirty favorite teen magazines, and back issues could be checked out. Posters were laminated and available for circulation, as were records. Another popular collection were the comic books. The exception to no programming at Orlando was their Youth Night. This event, which was held on all three floors of the library, featured continuous programs of rock and soul bands, magic, astrology, yoga, biking, judo, fashion shows, handwriting analysis, teen films, contests, and prizes.[59]

Libraries have found popularity in programs that pay tribute to minority cultures. The Ontario City (California) Library observed holidays of importance in Mexico, such as Cinco de Mayo and 16 de Septiembre. The Los Angeles Public Library participated in a three-night Las Posadas. The Queens Borough (New York) Public Library invited young adults to "Have Fun in Fun City," which involved attending street festivals honoring Italian saints' days and other minority events. The Boston Public Library made plans to decorate parade floats to celebrate Puerto Rican Independence Day, July 25, and the Chinese New Year.[60]

The Oak Park Branch Library in Sacramento, California, created a "soul shelf" of books on black history, which developed into one of the largest black history collections in the Sacramento area public libraries. For their Black History Week Program, the guest speaker was from the Watts Writers' Workshop, and local high school students performed African dances and presented an African fashion show. The library also participated in an Afro-American Unity Festival with another library. This involved an exhibit of books and a bibliography on black history, as well as works by local artists.[61]

A number of libraries have played upon topics of current interest in an attempt to attract young adults. At the Haydon Burns Library in Jacksonville, Florida, a series of occult programs were presented as a Halloween special for young adults. The staff scheduled a five-round program that included the showing of the film *Dracula* and lectures on witchcraft, yoga, palmistry, and spiritualism.[62]

Oxon Hill Branch of Prince George's County Memorial Library (Maryland) sponsored a series on drugs that featured a senator's representative who spoke on drug legislation. Films on drug use were shown, and there was a speaker whose topic was "Working with the Addicted." Boston's Brighton Branch Library presented a drug series with a street priest and a panel of former teenage drug users. The Free Library of Philadelphia named its drug program "How Was the Trip?" and gave a play that showed the effects of drugs on an average family.[63]

Prince George's County Memorial Library System (Maryland) invited the 1976 Olympic Gold Medal Winner in boxing, Sugar Ray Leonard, to the Fairmount Heights and Oxon Hill Branches. He met with groups, discussed what it was like to win in the Olympics, and related his experiences in early training and fights. Afterwards, young adults could get his autograph and ask questions.

This particular program sparked interest in young adults who had not been to the library previously. As a follow-up, the library provided materials on boxing, the Olympics, and sports in general.[64]

The Maplewood Community Branch Library of the Rochester Public Library (New York) offered six weekly, one-hour workshop sessions on babysitting. They used a 4-H program specialist with the Cooperative Extension Association of Monroe County, a nursery school teacher, a registered nurse, a Red Cross instructor, a policeman, and a fireman to discuss topics such as "Role of the Babysitter," "What Children Are Like," "Child Care," and "Safety and Emergencies."[65]

The Alameda County Library of Hayward, California, held "Valley Funk and Flash," a jean decorating contest for teens and adults at the Dublin and Pleasanton Library Branches. Local merchants donated prizes.[66] One of the most unique attention-getters was found at Fremont Main Library, also in Hayward, where the staff got a local firm to donate a water couch for use in the library.[67]

In Columbia, Missouri, the Fulton Public Library Service Center had an evening during which local distributors exhibited 28 different models of motorcycles outside of the entrance to the library. At the same time, films borrowed from motorcycle companies were shown inside the library.[68] Other unusual program topics that have centered on teen interests are skateboarding (New York's Westchester Library System); hairstyling, with curling irons and blow dryers (Indiana Lake County Public Library); and underwater search and rescue (New York's Long Beach Library).[69] The New York Public Library has presented such varied programs for teens as holography; magic show; zoo day, with a fifteen-foot python; a tai chi chuan demonstration; camping and outdoor survival; instruction in camera use; T-shirt silk-screen printing; kite making; bicycle care, repair, and safety; macramé; mobiles; horse care; and a 747 pilot training demonstration.[70]

Teens enjoy exploring new and unknown places. Libraries have attracted young adults by offering opportunities for them to visit points of interest in surrounding areas. The Boston Public Library has presented "encounters with the unfamiliar" through field trips. As part of a "Library Inside-Out Program," teens visited the airport, the Isabelle Stuart Gardener Museum, the Massachusetts legislature, and a beauty culture school.[71] Teenagers who were selected for the Enoch Pratt Community Action Program were taken on field trips to the FBI building in Washington; a NASA rocket launching facility in Wallops Island, Virginia; Gettysburg; and the Pennsylvania Dutch country.[72]

Programming and selection of materials for young adults is a wide-open area, with possibilities as vast as the ideas teenagers can conceive. The key to successful programming seems to be the development of programs that are closely attuned to the interests and desires of youth. Librarians should not seek to "reform" young adults and return them to "the good old days," but rather capitalize upon their present lifestyles and ideas as sources of program topics.

NOTES

[1] Margaret A. Edwards, *The Fair Garden and the Swarm of Beasts* (New York: Hawthorne Books, 1974), p. 88.

[2] Susan Uebelacker, "Rent a Hippie," *Top of the News* 94 (June 1968): 420-29.

[3] Regina Minudri, "What's a YAP?," *Top of the News* 26 (November 1969): 64.

[4] Ibid., p. 65.

[5] Ibid., pp. 66-68.

[6] "Where the Action Is: A Report on a Unique YA Facility," *American Libraries* 6 (June 1975): 362.

[7] Rose Marks, "What You Always Wanted to Do in Your Library but Were Afraid to Try," *Kansas Library Bulletin* 41 (1972): 14-16.

[8] Ruth M. Kaufmann, "The Mystery of the Room," *Wilson Library Bulletin* 47 (September 1972): 59-61.

[9] Edward N. Howard, "Terre Haute: No One Asked," *Wilson Library Bulletin* 43 (May 1969): 888-92.

[10] Jane Manthorne, "Provisions and Programs for Disadvantaged Young People," *Library Trends* 20 (October 1971): 421.

[11] Ibid., p. 425.

[12] "High Point Public Library Sponsors the Young in Touch Series," *North Carolina Libraries* 28 (Fall 1970): 146.

[13] Mary K. Chelton, "YA Programming Roundup," *Top of the News* 32 (November 1975): 45.

[14] "Program Notes," *Library Journal* 95 (March 15, 1970): 1155.

[15] Don Roberts, "Listen, Miss, Mrs., Mr. Librarian," *Library Journal* 95 (November 15, 1970): 3965-67.

[16] Manthorne, p. 421.

[17] "For Kids and YAs: Story Festival, Disco and Sex," *Library Journal* 102 (July 1977): 1448-49.

[18] JoAnn V. Rogers, "Town and Gown Present a Pilot YA Program," *Top of the News* 33 (Summer 1977): 369-73.

[19] "Program Notes," p. 1155.

[20] Manthorne, p. 421.

[21] "For Kids and YAs: Story Festival, Disco and Sex," p. 1449.

[22] "Spotlight on Young Adult Services: Boston," *Top of the News* 28 (June 1972): 476.

[23] "Spotlight on Young Adult Services: Columbia, Mo.," *Top of the News* 28 (June 1972): 378.

[24] "NYPL Videotape Workshop," *Library Journal* 97 (February 15, 1972): 724.

[25] Patty Campbell and Jane Brooks, "The Media Novice Plans a Young Film-maker's Festival," *Wilson Library Bulletin* 47 (January 1973): 440-45.

[26] Manthorne, pp. 424-25.

[27] Faith H. Hektoen, "Film-making by Youth," *Wisconsin Library Bulletin* 69 (May-June 1973): 171-72.

[28] Chelton, p. 45.

[29] Ibid., p. 46.

[30] "Spotlight on Young Adult Services: Boston," p. 376.

[31] Catherine Monnin, "YAs Sell Paperbacks to YAs," *Top of the News* 34 (Fall 1977): 85-86.

[32] "The Movie Box," *Wilson Library Bulletin* 44 (June 1970): 994.

[33] "California Library Uses Cable TV," *Library Journal* 98 (October 15, 1973): 3100.

[34] Manthorne, p. 421.

[35] Ibid., p. 424.

[36] Chelton, p. 45.

[37] Manthorne, p. 423.

[38] Chelton, p. 45.

[39] Joseph L. Buelna, "Creative Writing: The Inner Eye," *Wilson Library Bulletin* 45 (April 1971): 750-53.

[40] Manthorne, p. 424.

[41] "Spotlight on Young Adult Services: Orlando," *Top of the News* 28 (June 1972): 387.

[42] Andrea Brooks, "No Magic Formula," *Top of the News* 30 (June 1974): 410-14.

[43] "Spotlight on Young Adult Services: Boston," p. 476.

[44] Manthorne, p. 424.

[45] "Spotlight on Young Adult Services: Orlando," p. 382.

[46] Manthorne, p. 424.

[47] Ibid., p. 426.

[48] Ibid.

[49] Patricia Glass Schuman, "SLJ News Roundup," *School Library Journal* 97 (December 1972): 4030.

50 Manthorne, p. 421.

51 Ibid., p. 428.

52 Ibid.

53 "For Kids and YAs: Computers to Skateboards," *Library Journal* 102 (August 1977): 1550.

54 Chelton, p. 46.

55 "For Kids and YAs: Computers to Skateboards," p. 1550.

56 Arthur Myers, "Enoch Pratt's Community Action Program," *Top of the News* 26 (April 1970): 273-81.

57 "Backpedalling to a YA Shelf: The Warwick, R.I. 'Bike Rack.' " *Library Journal* 101 (February 1, 1976): 472.

58 Ramon R. Hernandez, "Youth Choices and Simple Processes: The Young Adult Compact Media Project at Merrill," *Wisconsin Library Bulletin* 68 (January-February 1972): 32-36.

59 "Spotlight on Young Adult Services: Orlando," pp. 382-87.

60 Manthorne, p. 422.

61 Marks, pp. 15-16.

62 "Florida Library Rebuffs Critics, Goes on with Occult Series," *Library Journal* 97 (January 15, 1972): 236.

63 Manthorne, p. 420.

64 "Olympic Boxing Champ at Two PGML Branches," *School Library Journal* 23 (February 1977): 24-25.

65 "Babysitters par Excellence," *School Library Journal* 22 (May 1976): 43.

66 Chelton, p. 48.

67 Ibid., p. 49.

68 "Spotlight on Young Adult Services: Columbia, Mo.," p. 378.

69 "For Kids and YAs: Computers to Skateboards," p. 1550.

70 Chelton, p. 45.

71 Manthorne, p. 423.

72 Myers, p. 277.

BIBLIOGRAPHY

"Babysitters par Excellence." *School Library Journal* 22 (May 1976): 43.

"Backpedalling to a YA Shelf: The Warwick, R.I. 'Bike Rack.' " *Library Journal* 101 (February 1, 1976): 472.

Brooks, Andrea. "No Magic Formula." *Top of the News* 30 (June 1974): 410-14.

Brown, Mary A. "Teen-Age Videotape Workshop." *Film Library Quarterly* 5 (Summer 1972): 16-21.

Buelna, Joseph L. "Creative Writing: The Inner Eye." *Wilson Library Bulletin* 45 (April 1971): 750-53.

"California Library Uses Cable TV." *Library Journal* 98 (October 15, 1973): 3100.

Campbell, Patty, and Jane Brooks. "The Media Novice Plans a Film-maker's Festival." *Wilson Library Bulletin* 47 (January 1973): 440-45.

"The Care and Feeding of Young Adults."   Orlando, FL: Young Adult Department, Orlando Public Library, 1975.

Cheatham, Bertha M. "SLJ's 1977 News Roundup." *School Library Journal* 24 (December 1977): 17-23.

Chelton, Mary K. "YA Programming Roundup." *Top of the News* 32 (November 1975): 43-50.

Edwards, Margaret A. *The Fair Garden and the Swarm of Beasts.* New York: Hawthorne Books, 1974.

"Florida Library Rebuffs Critics, Goes on with Occult Series." *Library Journal* 97 (January 15, 1972): 236.

"For Kids and YAs: Computers to Skateboards." *Library Journal* 102 (August 1977): 1550.

"For Kids and YAs: Story Festival, Disco and Sex." *Library Journal* 102 (July 1977): 1448-49.

Guiliano, Lillian. "It's Fun to Make Movies at the Library." *Top of the News* 33 (Fall 1976): 79-81.

Hektoen, Faith H. "Film-making by Youth." *Wisconsin Library Bulletin* 69 (May-June 1973): 171-72.

Hernandez, Ramon R. "Youth Choices and Simple Processes. The Young Adult Compact Media Project at Merrill." *Wisconsin Library Bulletin* 68 (January-February 1972): 32-36.

"High Point Public Library Sponsors the Young in Touch Series." *North Carolina Libraries* 28 (Fall 1970): 146.

Kaufmann, Ruth M. "The Mystery of the Room." *Wilson Library Bulletin* 47 (September 1972): 59-61.

"Kenneth H. Sayers: YA Librarian with a Do-It-Yourself Flair." *Wilson Library Bulletin* 49 (January 1975): 344-45.

"Library Opportunity Room." *New Jersey Libraries* 5 (September 1972): 4.

Madden, Susan. "Library in Lock Up." *Illinois Libraries* 56 (September 1974): 562-64.

Manthorne, Jane. "Provisions and Programs for Disadvantaged Young People." *Library Trends* 20 (October 1971): 416-31.

Marks, Rose. "What You Always Wanted to Do in Your Library but Were Afraid to Try." *Kansas Library Bulletin* 41 (1972): 14-16.

Minudri, Regina. "What's a YAP?" *Top of the News* 26 (November 1969): 62-68.

Minudri, Regina, and Reed Coats. "Two Years after . . . Reflections from YAP." *Library Journal* 98 (March 15, 1973): 967-71.

"The Movie Box." *Wilson Library Bulletin* 44 (June 1970): 994.

Myers, Arthur. "Enoch Pratt's Community Action Program." *Top of the News* 26 (April 1970): 273-81.

"NYPL Videotape Workshop." *Library Journal* 97 (February 15, 1972): 724.

"Olympic Boxing Champ at Two PGML Branches." *School Library Journal* 23 (February 1977): 24-25.

"Program Notes." *Library Journal* 95 (March 15, 1970): 1155.

Roberts, Don. "Listen, Miss, Mrs., Mr. Librarian." *Library Journal* 95 (November 15, 1970): 3965-67.

Rogers, JoAnn V. "Town and Gown Present a Pilot YA Program." *Top of the News* 33 (Summer 1977): 369-73.

Schuman, Patricia Glass. "SLJ News Roundup." *School Library Journal* 97 (December 1972): 4027-33.

"Spotlight on Young Adult Services: Boston." *Top of the News* 28 (June 1972): 374-77.

"Spotlight on Young Adult Services: Columbia, Mo." *Top of the News* 28 (June 1972): 378-81.

"Spotlight on Young Adult Services: Orlando." *Top of the News* 28 (June 1972): 382-87.

"Teen 'Underground' Library Withstands Attack." *Library Journal* 94 (March 15, 1969): 1284.

Uebelacker, Susan. "Rent a Hippie." *Top of the News* 24 (June 1968): 420-29.

"Where the Action Is: A Report on a Unique YA Facility." *American Libraries* 6 (June 1975): 362.

DEVELOPMENTAL NEEDS OF
YOUNG ADULTS AND
LIBRARY SERVICES

Marilyn W. Greenberg

Adolescence is a period of transition and rapid change, a period character-ized by accelerated physical, physiological, and cognitive development, and by new and changing social demands and expectations. The physiological changes of pubescence are frequently used to determine the beginning of the period known as adolescence, while sociological criteria are used to define its end and a person's passage to adult status. Such events as the end of education, economic independence, and marriage are considered evidence of adult status.

During the period of adolescence, the young adult must accomplish five developmental tasks. Havighurst defined a developmental task as,

> a task which arises at or about a certain period in the life of the individual, successful achievement of which leads to his happiness and to success with later tasks, while failure leads to unhappiness in the individual, disapproval by the society, and difficulty with later tasks.[1]

These developmental tasks, which define the structure, nature, and milieu of adolescence are:

1) adjustment to the physical changes of puberty and later adolescent growth and the flood of new impulses brought on by genital maturity;

2) development of a sense of identity and a system of values;

3) development of independence from parents or other caretakers;

4)   establishment of effective social and working relationships with same- and opposite-sex peers;

5)   preparation for a vocation.[2]

Understanding these tasks is necessary for an understanding of the needs of young adults, and it makes possible the structuring of library services to meet these needs. Thus each is examined in detail in the following pages, and is further considered for its implications for library service.

   Adjustment to the physical changes of puberty and later adolescent growth and the flood of new impulses brought on by genital maturity.   The period of adolescence begins with puberty, when sexual maturation becomes evident. This maturation of sexual organs is accompanied by an acceleration in the rate of increase in height and weight, a rate that varies widely in its intensity, duration, and age of onset. The young adult is acutely aware of the entire growth process, as the rapid increases in height and weight, changing body dimensions, and changes related to sexual maturation threaten her or his feeling of self-consistency. No longer is the adolescent able to recognize the self of yesterday in the strange person of today. The young adolescent is very concerned with the physical aspects of the self and needs reassurance that she or he meets the norm, as well as time to integrate these rapid changes into a slowly emerging sense of a positive, self-confident identity.
   Case studies show that personal and social adjustment during adolescence may be influenced by the individual's rate of physical maturation.[3] It has been established that early-maturing boys command an advantage in social relations, not only during adolescence but in later years of life as well. Also, her level of mature physical development contributes to the kind of reputation that a girl has in adolescence. Thus, the young adult has to deal with a developing sexuality, which involves integrating sexuality meaningfully with the other aspects of a sense of self and in relationships with others. There is a significant increase in specifically sexual interests and behavior during adolescence. This takes different forms of expression, depending on the sex of the young adult and on a variety of psychological and cultural forces. In the young male, the drive is imperious and biologically specific, while among girls, sexual drive is more diffuse and ambiguous.
   The implications for library service are that it must provide materials on growth, sex education, birth control, pregnancy, abortion, and venereal diseases. Such information may be in the form of books, periodicals, films, filmstrips, crisis centers, and referral services. The young adult should have available as much information on these subjects as is needed. Regarding the inconsistent image that the young adult has of the self, the young adult to whom new-found sexuality seems strange needs the opportunity to compare notes with others in order to evaluate the normality of his or her own situation. Materials, both fiction and non-fiction, about young adults who are dealing with their own sexuality must be provided. Opportunities could be provided for group interaction in which young

adults could share feelings and fears; such sessions might be sponsored jointly with health and/or counseling services. The library is obligated to provide these programs for all young adults, including exceptional and homebound young people. The blind, the deaf, and the handicapped young adults are also growing and have concerns about their bodies and their sexuality. Programs must be provided for these young adults, too.

Development of a sense of identity. Erikson considers the essential task of adolescence to be the establishment of a sense of one's own identity as a unique person.[4] Erikson calls this concept "ego-identity." The young adult with a strong sense of ego-identity sees himself/herself as a distinctive individual. There is a feeling of wholeness, a separateness from others, and a unity of the self—and a self-perceived consistency over a period of time. It is not surprising that the search for identity should be particularly acute at the stage of development when rapid changes challenge any feeling of self-consistency. The rapid changes increase the difficulty of achieving and maintaining a perception of the self as clearly defined. At this time, when the individual is confronted with internal physical, physiological, and cognitive changes, that person must also deal with the intellectual, social, and vocational demands of adulthood. Erikson suggests that prolonged adolescence can be viewed as a psychosocial moratorium, during which the young adult, through free role experimentation, may find a niche in society. This moratorium is a period characterized by a selective permissiveness on the part of society and of provocative playfulness on the part of youth.

Erikson describes the specific tasks of developing a sense of identity as:

1) to maintain the most important ego defenses against the vastly growing intensity of impulses (now invested in a matured genital apparatus and powerful muscle system);

2) to learn to consolidate the most important and conflict-free achievements in line with work opportunities;

3) to resynthesize all childhood identification in some unique way and yet in concordance with the roles offered by some wider section of society.[5]

Implications for library service here involve the fact that stories of young adults passing through adolescence provide examples for adolescents of other people dealing with the same problems of adolescence. These stories may be fiction or non-fiction, and the format may be print, non-print, or real persons. Programs that provide opportunities for the young adult to identify with, discuss, understand, analyze, or merely enjoy the behavior of the subject should be developed. The library can provide additional opportunities for self-actualization by employing young adults in meaningful library work. This work has implications for the need to choose and prepare for a vocation as well as for developing a sense of identity.

Development of a system of values.   The dramatic progress in physical and physiological development that occurs during the adolescent years is accompanied by impressive gains in cognitive development.[6] During adolescence, many kinds of mental ability, especially those least dependent on experience, approach their peak. The young adult is able to master cognitive tasks that could be performed in middle childhood with great difficulty, if at all. Significant changes occur in the nature of young adults' mental processes, in the ways in which they are able to define problems and to reason about them. These cognitive changes influence the nature of parent-child relationships; of emerging personality characteristics and psychological defense mechanisms; of planning future educational and vocational goals; of mounting concerns with social, political, and personal values; and of a developing sense of ego identity. This increased cognitive growth enables the young adult to deal with increasingly complex educational and vocational demands.

According to Piaget, there are four major stages in cognitive development: the sensorimotor stage (birth to eighteen months), the preoperational stage (eighteen months to seven years), the stage of concrete operations (seven to twelve years), and the stage of formal operations (twelve years and up).[7] In the period of concrete operations, the child begins to extend thought from the actual toward the potential. Children in the concrete-operational stage become increasingly capable of dealing with the properties of objects and relationships among them. However, the starting point for the concrete-operational child is always the real rather than the potential, and the child can only reason about those things with which there has been direct personal experience. The advent of the stage of formal operations involves a shift of emphasis from the real to the possible. The young adult is able to approach a problem by trying to imagine all of the possible relationships that might obtain in a given body of data. The young adult becomes capable of hypothetico-deductive thinking, which makes his thought much richer, broader, and more flexible than that of the concrete-operational child.

The adolescent can take his or her own thought as an object and reason about it.[8] This newly acquired ability to reflect results in the young adult thinking about his or her own thoughts and analyzing his or her own actions. Formal-operational thought not only enables the adolescent to conceptualize personal thought, but it also permits conceptualization of the thoughts of other people. It is the belief that others are preoccupied with his or her appearance and behavior that constitutes the egocentrism of the adolescent.[9] The adolescent is continually constructing, or reacting to, an imaginary audience, but fails to differentiate the concerns of personal thoughts from those of others. Adolescent egocentrism passes as the young adult moves into adulthood and is able to differentiate between personal preoccupations and the thoughts of others.

The cognitive structures of the formal-operational stage are used to question parents' values; to become aware of the discrepancy between the actual and the possible; to criticize existing social, political, and religious systems; and to consider alternative systems. The level and complexity of the young adult's political thinking, value systems, and conceptions of morality all depend to a significant extent on the individual's degree of cognitive development.

The demands placed upon the young adult by society require a continuing reappraisal of moral values and beliefs, and the problem of developing a strong sense of ego identity is inseparable from the problem of values. Kohlberg suggests an orderly sequence of moral development, six stages of moral thought divided into three major levels: pre-conventional, conventional, and post-conventional.[10] Kohlberg stresses that attainment of an appropriate cognitive stage is a necessary but not sufficient condition for attainment of the corresponding moral stage. Conventional level stages are dominant during preadolescence, as the young person begins to approach the cognitive stage of formal-operational thought. With the onset of adolescence and the development of formal-operational thought, the young adult is likely to reach the post-conventional state of moral development, which is characterized by autonomous moral principles that have validity and application apart from the authority of the group or persons who hold them. At the beginning of this level of moral thought, moral behavior tends to be thought of in terms of general rights and standards that have been examined and agreed upon by society as a whole. Later, there is an increasing orientation toward internal decisions of conscience, but without clear rational principles. The next change is toward an effort to formulate and be guided by "abstract ethical principles appealing to logical comprehensiveness, universality and consistency."[11] They are universal principles of justice, of the reciprocity and equality of human rights, and of respect for the dignity of human beings as individual persons. The questioning of conventional morality and conventional reality associated with logical and moral stage development is also central to the adolescent's identity concerns. All accounts of adolescence stress both the sense of questioning and the parallel discovery of or search for a new self of the young adult.

The implications for library service are rather obvious: in the period of adolescence, the young adult is at the peak of intellectual capacity, capable of abstract thinking and able to handle complex thought. This enables the young adult to understand difficult concepts and subjects on an adult level. There is no limit (except individual interest) to the subjects that the young adult can explore. Combined with the development of moral thinking and the need to define a philosophy of life, the development in cognitive capability opens up the field of philosophy, political science, religion, ethics, government, economics, ecology, futurism, current events, sociology, anthropology, and literature. Programs and materials that stimulate intellectual curiosity or contribute to the development of a personal philosophy meet the need of the young adult to develop a system of values.

Development of independence from parents or other caretakers. Development of independence is important, not only in itself, but because of its relationship to the other needs of adolescence. Without the achievement of a reasonable degree of separation and autonomy, the young adult cannot achieve mature sexual or peer relationships, confident pursuit of a vocation, or a sense of identity.[12] All of these require a positive image of the self as separate, unified, and consistent over time. The severity of the young adult's independence-dependence conflicts, and the ease with which they are resolved in the direction of greater independence, depend to a large extent on previous and current parent-child relationships.

Establishing independence from parents is a complex matter because the motivations and rewards for independence and for continued dependence are both likely to be strong, thus leading to conflict and vacillating behavior. Complicating the matter further are likely contradictions in attitudes toward adolescent independence within individual parents. In addition, the years of adolescence are likely to be difficult ones for the family, because the marriage is most likely to be at mid-stage when the children are adolescents. The kinds of conflicts to which middle-aged parents are exposed during their children's adolescent years and the ways in which they cope with them can profoundly affect their children's changes of mastering the developmental tasks of adolescence. In addition, our society provides no clear pattern of transition from dependence to independence. In fact, the laws relating to the age at which adulthood begins vary among states and even within individual states.

As for implications for library service, the struggle to achieve independence is generally conducted away from the arena of the library, although work experiences in the library can contribute to the young adult's independence. A major thrust toward meeting this need can be achieved by programs and materials that focus the young adult's attention on the struggle for independence and lead to greater personal understanding of the person's own actions and motivations and those of the parents.

Establishment of effective social and working relationships with same- and opposite-sex peers. Certainly, peers play an important role in the psychological development of adolescents. Peer relations provide an opportunity to learn how to interact with age-mates, to control social behavior, to develop age-relevant skills and interests, and to share similar problems and feelings.[13] Peers play a more important role in adolescence than in childhood, as relations with same- and opposite-sex peers come close to serving as prototypes for later adult relationships. Ties with parents have become progressively looser as greater independence from them is achieved. Increased strain and conflict with the family may cause the adolescent to be less likely to share her or his inner life and outward behavior with parents.

The role of the peer group in helping the adolescent to define personal identity assumes particular importance at this age, then, because at no other stage of development is the individual's sense of identity so fluid. It is desirable that a major part of the young adult's experiences with peers be positive because, more so than at any other time, as the young adult needs to be able to share strong and often confusing emotions, doubts, and dreams.

The nature of the peer groups and the functions they serve change with age. During middle childhood and preadolescence, the child's peer relationships center around neighborhood play groups, which are likely to be composed of same-sex peers. As the young adult enters junior high school and spends less time at home, the range of his acquaintances broadens. However, the same-sex peer group continues into the adolescent period. The next stage is a movement toward heterosexuality in the group structure, which begins with interaction between one group of males and one group of females. Gradually heterosexual groups are formed, and the adolescent period ends with the development of loosely associated groups of couples.

Friendships perform a special function in adolescence, and close friendships contribute to a young adult's development in ways that the broader peer group cannot contribute. They are more intimate, involve more intense feelings, are more honest and open, and less concerned with self-conscious attempts at role-playing to gain greater popularity and social acceptance. The friendship offers a climate for growth and self-knowledge that the family is not equipped to offer. Friendships may help the young adult in dealing with complex personal feelings and with those of others. They allow the free expression of suppressed feelings of anger or anxiety and provide evidence that others have many of the same doubts, hopes, fears, and strong feelings.

During preadolescence and early adolescence, friendships tend to be more superficial. With the approach of middle adolescence, the relation becomes one that is mutual, interactive, and emotionally interdependent. The personality of the other and the other's response to the self become the central themes of the friendship. The opportunity for shared thoughts and feelings help to ease the gradual and initially uncertain transition toward heterosexual relations and a newly defined sex-role identity. By late adolescence, the passionate quality of the friendship recedes and is replaced by a more equable tie to the other. As the young adult begins self-definition, to find a basis for that personal identity, and to develop fairly secure psychological defenses, intense dependence or identification with close friends becomes less vital. More meaningful heterosexual relationships are likely to have begun, further diluting the exclusiveness of the young adult's reliance on same-sex friends.

Regarding relations with opposite-sex peers, the awakening of sexual impulses and related physiological and psychological changes in early adolescence are likely to provoke a temporary period of acute self-consciousness and anxiety both about sex in general and about peers of the opposite sex. As maturation continues, boys and girls begin to pay more attention to one another. In their early stages, heterosexual relationships still reflect many preadolescent characteristics. Self-preoccupation remains strong, and deep emotional involvement with opposite-sex peers is rare. At this time, group activities are common. Increasing familiarity with opposite-sex peers and confidence in one's ability to relate to individual peers of the opposite sex increases the maturity of heterosexual relationships.

The primary implications for library service in this area lie in young adults' interests in materials that describe and analyze the interaction of young men and young women. The level of maturity and the success of the young adult in developing competence in this area determine the level of maturity of the materials needed. Young adults are interested in same-sex interaction as well as opposite-sex interaction. They are interested in materials that deal with friendship as well as materials that deal with romance. Programs that bring young adults together in a setting that provides opportunity for social interaction are useful in meeting the need to establish effective social and working relationships with same- and opposite-sex peers. Even if the library does not intend to meet these needs by providing social situations, comfortable, informal library areas may soon become meeting places for young adults who would rather interact than read, view, listen, study, or work.

Preparation for a vocation. The problem of deciding on and preparing for a career represents one of the critical tasks of adolescence, and there are three distinguishable periods in the maturation of vocational choice: the fantasy period, the tentative period, and the realistic period.[14] Beginning with preadolescence is a progression into the tentative period, in which there are four stages: interest, capacities, values, and transition. At the beginning of the tentative period, the influence of the young adult's interests predominates. As the person matures, she or he begins to assess personal capacity for actually performing the jobs in which there is interest. Later, the young person attempts to integrate those interests and capacities into a broader value system. Once that happens, the young adult is ready for the transition to the period of realistic choice—to assess aspirational level and job objectives, and then make educational and vocational plans.

Two influences that greatly affect vocational goals are social class and sex group membership. Social class is a factor in determining the kinds of occupations with which the young adult is familiar and the social acceptability of a given occupation to the young adult, his family, and his peers. Although significant changes are occurring in the vocational orientation of increasing numbers of girls, identification with an adult role for many females still involves assuming primarily the role of wife and mother. The range of vocational choices among girls is more restricted than among boys and is less influenced by socioeconomic status.

Although numbers of contemporary young adults are disenchanted with the contemporary vocational world, a majority of American young people still hold to many traditional beliefs commonly associated with the Protestant work ethic. A major problem, however, is the number of young adults who currently want and need work, but who are unable to obtain it. Poorly educated young adults with few skills will be increasingly penalized in the future as automation and technical change produce significant shifts in employment patterns.

The implications for library service seem to be that libraries must provide many varied materials and programs about careers. Today, the young adult is often removed from a large number of vocations but needs as much information as possible about the potential choices. The library must provide information about schools as well as about careers. Programs that give information about counseling services, career guidance centers, testing services, careers, and schools are an essential part of library service to young adults.

■ ■ ■

Much of the time of adolescence is spent away from the library, away from reading, away from studies, and in interaction with parents and peers. The young adult is a passionate individual, and pursues activities with intensity. These years see intense personal interaction. But, there are also times of absorption in reading, viewing, and listening, times of comprehensive investigation, philosophical questioning, and exhaustive analysis. The library, with its personnel, materials, and programs, can stimulate such activities and be ready to serve when the demand is made.

NOTES

[1] Robert J. Havighurst, *Developmental Tasks and Education*, 2nd ed. (New York: David McKay, 1952), p. 2.

[2] John Janeway Conger, "A World They Never Knew: The Family and Social Change," in John Janeway Conger, ed., *Contemporary Issues in Adolescent Development* (New York: Harper and Row, 1975), pp. 86-104.

[3] Paul Henry Mussen and Mary Cover Jones, "Self-Conceptions, Motivations, and Interpersonal Attitudes of Late- and Early-Maturing Boys," in John Janeway Conger, ed., *Contemporary Issues in Adolescent Development* (New York: Harper and Row, 1975), pp. 4-16.

[4] Erik Erikson, *Identity: Youth and Crisis* (New York: Norton, 1968).

[5] Ibid.

[6] John Janeway Conger, *Adolescence and Youth: Psychological Development in a Changing World* (New York: Harper and Row, 1973).

[7] B. Inhelder and Jean Piaget, *The Growth of Logical Thinking from Childhood to Adolescence* (New York: Basic Books, 1958).

[8] David Elkind, "Cognitive Development in Adolescence," in J. F. Adams, ed., *Understanding Adolescence* (Boston: Allyn and Bacon, 1968), pp. 128-58.

[9] Ibid.

[10] Lawrence Kohlberg and Carol Gilligan, "The Adolescent as a Philosopher: The Discovery of the Self in a Post-Conventional World," in John Janeway Conger, ed., *Contemporary Issues in Adolescent Development* (New York: Harper and Row, 1975), pp. 415-43.

[11] Ibid.

[12] Conger, "A World They Never Knew."

[13] Conger, *Adolescence and Youth.*

[14] Ibid.

BIBLIOGRAPHY

Adams, J. F., ed. *Understanding Adolescence.* Boston: Allyn and Bacon, 1968.

Conger, John Janeway. *Adolescence and Youth: Psychological Development in a Changing World.* New York: Harper and Row, 1973.

Conger, John Janeway, ed. *Contemporary Issues in Adolescent Development.* New York: Harper and Row, 1975.

Erikson, Erik. *Identity: Youth and Crisis.* New York: Norton, 1968.

Havighurst, Robert J. *Developmental Tasks and Education.* 2nd ed. New York: David McKay, 1952.

Inhelder, B., and Jean Piaget. *The Growth of Logical Thinking from Childhood to Adolescence.* New York: Basic Books, 1958.

ROADBLOCKS TO YA CRISIS SERVICE
IN THE PUBLIC LIBRARY

Rosemarie E. Falanga

The scene was the 1977 Midwinter meeting of YASD's Intellectual Freedom Committee. The speaker was a public librarian who had responded to the new wave of service philosophy by taking inventory of her community and developing a proper information and referral (I&R) file. She told of waiting at her desk in vain for those sensitive questions to begin. No one seemed to be asking for the service that she was so prepared to give. When she finally was confronted with her first crisis—a teenager's plea for help with an unwanted pregnancy—it was not presented in person or even called in to the library. The librarian, quite by accident, found the crisis scrawled on the wall of the public toilet. Staring at that wall, she experienced a sense of total frustration and failure. The information, so neatly arranged on her desk, was not enough.

I was present in the audience that evening. And even though the story I heard was not new to me, the telling of it helped me to resolve a personal existential dilemma about the giving of crisis information service in a public library setting. I have been working as a peer counselor and an information and referral specialist in hotlines for as long as I have been working as a young adult specialist in public libraries. At one time, the hotline was only a mile away from the library, and some of the same kids I saw reading *Sports Illustrated* in the library at 3:00 p.m. would show up spaced out and panicked at the hotline center at 3:00 a.m. In the two different environments, they became different people, and I underwent a similar metamorphosis. I was Ms. Falanga to them in the daytime and Rose at night. It took me years to recognize what part the limitations of being a professional librarian played in these changes of attitude and, ultimately, of service. At the hotline, which was sponsored by a local college and located in a private house off-campus, I had all of New York City at my fingertips, including a doctor, a lawyer, and a psychologist on 24-hour call. There I learned to expand my concept of what was and was not available beyond on-site resources. But if people had brought their problems to me at the public library, how could I have helped them? At that time, the library was so caught up with its own priorities and fiscal crises that it didn't even permit staff to make outgoing telephone calls. If that had been my only training ground, I would have learned very early a thousand-and-one ways to say "no."

The two approaches to service seemed irreconcilable, and despite five years of attempting to fit crisis services within the framework of the library as a public institution (which included two years with the federally-funded Neighborhood Information Center Project), I am still left with the image of the unused I&R file versus the cry on the bathroom wall. It represents to me a gap that has never been bridged. I've gone back over the speeches and reread the literature that speaks of the library as the perfect information center. But based on my experiences, I conclude that the same rationale can be used to depict the library as the worst possible source of crisis information.

To begin, I would like to get the terminology straight. Crisis information is, by and large, community information, but the reverse is certainly not true. In crisis service, the need for accuracy, immediacy and humanity, though always present in any referral service, is raised to a life-and-death level. And crisis information deals with difficult, sensitive areas, from abortion to transvestism, where there is a necessity to concentrate on the needs of the client to the exclusion of strong personal and community prejudices. This problem is heightened when minors are involved. We are just beginning to become aware of the traditional practice of denying the young access to crisis information, despite laws guaranteeing their rights to it.

The following is a distillation of reasons frequently given by Croneberger, among others, to explain why librarians should take an interest in developing an information and referral service, and why libraries can manage this kind of information system better than any other organization:

WHY?

People need information to solve their problems.

People don't know where to go to get help.

No one else is doing it.

WHY LIBRARIANS?

We have the necessary reference and information organization skills.

We are trusted and believed.

We are people-oriented.

(Quote continues on page 102)

WHY LIBRARIES?

Libraries are neutral spaces in the community.

Libraries already have the necessary resources.

Branches are convenient places to disseminate information.

Libraries already have an established clientele.

Libraries have a stable financial base and know how to get additional funding for special services.

Libraries are accountable to the community.

In the face of declining book circulation, libraries need to look elsewhere for a reason to continue to exist.[1]

On the face of it this is an impressive list. But over the years, I have seen the other side of each argument.

People need information to solve their problems. In their surveys and analyses of community informational needs, both Dervin[2] and Childers[3] have concluded that most people in crisis are there not so much because they don't have information, but because: 1) they don't know that they need information; and 2) they don't know how to use information even when they have it. There are other psychological barriers that exist when you deal with young people. A large percentage of young girls who get pregnant had the necessary birth control information available beforehand, but chose not to use it because: 1) they felt it would make them look "easy" if they were prepared; 2) they didn't really believe that they could get pregnant;[4] and 3) they subconciously wanted to get pregnant.[5] In the drug abuse prevention field, it has been demonstrated that an increase in drug information correlates, up to a point, with an increase, not a decrease, in drug use.[6] Providing information alone without helping a person to create a context in which the information can be used is the same as providing no service at all.

People don't know where to go to get help. This is a very subjective statement, and most people would deny that they were without their own resources. Childers speaks of unofficial community/peer networks that are regularly turned to for information.[7] The reliability of these networks may be in question, but it is nonetheless true that people are generally satisfied with them. We become distressed when few people use the library because, as librarians, the library is part of our own personal network. It is where we would naturally go if we had a problem. This statement also implies that the librarian with a community information file has a better notion of where to go than a client, which may be true in ordinary circumstances but does not hold when the client is a minor in trouble. How many libraries evaluate their referrals from a young person's point of view? Treatment of runaways, for instance, differs from state to state and from facility to facility. How do librarians know if they are referring someone to a runaway center with the capability of intervening in the crisis, as opposed to one that will just turn the youth immediately over to the police? Young people turn to their friends for answers, partially because we adults don't even ask the right questions.

No one else is doing it. It seems silly in these days of increasing emphasis on fiscal economy to talk of the necessity of surveying the community for existing I&R services. Yet I know of a county library system that recently overlooked the existence of a 24-hour community/crisis information service and started its own project. The result? The now competing service, also county funded, threatened to sue because of duplication of effort. Surveys often find what they want to find, and the community is rarely evaluated from the point of view of the young adult. Are courses in "survival" being given in the local high school, for instance? What part do gangs play in the unofficial flow of information?

As libraries enter into the I&R field, they have been known to raise hostile feelings on the part of social workers, who ask, "what are you doing in this business?" At this point, proponents often modify the above statement to read: No One Else Is Doing It AS WELL AS WE COULD. This leads us to the next ten justifications.

We have the necessary reference and information organization skills. Here we are apparently on solid ground, for reference is our business. But are reference skills and crisis information skills the same?

> It is difficult . . . to equate the reference interview and the astute librarian zooming in on the "hidden reference question" with the situation where a woman asks for a place to stay the night when what she really needs is financial assistance and counselling because she has no job, has had a row with her family, and is pregnant with a child she does not want.[8]

One of the ways in which traditional reference service differs from crisis interviews is in the kinds of questions that must be asked. At the hotline, for instance, a request for an abortion referral was routinely countered with, "how do you know you're pregnant?" In order to make the proper referral, it was necessary to know: 1) whether there had been a pregnancy test; 2) how long since the last menstrual period; and 3) the extent of the client's knowledge of her own body and of birth control methods. Pregnancy tests given at the abortion clinics often showed results that were to the clinics' financial advantage. We had to know approximately how many weeks along a client was, because different clinics specialized in different methods of abortion. And some clinics gave better birth control follow-up than others. Many skilled reference librarians are not comfortable with such a personal approach with clients. They find these questions embarrassing, of the "none of our business" type. But if our business is crisis information, these questions are necessary.

Another difference is the emotional state of the client in trouble. People do not always behave rationally at the best of times. The ability to handle someone who is screaming or crying or just nervous should be part of our reference training, but for most of us, it is not.

Evaluation of referrals is also not included in most master's degree programs. Looking at an agency from the point of view of a young person is a necessity. A service agency run by fallible human beings must be evaluated with a cautious eye, but we tend to accept self-reported descriptions of such agencies' capabilities. Most librarians do not know how to conduct a telephone interview, how to decide when an on-site visit is called for, or how to elicit and use client feedback.

Five years ago, when interest in I&R services was beginning to take hold in public libraries, *Library Journal* printed an article about a store-front Canadian information center run by a former librarian, Bettie Armitage, who was adamant about hiring people specialists, not information specialists:

> When *LJ* asked whether her library training helped in the development of the Contact Centre program, Bettie smiled. "Sure, it helped a lot. I learned a lot about writing proposals. And certainly in a place like this where we are creating our own information files, training in the organization of information is essential." Would she hire librarians, we asked. "No, there is really a need for some new kind of information profession."[9]

We are trusted and believed. During my seven years in the profession, I have discovered only two instances when it is invariably to my advantage to describe myself as a librarian: signing a lease and selling a car. Our image in the community-at-large is one of respectability to the point of dullness. We are trusted to suggest a good romantic novel, to balance our budget, and to maintain relative order in our domain; but this is not the kind of trust necessary when someone, particularly a teenager, is in trouble. "Librarians frequently give advice; but advice in the context of an individual in crisis is quite different from the readers' advisory function."[10] If whether or not we should act *in loco parentis* is still a moot question in the profession and the community, how can we expect the teenager to view us as anything other than an extension of authority figures from home and school?

It can be argued that this is what YA librarianship is all about: an attempt by someone who really cares for kids to break down their resistance and gain their trust and love. (I am assuming that the YA specialist is someone with an aptitude for the job, not someone "volunteered" by supervisors because no one else wanted to do it.) What if all of the suspicions and barriers are surmounted, and the young adult is standing before your desk telling all: his best friend ran away from home and is hiding in his family's garage; she needs a book on artificial lighting to grow marijuana in her closet; his fifteen-year-old girlfriend is pregnant and is scheduled for an abortion tomorrow—will you drive her to the clinic?

What do you do now? First of all, many librarians have no idea of what their legal position is in such situations. They assume that, like doctors, lawyers, and clergymen, they cannot be compelled to divulge confidences. But there is no legal precedent supporting such privileges of confidentiality for librarians. Circulation records may be safe, although this, too, is debatable. Verbal revelations are not. Are we legally or ethically mandated to tell parents and police about any illegal action that we know a minor is committing? Even when the action is legal, in the case of the abortion, for instance, must the parents be informed? What if you drive that young person to the clinic? Even though you do it on your own time, how would your board of trustees feel if they heard of it?

I do not know of any case where a librarian was successfully compelled to reveal the confidences of a patron. But we are inviting danger if we encourage those confidences without first knowing where we stand.

We are people-oriented. While the previous statement dealt with the image that others have of librarians, this statement involves the way we see ourselves. Both are, to come extent, unfair stereotypes of a large and varied body of people. There are kind, giving, socially aware librarians, and there are bigoted recluses. There are many people-oriented librarians, but did they get that way because the profession demanded it of them? Did they choose to become helpers, counselors, activists, and then choose libraries as the best place to express their social conscience? I believe that, although some fine librarians are truly people-oriented, at bottom line what distinguishes us as librarians from other professionals is that we are book-oriented and institution-oriented. Gordon McShean, comparing personnel at a community switchboard to public libraries, comments:

> Training and education for library service has often idealized our purposes to the extent that some of us entered the profession believing that we had an obligation to discover and serve the community's information needs. In practice, we simply regurgitate what appears in print . . . disclaiming responsibility for the rest, justifying our existence as a custodian of public property.[11]

We have chosen the library because we believe in its power for social change. While others picket, march, and run for office, we make speeches at library conferences and compile bibliographies. The library as institution is a haven to many of us and fits our personalities. It is safe, secure, organized, and provides the kind of answers that we, as librarians, can best understand. But people in trouble often see themselves at odds with institutions and apart from the general public. If we are to give crisis service, we must ask ourselves where our primary commitment is. As McShean notes,

> The dynamic factor . . . is motivation . . . A person committed to a contribution of *personal aid and assistance* to the community will seldom hide behind the bureaucracy to avoid responding to a request.[12]

Libraries are neutral spaces in the community. In *West Side Story*, when the Jets and the Sharks were trying to find a place to have a council of war, they ruled out the gym because it was "neutral territory."[13] Neither gang claimed it as "turf," and thus it was a safe space, but also, in a sense, an uninteresting, even sterile space, not even good enough to be used as a place for settling disputes (in whatever manner).

Looking at the library's oft-toted neutrality, several questions occur: are we really neutral? are we neutral in terms of young adults? is neutrality what is needed in crisis information service? The concept of the library's neutrality first came to my attention when I was working in the Neighborhood Information Center Project (NIC), and I was in total agreement with it. Within New York City's vast and highly political social service arena, we certainly had greater flexibility in making objective, quality referrals than in many other institutions. What becomes increasingly apparent, however, was the bias that we had as an established, respectable municipal institution for other institutions of like kind. We referred people to Community Councils, not hotlines; to city-run shelters rather than student-run crash pads. Our evaluations were subtle and not for quality of service. Apparently other NICs did the same:

> Controversy exists . . . over Cleveland's practice of indicating on the agency cards those organizations which are regarded as good services to make referrals to since they are more stable financially, older, and generally well known. Designed to ease the job of a librarian operating the service with little experience, it was argued that this may lead to difficulties with non-recommended agencies.[14]

A friend of mine describes this tendency as "stocking the standard condiments."

Does the public library, as an institution, feel comfortable dealing with requests from people whose world views are somewhat different? We refer people without qualms to hospitals and roller rinks, but what do we do when someone asks for an exorcist, a macrobiotic restaurant, or a leather shop for sadomasochists? What about unpopular political stands? Did libraries keep a list of draft counseling centers at the beginning of the Vietnam War dissension, when draft dodging was looked upon as un-American? Do I&R centers today have cards in their files for fascist parties or pro-marijuana lobbies? These hypothetical requests are all for legally existing services and organizations. But most libraries do not feel obligated to serve those whom the community feels to be weird or offensive.

Lack of library neutrality has a special meaning for young adults. Open access to the entire collection is still being debated. Even in systems that nominally have open access, other restrictions are imposed (like asking for additional identification or denying access to AV materials) that have the effect of making young people feel that the library is not exactly their territory. Many libraries still routinely deny teenagers certain books at their parents' request. After all, they argue, parents are taxpapers who often have a protective attitude toward their children and expect the library to share it. And parents are much more capable and likely to take action against the library if they are displeased.

So where does that leave us in terms of I&R? What if the young person asks for a referral without parental knowledge and consent? Is your library prepared to handle an irate parent who has just discovered that his child is homosexual and was referred by the library to a gay teens' group? YA librarians often have to ask themselves whom they are serving—parent or child?—as they choose books and plan programs. How much more relevant this question becomes when the service has impact at crisis points in peoples' lives.

Crisis service is never neutral, because a person in crisis sees himself or herself as being alone against the world. That psychological disposition is one of the things that makes it so hard to ask for help in the first place. The person offering assistance must feel committed to the individual's priorities. Yet time and again, I see libraries pulling back from that commitment:

> In every aspect of service, the public librarian serves as ombudsman or expeditor, not advocate. . . . the library is not designed, by definition or purpose, for direct social action. . . .[15]

> Why is it that a patron can usually obtain historical information about the community from the librarian . . . but current, immediate needs go unattended?[16]

For libraries, the opposite of neutrality is not advocacy, but selective response to questions through an uneven allocation of resources and time.

Libraries already have the necessary resources. To justify their entrance into I&R, libraries point to an impressive display of resources: trained information specialists, books on appropriate subjects, seating capacity. But are the resources they have of the kind that will actually be of help to someone in crisis? We have already considered staff capabilities. A large collection of reference and popular books in crisis areas may actually be a disadvantage, as we are conditioned to rely on a book and believe what it tells us. Too often, directories of social agencies on library shelves are from two to ten years out of date and virtually useless. There are ways to use such books safely, but how many reference librarians can take the time?

Outdated directories can be frustrating; outdated factual materials can be dangerous and misleading. We are usually not ruthless enough with our library collections. Do your books on sex list the latest discoveries about oral contraceptives and IUDs? Do they say that abortion is illegal? Do they claim that masturbation causes warts? Is homosexuality in the same chapter as bestiality? Since a crisis service's first duty is to provide up-to-date, accurate information to the client, tossing out a ludicrous book or penciling in corrections and new data do not pose the same problems as the weeding of a more static library collection.

There is also a question about how much emotional help YA fiction and non-fiction are to most teenagers in trouble. It is not impossible for a book to help someone in crisis. I was once assisted through a difficult period of mourning for a friend who had committed suicide by hearing Julius Lester read Aldous Huxley's description of his first wife's death. But who could have anticipated the link my mind made between those two events? Such epiphanies are rare and cannot be forced. Handing out *Life after Life* to a teenager whose mother is dying of cancer will not really help him cope with the complex feelings of terror, sorrow, hatred, and guilt that accompany such a crisis.

The library building itself can be another barrier to good crisis service. The reference desk is not designed to promote intimate, lengthy, private interchanges. Often, there is not even a chair for the patron. Scheduling that is designed for maximum staff efficiency frequently leaves only one librarian at a time on desk duty. This means that phones have to be answered and bathroom keys given out while trying to concentrate on a distraught patron. Yet, at the hotline, we had from two to eight people on duty at a time. There were six completely private spaces in which we could be physically isolated with a client. And nothing short of a fire was allowed to interrupt us.

Branches are convenient places to disseminate information. This is another variation of the above argument. Libraries appear to be convenient to us because they are frequently designed to be convenient for library administrators and staff. Locations are chosen as much for fiscal considerations as for closeness to population centers, and hours are compromises between community and staff demands. I am not suggesting that a service must be 24-hour to be effective. In a self-help crisis center that served mostly middle-class housewives, we found that the large majority of our calls came between 10:00 a.m. and 3:00 p.m., a very depressing time of the day when many women found the space to seek assistance. An excellent time for young adults to seek help is right after school. Libraries are open and fully staffed, but also usually doing a booming homework business, and a crowded, hectic atmosphere is discouraging to someone with a personal question. Librarians' minds are somewhere between a haiku and the Ice Age; a young girl is surrounded by her friends and cannot find a moment alone; a young man approaches the I&R desk only to find that it has been placed directly in front of the circulation desk and the clerk on duty is his mother's best friend. All of the ingredients for help may be present, but the library setting prevents them from getting together.

Libraries already have an established clientele. This is true, but are they the clientele that have the greatest need for crisis service? With only one poster on runaway centers and the need to decide where to post it to reach the largest number of kids in trouble, the library would not be my first choice. Bus depots, pizza parlors, and subway stations would be much more appropriate. But how many young people never come to the library and may not even know where it is located? Surveys have been done of library patrons to determine their use of I&R services. YA specialists need a survey of kids in trouble who are in runaway homes, juvenile halls, and prisons to find out how many of them were regular library patrons or ever even thought of coming to the library with a problem. Access to crisis information means more than putting up a display or hanging up a sign. If we take our responsibilities seriously, we have to go beyond the building and its clientele and take our resources where they will do the most good.

Libraries have a stable financial base and know how to get additional funding for special services. Libraries are accountable to the community. In the face of declining book circulation, libraries need to look elsewhere for a reason to continue to exist. These last three justifications are so interrelated that they can be considered together. There is no doubt that stable funding is necessary, up to a point, for any community service. The less time spent writing grants, having bake sales, and soliciting donations, the more time there is for clients. But the more financially secure an institution is, generally, the less responsive it is to the community. Most libraries are accustomed to reporting to an intermediary (a board of trustees), not to the community as a whole. Those that have their budgets approved every year by direct popular vote are probably most sensitive to needs and issues. But whose needs? Undoubtedly the vocal, politically involved, adult minority rather than the relatively powerless young adult and counter-culture groups.

Libraries have repeatedly demonstrated that they do not consider even community information services, let alone crisis information services, to be part of their basic responsibilities. These are something special, extra, to be paid for out of special funds and to be discontinued when those funds run out. Most administrators do not even give crisis information the same priority in their budgets that they give children's story hours. Crisis services are looked upon as a new gimmick that will lure to the library people who, after they get their problems neatly and quickly solved, might even take out a few books. Book circulation is still the prime *raison d'être* in the minds of most people, librarians as well as fiscal planners.

When because they are established institutions, libraries receive federal, state, and private funding to implement crisis services, and when their real interest is in maintaining staff who are no longer needed, increasing book circulation, and getting kudos in the local and national press, they are diverting these funds from less stable, grassroots organizations that are more committed to people in trouble.

The key word is commitment. Every psychological, emotional, financial, and political barrier that I have mentioned that hinders young adult crisis service in the public library can be overcome—if we are prepared to devote the time, energy, and financial resources necessary to do so. The library as an institution is no worse than other service institutions and sometimes a great deal better than most. But it is not the perfect, ready-made crisis center. We have to be reconditioned and retrained. We have to learn how to make use of official and unofficial communication networks.

After attending that YASD Intellectual Freedom Committee meeting in Washington, D.C., I returned to my job in the suburbs of Cleveland and began looking around for natural information centers where young people meet and exchange problems and solutions. I found a few: a low-keyed vegetarian restaurant specializing in student poetry reading and jazz, and a bulletin board in a feminist book store. My favorite was the bathroom of the Agora Ballroom, an immensely popular rock/jazz joint specializing in weak beer and towering amplifiers. That's where the young people were. If we are really interested in crisis information service, then, we must leave the safety and security of the library womb and take our skills where they can be put to better use. This article is not intended as another roadblock, but as a checklist and self-evaluation tool. Perhaps someone can show us how a library has accepted the challenge and does provide the dedicated, high quality service that is needed. It isn't easy to turn priorities, assumptions, and training upside down. But it can be done.

NOTES

[1] Robert B. Croneberger, "Public Library—Library for the People," *RQ* (Summer 1973): 345.

[2] Brenda Dervin, et al. *The Development of Strategies with the Information Needs of Urban Residents. Phase I. Citizen Study. Final Report* (Seattle: University of Washington, School of Communications, 1976). [ERIC ED 125 640].

[3] Thomas Childers, *The Information-Poor in America* (Metuchen, NJ: Scarecrow, 1975).

[4] G. Cvetkovich, et al. "On the Psychology of Adolescents' Use of Contraceptives," *The Journal of Sex Research* 11 (August 1975): 256-70.

[5] S. Fischman, "Delivery or Abortion in Inner-City Adolescents." *American Journal of Orthopsychiatry* 47 (January 1977): 127-34.

[6] Eric Schaps, et al. *Balancing Head and Heart. Book I: Prevention in Perspective* (Lafayette, CA: Prevention Materials Institute Press, 1975), pp. 26-29.

[7] Childers.

[8] Mairead Brown. "The Territorial Stake-Out," *Australian Library Journal* 25 (November 1976): 386.

[9] John Berry. "The Contact Centre," *Library Journal* 97 (December 15, 1972): 3957.

[10] Brown, p. 386.

[11] Gordon McShean, "Switchboard . . . A Threat to Libraries?," *California Librarian* 34 (January 1973): 54.

[12] Ibid., p. 51.

[13] Leonard Bernstein, et al. *West Side Story*. New York: Random House, 1958 [Act I, scene I, p. 14].

[14] E. D. Walley and D. E. Davinson, *Developments in Community Information Services in Public Libraries in the U.S.* (Leeds, U.K.: Leeds Polytechnic Department of Librarianship, 1976), p. 34.

[15] John Berry, "A Tip from Detroit," *Library Journal* 100 (July 1975): 1287-90.

[16] Sue Critchfield, "Information Wanted! Dead or Alive?," *Synergy* 41 (Summer 1973): 12.

BIBLIOGRAPHY

Bernstein, Leonard, et al. *West Side Story.* New York: Random House, 1958.

Berry, John. "The Contact Centre." *Library Journal* 97 (1972): 3957.

Berry, John. "A Tip from Detroit." *Library Journal* 100 (1975): 1287-90.

Brown, Mairead. "The Territorial Stake-Out." *Australian Library Journal* 25 (1976): 386.

Childers, Thomas. *The Information-Poor in America.* Metuchen, NJ: Scarecrow, 1975.

Critchfield, Sue. "Information Wanted! Dead or Alive?" *Synergy* 41 (1973): 12.

Croneberger, Robert B. "Public Library—Library for the People." *RQ* (Summer 1973): 344-45.

Cvetkovich, G., et al. "On the Psychology of Adolescents' Use of Contraceptives." *The Journal of Sex Research* 11 (1975): 256-70.

Dervin, Brenda, et al. *The Development of Strategies with the Information Needs of Urban Residents. Phase I. Citizen Study. Final Report.* Seattle: University of Washington, School of Communications, 1976.

Fischman, S. "Delivery or Abortion in Inner-City Adolescents." *American Journal of Orthopsychiatry* 47 (1977): 127-34.

McShean, Gordon. "Switchboard . . . A Threat to Libraries?" *California Librarian* 34 (1973): 54.

Schaps, Eric, et al. *Balancing Head and Heart. Book I: Prevention in Perspective.* Lafayette, CA: Prevention Materials Institute Press, 1975.

Walley, E. D., and D. E. Davinson. *Developments in Community Information Services in Public Libraries in the U.S.* Leeds, U.K.: Leeds Polytechnic Department of Librarianship, 1976.

LIBRARY COOPERATION TO
SERVE YOUTH

Peggy A. Sullivan

In a time when we are more keenly aware than ever of the need for libraries to work cooperatively as parts of systems, networks, or as units cooperating with other social and educational agencies, the need for cooperation to provide better service to young people is clearly recognized. What is not so clearly recognized are the varieties of cooperation that are possible, the numbers and kinds of libraries that need to adjust to provide that cooperation, and the need to recognize the fact that many aspects of cooperation may affect service to youth even if they are not designed for that particular purpose. Library cooperation is an easy answer to problems, rather like the comment that communication can solve everything, but much thought and much planning are required if cooperation is to be effective as a part of service.

There is a form of active cooperation in which libraries set patterns for themselves that recognize the patterns of other libraries, and plan within those patterns for active inter-library cooperation. I distinguish this from passive cooperation, which is intended rather to set aside different parts of the "library turf" for different kinds of library programming. An example of the latter is the decision that may be made between school and public libraries to have one kind of service provided by one of those libraries to young people, and that same kind of service omitted or provided to a lesser extent by the other kind of library. Sometimes, of course, these decisions are made unilaterally, and when they are, they are not really examples of cooperation. This, as I see it, is one of the biggest obstacles to true cooperation. What happens is that a high school librarian responds to an inquiry by saying, "No, of course we don't have that. You should get that at the public library." But the librarian makes the comment without having checked the resources of the public library and without being sure of having good grounds for making such a statement. Active cooperation requires extensive communication, and it should be based on active participation in decision-making on the part of librarians from various kinds of libraries. For example, when a public library decides to provide a book catalog for its users, the initial decision must be made at the public library by its own staff. However, early information about the decision and discussion of its effect on school libraries in the area will have much to do with what service to young people in the community can really be. The opportunity to provide a union catalog of public library materials in every school library has been eagerly accepted in many places; but it is most attractive when it is based on full information provided at an early stage of the planning, and when the needs of other libraries in the area for information are fully considered and incorporated into the planning for the change in cataloging.

Cooperative programming may be direct or indirect, as far as service to the public is concerned. Provision of inter-library loan materials, cooperative film centers, and other services that affect what is available to individual borrowers in a very direct way are examples of the former kind of cooperation, while in-service education, cooperative purchasing, selection clinics, etc., may be examples of indirect cooperation. It is possible for two or more kinds of libraries to be cooperating very effectively without their respective publics' being aware of it. The opportunity of bringing speakers or media presentations that may have great positive impact on the in-service programming of libraries may be increased when they are willing to plan, finance, and conduct such programming cooperatively. This happens all too seldom. One reason is the perennial problem that librarians representing one kind of library service find it extremely difficult to empathize with those in other kinds of libraries. They fail to appreciate that a program that might be of primary interest to them may well be of secondary, although considerable, interest to librarians in another kind of library. Compromising by choosing a program of limited interest to both is not the answer. Planning together so that the best of one area of interest can be provided at one time and possibly something of greater interest to other librarians provided at another time may be the best solution.

In addition, one of the problems is that the planning is customarily done by individuals at the supervisory or leadership level. Their opportunities to participate in programs in regions, states, or associations on a nationwide scale are usually greater than those of librarians in branch libraries, small community libraries, high school libraries, etc., and they may be insensitive to the needs and interests of those individuals. The kinds of programs of which I am thinking here include presentations by authors who write for young adults, critical screening of media for young adult audiences, panel presentations by librarians and media specialists themselves, and the kinds of inspirational and controversial programs that can often be effectively presented by expert librarians who have extensive experience in work with young adults. These programs may be carried out without the young adults in the community even being aware of them, but they can certainly increase the library's contributions to those young people.

As far as direct service to youth is concerned, cooperation is important to practically the same extent that it is in all other aspects of improvement of direct public services. One problem is that sometimes only one aspect of a cooperative endeavor may be considered at the time it is first discussed or first planned. An example is the major change in cataloging mentioned above, when a library drops its present system to provide a book catalog, COM catalog, or some other new format. Young people will certainly be affected by the change, and those who serve them need to be aware of the implications for their use and aware of ways to communicate to young people the information they will need to make the best use of the new technology available for them. Those who serve youth should also be concerned with communicating to other decision-makers what young people want and need in a cataloging system. It goes without saying that the often discriminatory services provided to young adults—through limitations of their opportunities to request materials on inter-library loan, limitations of their rights to reserve materials, etc.—need to be reviewed carefully and usually resisted by those who are dedicated to service to young adults. Their presentations along this line will be effective to the extent that they are truly informed about what the impact of such service can be and helpful in providing ideas for the best kind of direct service to young people.

In the examples given here, I have been as guilty as others of implying that if school libraries and public libraries would cooperate, then service to young adults will be considerably improved. This may be true, but more important is the fact that many kinds of libraries need to be concerned about service to youth. State libraries that receive numerous mail requests for documents or free materials from young people writing papers in school, special libraries that provide through parents or others the materials desperately sought by young people, college libraries that often feel threatened by the onslaught of young users, and other libraries know what it is like to receive the requests of youth. Often, this activity goes on without the local librarian who serves those same young people in the school or public library having any inkling of their needs in this regard. Even when they do, they sometimes dismiss them rather casually with such comments as, "Oh, Charlie did well at the science fair because his father got all that stuff from his plant library," or, "I was so impressed with the way Ellen found all those documents from all over the country for her paper in social studies." The fact that young people triumph over the obstacles of communication among libraries should not be an excuse for lack of cooperation among those libraries.

One of the most serious obstacles to cooperation that I see is the frequent psychological isolation of school librarians who are reluctant or shy about becoming a part of the library community when they know how important it is in terms of their own positions and in terms of library service for them to be strongly identified with the school community. Communication with other kinds of librarians in their areas is important for them, and it would be a major breakthrough if more of them became aware and articulate about the libraries that serve their young people as individuals, and also if more became equally aware and articulate about the needs of their young people as they relate to other kinds of libraries.

Actually, cooperative efforts go beyond libraries themselves. A significant contribution has been made in service to youth by representatives from programs of library education, who often provide the leadership at regional or state or national levels that is necessary to bring together those librarians whose major public is young people. Less significant, unfortunately, is cooperation among library education programs or among them and the schools and libraries of their areas. Too often, such programs as summer workshops featuring emphasis on service to young people are planned to be competitive rather than cooperative with other similar programs elsewhere. I remember visiting a state where two summer workshops, both of them featuring nationally-known speakers and dedicated to library work with young people, were being scheduled in the same summer. It was clear that anyone in the area planning to attend would have to choose between the two, and it was also clear that there would be a long period of time before any such similar opportunity would be offered. Cooperative planning might have made both of the programs richer and might also have enriched and stimulated the librarians of the area who were working with young people, rather than force them to arbitrary decisions about attendance at one or the other function. Generous leadership on the part of library school faculty might have averted that problem, just as that same kind of generous leadership has been a major asset in the improvement of library service to youth throughout this country and, indeed, throughout the world.

Some tempting mirages customarily fool people who are concerned about better library service to young people, and they also are related to cooperative endeavors. One is the mirage of the great school-housed public library facility. There was a time when, for political and economic reasons, a number of these facilities came into existence, usually where public libraries were under the supervision of the board of education of a locality. More recently, federal funds and other experimental grants have made it possible to plan for similar facilities. I know of no instance in which planning has been thorough and thoughtful from the beginning and where a school-housed public library that is appropriate for both purposes has emerged. It may be that one may do so in the future, but until then, it is only fanciful to think that such a plan will provide better service to young people. What tends to happen instead is that the facility is operated as part of either one library system or the other, but never manages to achieve the best of either. Perhaps by planning for such a facility in a community that is small and/or isolated, where there is one high school serving an area, and where it is difficult to recruit librarians, it would be possible to test this idea in the best of circumstances. Ironically, it is not localities of this kind that have usually been interested in such experimentation. I recall giving a series of workshops about ten years ago in a state where, on the first day of the workshops, I commented that some of the small towns in that state might benefit from considering such a plan, since it was extremely difficult for them to maintain both a high school library and a public library. I was rather briskly but firmly told at the end of the day that comments like that were not welcome in the state, and that if I were to continue with workshops there, I should not discuss such a possibility. Yet, I still believe that a plan of this kind could be tried somewhere and service to youth could be provided in a more economical and carefully planned way than it presently is when both school and public libraries try to provide it on limited budgets.

Another mirage related to the question of cooperation among types of libraries is the idea that by serving schools, public libraries are reaching all young people. There are several levels to this mirage. One is the supposition often made that all young people are in schools, another is that they are all in public schools, and a third is that most of their social and intellectual relationships exist in schools. While the last statement is certainly true of most young people, it is not true of all, and they are the very ones whom the public library could and should serve extremely well. Instead, by concentrating its efforts on the schools, the public library tends to lose those whose social reationships exist primarily outside of the schools. I am thinking of the young people who are active in drama groups, social agency action groups, and similar community activities, but who simply are too busy at school to pay much attention to the efforts made there to encourage them to use the public library; and those whose interests are not immediately recognized as being related to libraries. Along this line, there are many young people enrolled in vocational and technical schools or similar special schools who attend these schools outside of their home communities. Often they are unaware of the possible service that a public library could provide for them, and little effort is made to reach them. Libraries communicate with schools to attract young people, which is reasonable and in most instances, efficient. But schools should be recognized as only one link, although the major one, in communication with young people. Similarly, the interests of young people who are parents, concerned citizens, members of militant action groups, job-holders, dissident unemployed, etc., need to be recognized if the library is to serve them effectively in the various roles in which they may be participating.

The third mirage relates to the level at which libraries communicate about their mutual concerns for service to young people. Too often, as public library systems become larger and more complex, the establishment of some formal liaison with other kinds of libraries serving young people is necessary. Similarly, school systems may have liaison personnel to be in close touch with public libraries and other educational institutions in the community. However, these high-level communicators should be only supplementary to the regular, day-to-day communication among library personnel at local levels. I remember that when I left one large public library system to work in a smaller one, one of the first questions that was asked was how soon I might establish a position for someone to be the library's liaison with the schools of the area. My answer was that, although such a position existed in the large system that I had left, it was established simply to expedite the continuous necessary communication from branches to schools and to other parts of the community concerned with young people. I said further that no single liaison person should have the responsibility or the authority to represent the library when there were more effective and immediate ways to achieve this. My views have not changed, although I hope for greater improvement in the relationships between local library agencies. These begin with someone's reaching out and talking with a colleague, and they become firm and useful when communication turns to cooperation, and when understanding of each institution's purpose, plans, and present activities develops.

There may be other mirages of which I am presently unaware, but these exemplify some of the problems which can impede better library cooperation. Perhaps we also need to ask what the purpose of library cooperation is. If it is not to provide better service for young people, including better access to more media in more convenient locations and/or formats, then it is not very effective cooperation. However, in this time of limited budgets and the prospect of further limitations, cooperation may be necessary simply to achieve the best of what is possible. Loans among libraries on a large-scale basis, loans of materials such as films for programming, exchange of information about programs and related activities, cooperative planning for book talks that might be given by public librarians in schools, are only a few of the possible aspects of cooperation that should help to make better service more accessible to young people.

Participation of young people on boards of education, and even their membership on college or university boards of trustees, have occurred more readily than their active participation in advisory groups to school or public libraries. There is research evidence to indicate that young people are not only willing but competent to discuss what their needs are in terms of library resources, but they are very seldom asked. It is, as with other groups, even more difficult to identify and to get reactions from young people who are not users of libraries, but both of those should be goals for future cooperative efforts. Whether reached through schools or through other means, young people should be invited to comment in a fairly formal way on what libraries should provide that would be useful to them. Their potentials as volunteers are customarily underrated or unrecognized also, but it may be that another silver lining in this time of economic adversity could be the availability of young people for volunteer efforts. Provision of service to shut-ins, offering programs to children, reading aloud for the blind or physically handicapped patrons, and similar activities are only a few of those in which young people could be quite valuable to public library programs. They already serve extensively in school libraries, and their work is generally quite appreciated and in most instances, much needed if quality in the program is to be maintained. In this area also, some of the school librarian's expertise might help public librarians to recruit and deploy young people as volunteers so that their skills are used to the best extent.

There are probably many more avenues for possible cooperation among libraries serving youth. What it comes down to, after all, is that young people need libraries, and libraries need young people; and the more libraries cooperate among themselves, the more and the better service they can provide to young people. This is true whether the cooperation is directed exclusively or primarily toward young people or not, and it is true whether it is a part of providing better service to them or of encouraging them to participate as planners and providers of that service. Better libraries and better library service are worth the cooperative efforts that may be necessary to achieve them. The fact that they will result in better library service to young people is an important consideration and a goal to be avowed and achieved.

YOUNG ADULT LIBRARY SERVICE:
The International Scene

Jean E. Lowrie

A survey of library service to youth at the international level is really a picture of every type of library service in existence around the world. It spans the gamut from sophisticated media centers under the auspices of a school system to fully developed young adult divisions in public libraries; from an emphasis on library service through a cooperative school/public system to a pattern as varied as an independent service center may wish to establish; from an emphasis on service to young adults to a special program that makes no age distinction between children and teen-agers (and indeed, may mean primarily the younger group). Because of the great variation in patterns of administration, service, and age group, this presentation will highlight points by specific examples. Readers will recognize that Western countries have similarities in their more sophisticated and varied efforts, and that developing countries, which are concerned with their total sociopolitical, economic, and cultural needs, support programs quite different from those to which Americans are accustomed. Furthermore, readers will realize that library service for youth (i.e., teen-age persons) cannot be practiced in those countries where the livelihood of the family is often dependent upon additional support from the young adult. Thus only a minority of the young adolescent group will continue in school and have access to a library, school or public, on a regular basis.

INTRODUCTION

Before looking at some of the specific programs, it is necessary to take a look at the overall problems that librarians and educators in many countries face. The competition for funds, whether local taxpayer's or federal government's, is intense. Each tribal village, each state, each metropolitan system is intent upon acquiring its share of naira, dollars, yen, cedi, etc. for all of the many needs facing that local government. Food, shelter, clothing, and jobs come first; education and library programs often are forced to take a back seat, even though all politicians and governments profess to believe that these are basic to the development of their countries. The need to educate the citizens of any country in order that they may have jobs and produce material goods, which will in turn assist the economy of a country, is paramount. But every country also faces the age-old question, which comes first, production or education? How much book knowledge is necessary? Can a person be taught to do a job satisfactorily even though he cannot read? Of what value are books? How does a government implement a policy of universal education when the population increases faster than the number of teachers, let alone the number of trained teachers?

The great efforts being made by many countries to leap into the twenty-first century are commendable and understandable. But the cost in many cases is almost prohibitive. For example, in Nigeria the concept of free primary education for all was promoted by the government in 1974. "For the scheme to take off by September 1976, it was estimated that some 163,000 additional teachers must be trained for the estimated 2.3 million pupils who would be enrolled for the scheme of that time."[1] Among the concerns stated by the federal authorities was the implication that Nigeria's Universal Primary Education Act would have for library services. Libraries are needed, but where to obtain personnel and materials for them remains an enormous problem for that country.

Parallel with the personnel problem in developing countries is the difficulty of obtaining books—text or trade. Where are they available in sufficient quantity to meet the reading needs of children and young people? The question of the language to be used in the books also presents a formidable question for many publishers. In Malaysia, for example, where Malay, English, Chinese, and Tamil (in that order of priority) are the official languages, how does a publisher decide what books should be printed in which language and how many? Where can he find an author or translator who will do justice to indigenous material? And this says nothing of the effect of heat and dampness on the preservation of materials, or of the problem of importing books from other countries with ever-present currency difficulties.

We who live in more industrialized countries can scarcely grasp the enormity of these problems. And we stand in awe at the progress that *is* being made in many countries where teachers, ministers of education, and parents are determined that their children will have schools and will have access to reading materials.

Educational patterns vary around the world. Generally speaking, there is a concerted effort to promote universal primary education for youngsters up to eight, ten, or twelve years of age; but following that, education is not easy to acquire in many countries. Secondary school programs are often privately sponsored, and the entrance examinations are most difficult. Certainly, in developing countries, the need for laborers outranks all other needs. Some countries follow the "American" school pattern of elementary, middle (junior), and secondary school with no divergence in program until college. Other countries use modified British or European plans, where an examination given around the age of eleven or twelve separates children into various educational tracks, either for further study or to track those failing into trades or labor.

Similarly, one finds great variation in public library service to these age groups. The great traditional, free public library concept (with branches and various forms of outreach services) exists to a greater or lesser degree in most developed countries. But in developing or Third World countries, the national library alone may be responsible for all public library programming. In a country like Sierra Leone, the entire country is served by three regional libraries and seven branches working out of the National Library. There are bookmobiles and book boats, which bring a semblance of service into the remote rural areas. The collections are still infinitesimal by our standards, but the effort is being made to bring books and people together so that the people may realize that reading can be of practical help to them in their family and community life as well as a possible source of enjoyment.

Although no comprehensive international survey has been made of library service to youth, a survey of the literature indicates that library service to children is better developed than that for the teen-ager or young adult, and that such service is fairly equally balanced between school and public library programs. Probably more service to the young adult is given through secondary school libraries than through public, since the latter often have well-developed children's services but put little emphasis on the needs of the older group. Indeed, socialist countries, for example,

> do not regard the establishment of independent youth libraries as a universal necessity. In Poland and in Yugoslavia experimental independent youth libraries are functioning. In Bulgaria youth libraries are in youth and pioneer homes. In Zagreb and in Bucharest libraries are functioning in youth clubs; in Sofia, Bucharest, Slovakia and Poland youth sections of public libraries can be found. The arrangement of stock for young people depends on local circumstances. Youth shelves are used very often. Uniform rules for the compilation of a special stock are nowhere in the world developed. The selection of stock is influenced everywhere by the young person's general field of interest. In Bulgaria the stock for young people is not separate.[2]

It is interesting to note that evidence gathered within the last decade points to growing awareness of the need for library service to this pre-adult group. The need for a forum that could bring international bodies together to discuss problems and to share supportive ideas promoted the formation of formal organizations such as the International Association of School Librarianship (IASL—organized in 1970 and independent of, but still affiliated with, the World Confederation of Organizations of the Teaching Professions). More recent has been the acceptance within the International Federation of Library Associations (IFLA) of a Standing Committee on School Libraries within the new Division of General Library Science. (IASL is also affiliated with IFLA.) Newsletters and other publications are being developed to serve as communication channels. It is hoped that ever-widening contacts among school and public librarians will develop, for all learn from each other, and patrons in turn should benefit both culturally and politically from such international relationships.

Since programs in Canada and the United States have a marked similarity in design, the presentation of efforts in Western or developed countries will focus on European and Australian programs. Among developing nations, plans, projects, and problems in the Caribbean, Middle East, Asia, and Africa will be reported. There is a common pattern in all these efforts even as there are inevitable variations, because the efforts are appropriate for particular countries. The common aspects fall into three familiar areas—a collection of materials that will appeal to the users; a staff trained in library administration and concerned with service appropriate to the users; and facilities accessible to users who live in the community. The variations are affected by the socioeconomic levels in the individual countries.

PROGRAMS IN DEVELOPED COUNTRIES

In the 1920s in Walthanstow, England, a separate young people's library division was established, and by 1930, 8 percent of London's public libraries had separate youth divisions.[3] This separate program of service has served as a model for young adult services up to the 1970s. A Youth Libraries Group is a section within the Library Association, and the term "youth" here includes both children and adolescents. This group attempts to encourage discussion of and promote an interest in all matters relating to young people's libraries, literature, and all resources in recorded form. It also attempts to collect and disseminate information relating to young people's literature and other recorded resources to raise the standard of book and resource production and selection. It should also be noted that

> the personal and organizational problems of library work with young people, professional training and personal qualities of youth libraries, the intermediate department isolated completely from the children's and adult libraries provided for the first time in 1924, in Walthanstow, is still a model for libraries in surmounting the gap between children's and adult libraries.[4]

A modern effort in the area of young adult library service is that of the North Bedfordshire district's librarian, who believes in cheap and not necessarily orthodox ways of making his service known—including a stock of around 3,000 comic books to tempt the more reluctant customer. Furthermore, "Bedlam" is a youth theater and film group that he runs at Bedford Library, an amalgam formed of a former theater workshop and the library's own film group.

As in so many countries at the moment, there continues to be much discussion as to whether children and young people should be served through the public library, through the school library, or jointly (for example, see Christine Kolet's "Working It Out . . . ," *YLG News* 16 [1972]). Where does the public library fit in? First and foremost, the local public library authority gives provision in the way of materials, including audiovisual resources, to the school through a school library service that is an important link for the school librarian with the profession. The helpful advice that the public librarians can give makes their visits to schools welcome. It is easy to become involved in the day-to-day life of the school if its library is timetabled, and if the librarian can get out of school then to see books, talk to other librarians, and visit the local branch library through regularly organized meetings with the school library service. The librarian thereby can retain current awareness and, incidentally, professional integrity.

The local branch library may also be a good link, because it helps make the school librarian less isolated professionally in demonstrating to teachers and pupils how varied and accessible the resources of a public library are. The school library is a part of a resource center and reprographic unit in the school and should function as a sort of satellite of the local branch library. Telex or computer links, regular book deliveries between the two places, joint book selection meetings, cooperative purchase of periodicals and bibliographic tools, joint production of book lists, interloan of display materials—all are examples of cooperation that are endless.

A 1971 international survey presented some interesting background on the Hungarian situation. A 1965 leisure-time decision affected library services, necessitating a "differentiated" program. In 1968, the executive committee of the Young Communist League's Central Committee joined the movement "For a Reading People" and announced a program "For a Reading Youth." They published methodological guidelines to further cooperation between the Young Communist League and libraries. In 1970, the Communist Party's decision on youth policy affirmed the importance of "differentiated" library services for young people and declared that "institutions and organizations should exert an increasing educative effect on the life of young people in schools, in working places and during their leisure time alike." The National Conference for Public Education in 1971 and the third conference for librarianship both took a strong stand in the organization of young adult library services.[5]

The library department of the Hungarian Ministry of Culture prepared guiding principles for the improvement of library services for children and young adults, and in 1971, these were outlined in relationship to the age group of fourteen to eighteen. From then on there was a strong tendency to organize public library services for young adults. One staff member of the Center for Library Science and Methodology was made responsible for the organization of methodical solutions to problems of library work with young people, to set up the limits and content of youth service, and to elaborate a uniform attitude in connection with it. Librarians in Hungary maintain that young adults expect the library to offer adult services in specialization on an intellectual level designed for teenagers, but young people visiting the adult library are also free to use the whole stock. There appears to be a tendency to consider building new libraries with a youth area adjoining the adult area, but whether or not this has been actually accomplished is not known. Hungarian librarians are concerned about their information work in answer to young readers' demands, and they work particularly with pupils who come from limiting cultural surroundings. They prepare bibliographies for individual youth groups and guides on library use by young people, and they also plan group activities in larger libraries.[6]

In West Germany, school and public libraries are often being built together. For example, in a newly developed suburb of Hanover, the school and public library were designed to be in one building. It is a joint program, however, planned with three professional librarians, two assistant paraprofessionals, and clerks. The school classes come to the branch library both for instruction and for general circulation of materials, although this has been somewhat difficult to develop because public libraries are under the jurisdiction of the Minister of Culture while school libraries are under the Minister of Education.

One of the most significant combined programs is to be found in Bremen, where the former librarian of the city library developed a prototype for school libraries in this area. In West Germany, since there is no unilateral legislation in regard to the development of school or public libraries, states as well as city-states have determined their own particular programs. The individuality of the librarian comes through very clearly in each of these cities as to the direction in which the plan will move. The Bremen librarian indicated that librarians and administrators supported a combined school/public library located in the school, although the teachers preferred the libraries for school use only. The combined program was developed somewhat by chance, with an annex being added to a school building built after World War II to serve both as a public and as a school library. Since then, they have combined these and now have a comprehensive school, the adult education school, and the public library together. It should be noted that the public library and the school library border on each other in most of the new school buildings, so there are separate collections, although they are housed under the same roof. The state of Bremen has a sub-department for youth library work, where the librarians who work in school and public libraries meet once a month for meetings and discussions. The public library has a separate entrance, with direct access from the street. The opening hours of the library can then be extended regardless of the school's hours or school vacations. Since both libraries are housed in the same building, often the cultural activities of the immediate area are planned as a part of the community library program as well.[7]

In Australia, a survey done by Helen Modra in the early 1970s revealed some important implications for aspects of public library service to teen-agers: libraries often represented outmoded institutions to the majority of teen-agers, yet many dropouts and graduates remain undiscerning and illiterate in the broadest sense. Modra believes that the educational system must involve public libraries as a part of the total educational network, but the library as presently constituted gives no opportunity for involvement and youth participation. In Western Australia, public libraries are providing more service in some of the suburbs. Secondary school library services have been expanding. Certainly the movement toward cooperative school and public library facilities with combined staff and program has gained momentum within the last two or three years. Young adult librarians there, as in many other "developed" countries, are attempting to make available materials that young people consider relevant, including more new books, films, cassettes, and other formats. They are looking for new types of centers where they can relax and enjoy new forms of group activities such as poetry discussions, pop films, and "how to cope" programs.

An experience in an industrial area of the state of Victoria may seem familiar to many librarians. The setting is a library center that houses primarily migrants, non-readers, and troublemakers and, in the winter, those needing a place to keep warm and comfortable. Finally, instead of a policy of tossing out, the staff tried an approach of "talk-on-equal-terms." They discovered that not all were non-readers, but that the readers only read when at home or alone, so the problem of disruption continued.[8] Little understanding or financial support came from the shire council. Obviously the problem lies in the fact that a small staff and limited facilities simply cannot tame or entertain all teen-agers. It is reasonably easy to work with readers, but not with the great block of young adults who come to the library only to escape school. Australia's young adult librarians are moving in a new direction, reacting to public opinion, employing more professionals, and trying (as are librarians in every country) to understand this age group and provide them with library services they are currently demanding.

EFFORTS IN DEVELOPING COUNTRIES

Programs in developing countries primarily concentrate on school library development. Nevertheless, there has been growth in public library service to children and, to a lesser degree, for young adults. Concern for such services has been evidenced from Unesco and Unicef, particularly in Asia and Africa during the last decade.

A regional seminar on "Planning, Production, and Distribution of Books for Children and Young People in Asia" was organized by the Unesco Regional Centre for Book Development in Asia [office in Karachi] and held at Kuala Lumpur, Malaysia, from December 8-13, 1975. This seminar was in response to the continued emphasis placed on the need for suitable literature for children and young people, a very weak area in the publishing efforts in the developing countries of Asia. Some stimulus is clearly needed to focus attention on the dire necessity to plan, produce, and distribute attractive low-cost books, and thereby to promote and maintain the reading habit in the new generation.

There were 21 participants representing 13 countries of Asia, namely, Afghanistan, Bangladesh, India, Indonesia, Iran, Republic of Korea, Malaysia, Nepal, Pakistan, the Philippines, Singapore, Sri Lanka, and Thailand. In addition, there were eleven observers from various professional associations in Malaysia. The Asian Cultural Centre for Unesco/Tokyo Book Development Center was represented also. Although the seminar intended to emphasize mainly general books for children and young people, there was a tendency among countries represented to place emphasis on textbooks, which apparently form the main bulk of reading material for children. Nevertheless, strong recommendations were drafted, among them:

1. each Asian country should establish a National Book Develop-ment Programme as an integral part of its overall national development programme;

2. a Children's Book Council or a Children's Book Committee should be established in each Asian country by the national body for book development, to ensure the healthy develop-ment of books for children and young people. Regular meet-ings of publishers, writers, illustrators, printers, booksellers, librarians, and all those connected with the planning, produc-tion and distribution of books, as well as teachers and parents and the government, (if and when required), should be held as a substantial joint national effort towards promoting books and the reading habit among children and young people;

3. extensive surveys and research into the reading tastes of children and young people should be regularly conducted in each country of the region, particularly in the rural areas, in order to provide information and guidance for the formula-tion of the national book programme;

4. every Asian country should have a library not only in each school, but in each classroom as well, to help promote and sustain reading interests, as well as to provide an effective channel for the distribution of books for children and young people. All public libraries should have special sections for children and young people. The government in each country of the region should consider setting up mini-libraries in villages and remote places with the cooperation of the local people;

5. a central body should be set up in each country of the region to evaluate and recommend suitable reading material for children and young people through the regular publication of bibliographies. This body could also become the central pur-chasing agency to procure in bulk the book requirement of libraries throughout the country including those in the schools;

6. parents should be urged, through incentives and other forms of encouragement, to establish a book collection at home for their children. Adequate time should be provided for children to read books other than their textbooks. It is

suggested that educational authorities in the countries of the region consider reducing the curriculum load which would appear to be heavy at present;

7. reading materials for children and young people in Asia should be geared to meet the needs of the child's growth and development. Since children and young people everywhere like to read comics, this medium should be well exploited and fully utilized effectively to stimulate reading interest, but it is essential that the contents of these comics be of good quality;

8. each country of the region should intensify its research into and publication of traditional literature for children and young people, and introduce more stories with local themes. Traditional stories should be rewritten for children either in prose, verse, or made into cartoons;

9. there should be sustained regional collaboration in the production of books for children and young people and this should include regular exchanges of new publications among the countries of the region.[9]

Among the African countries, Nigeria, Kenya, and Ghana are perhaps the most active in promoting service to youth. Tanzania, the Union of South Africa, the Ivory Coast, and Ethiopia, up until a few years ago, have also endeavored to begin and expand book collections and personnel to support what they consider a basic need in their socioeconomic development plans. Again, only a few examples can be mentioned, but they reinforce the national trends. In Kenya, it should be pointed out, the majority of children's books not directly related to school educational curricula are books published outside Kenya. Very little is published in Kenya that is not textual material. A similar general comment can be made about publishing for young adults in Africa. The majority of the young population in Kenya is of African origin. But there are also Asian, Australian, and European readers, and they fall into two main categories—the rural population and the urban (and to a large extent cosmopolitan) population.[10] Actually, even in the cities, few children have any concept of the use and enjoyment of books, while folk material is particularly enjoyed, a distinct connection with the oral culture that still prevails.

Most African books are published in English, although more effort is now being made to print in each country's vernacular. Little, for example, is published in Swahili, the national language of Kenya. West African publishers have done more to correct this, and many of those titles will also be found in East African countries, since local experiences are quite similar—even though the native languages are quite different. The emphasis is on making children aware of their immediate surroundings and then on developing their curiosity about the rest of the world.

A program for companies producing children's books in the area south of the Sahara has been promoted by Unesco. This is similar to the highly successful program of the Tokyo Center for the Development of the Book in Asia. The aim is to publish large editions of texts in the languages of those countries participating, prepared by authors of the region and complemented by native illustrators and artists. This effort is based on the fact that reading habits are developed at an early age and can determine the future behavior of young adults. Such stories should arouse interest in international understanding as well.

It is interesting to note that public library service, bookmobiles, library education, and school library service developed early their independent status among the English-speaking countries of Africa. This was not so in the former French colonies. Some of this can certainly be traced to the attitude toward library service for children and youth in the respective European colonizing countries. Although this is changing now, there is still great unevenness in library service among African countries.

Nigeria and Ghana lead among the West African countries in the development of library service to schools, particularly at the secondary level. In Ghana, school library service is coordinated at the Central Library in Accra, and a bookmobile carries current materials around to regional centers. This remarkable program of selection, processing, etc. is carried on by a staff of three at the main office. Although the Central Library itself has a stronger public program for children than for young adults, there is concern to serve this age group, as witness the many older teen-age students who come to the library for study and reference work. Formal young adult service, not school affiliated, is an area still to be developed.

In Nigeria, an increasing number of urban families are literate, but the actual acquisition of reading materials for the home is seldom realized.[11] Generally, children in both rural and urban homes do not read until they enter school. The Universal Primary Education Act not only has impelled Nigerian children into school but has increased the problem of having enough reading material. Too often, it is a case of "read and pass on to the next person." There is, therefore, no reading tradition on which to build, and little is available for older youth to read. Furthermore, this group is out in the streets and fields attempting to earn money rather than going on to secondary schools and higher education programs. As mentioned in connection with Kenya, the national language in Nigeria is a second language, English remaining the common reading language; and there is little written material in the vernacular. However, experimental centers are being established and books in Yoruba, Ibo, etc. are being published, which encourages expansion.

Public library services to children began in Lagos (capital of Nigeria) in the 1950s and have spread to other regions. Most of the nineteen state libraries support the expansion of children's programs within their systems. Service for teen-agers is conducted primarily through the secondary schools, which far outnumber public libraries even though their programs and facilities are often minimal.

An outstanding program of school library service has been developed in the state of Lagos. This was started as a Unesco Pilot Project and included an education library for teachers, demonstration libraries for both primary and post-primary schools, centralized school library service, and training programs for teacher/librarians. Today, services to schools are being operated in some other Nigerian states. An effective model demonstration media center is the Abadina School Library Project in Ibadan, operated by the Department of Library Studies, University of Ibadan. The Bendel State Library Board also operates an effective book depot for school and public libraries, one of the most efficient programs for acquisition and dissemination of materials to librarians in the country.

Several states have organized school library associations, and the Nigeria School Library Association was formally organized in October 1977. These associations are pushing for minimum standards for school libraries, for government support, and for qualified staff and materials in sufficient quantity for every Nigerian child to read. African librarians are cognizant of the need for expanding public library service not only through existing children's rooms, but also for the older readers. But motivation for support of such programs has still to be developed; the library spirit is willing, but often the governmental flesh is weak.

In Malaysia, the educational system is centrally administered by the federal government. All primary and secondary schools follow the same curriculum, drawn up by the Ministry of Education. Librarianship is a comparatively young profession in Malaysia. The professional association is the Persatuan Perpustakaan Malaysia (Library Association of Malaysia). Originating from the Malaysian Library Group (first inaugurated in 1955), this association is very active and has made a significant contribution to the development of Malaysian libraries. Its Steering Committee on School Libraries prepares booklists for the schools, and in cooperation with the Ministry of Education, it has organized a National Progress Award for school libraries. Recently, several Malaysian states have organized state school library associations for teachers and heads of schools.

The National Library of Malaysia was officially established in 1971, although the nucleus of the staff was developed in 1967. It hopes to offer public library services to the Federal Territory of Kuala Lumpur. The National Library is actively involved in assisting state governments to set up a network of public library services in peninsular Malaysia. All eleven states in peninsular Malaysia offer public library services—some include branch and mobile services; eight of these have legislation for State Public Library Corporations.[12]

A general survey of some 4,592 Malaysian schools was made in 1973. Only 19 percent of the primary schools had centralized libraries. On the other hand, only 2.5 percent of the secondary schools surveyed did not have library facilities, and 82.2 percent of them had centralized libraries. Most of the librarians in these schools also carry a normal teaching load (25 to 30 teaching periods). About 63.8 percent of the secondary schools had between 1,000 and 5,000 volumes, but many of these could have been duplicates, obsolete textbooks, etc. About 25 percent of the primary schools and 36 percent of the secondary schools provide library periods, mostly for silent reading and borrowing materials. The majority of the libraries are only open during recess and after school hours for a short period. It should also be noted that there is great contrast between rural and urban schools.[13] Since 1973, a School Library Service Unit has been a part of the Schools' Division in the Ministry of Education. The federal organizer is responsible for planning and implementing school libraries in peninsular Malaysia and for in-service training programs.

Again as in many developing countries, the lack of a good book distribution network is a problem in developing library service for youth. The level of production is low and indigenous writers are limited in number. Although English books are available, books for general reading in Malaysia are not adequate in number at present. However, since 1956 a federal movement to publish Malaysian materials (such as encyclopedias, dictionaries, fiction, and non-fiction) has been evident. Furthermore, all primary and secondary schools are now given an annual library subsidy, which should stimulate both the production and acquisition of Malaysian material. As materials begin to proliferate, and as students and teachers become aware of library values, it is to be expected that there will be an increase in programs developed by public libraries. But again, until there is a reading public (which is dependent upon the educational scheme), there will be neither the demand nor the support for broad public library access.

The program for library services in New Zealand falls between the quite well-developed Australian system and the efforts of the developing countries in Southeast Asia. The New Zealand Library Association includes a Children's and Young People's Section designed to provide a meeting ground for those professionally involved in providing library service to children, whether through public libraries, the centers of School Library Services, teachers' colleges, or the libraries of individual schools. Present targets are to implement recommendations made by Sara Fenwick in her 1974 report on her visit to New Zealand, and to ensure that any courses for school librarians meet a standard approved by the New Zealand Library Association. The Children's and Young People's Section is responsible for sessions at the New Zealand Library Association's annual conference, which holds a regional seminar annually, and prepares an annual booklist for parents.

The National Library of New Zealand, through its School Library Services, has provided bulk loans of books to schools, as well as special loans on request. The bulk exchanges are gradually being replaced by repository loans, while demands on the request service are steadily increasing. There is a field staff of fifteen itinerant library advisors who are much appreciated by the untrained people working in school libraries. However, there are also about 1,500 school libraries, so the advisors' influence is necessarily limited. There are school library associations in the three largest cities but no national school-related association. Discussions are going on about the relative advantages of forming such a national association or forming a school library section within the New Zealand Library Association.

All recent reports on New Zealand's education system have recommended the provision of trained full-time staff in school libraries. It is now government policy to extend the training of librarians to ensure that courses are open to teachers and librarians to qualify as school librarians. Approval to set up these courses has not yet been given, but planning is underway. Teachers in charge of libraries, helped by School Library Service librarians and supported by parents, have provided a service to pupils and teachers that is remarkable when the shortages of training, time, and money are considered.[14]

It is particularly interesting to note the recognition of the need for library services in the islands of the South Pacific. The Kingdom of Tonga, for example, consists of 200 islands clustered in the South Pacific Ocean as the southern point of a triangle of independent island states, the two others being Fiji (80 miles west) and Western Samoa (about the same distance to the north). They are about 1,800 miles due east of the northern Queensland coast of Australia, and 1,100 miles north of New Zealand. Tonga's population is 90,000. The government of Tonga, in the 1950s, established a Tonga Traditions Committee to collect, record, and interpret the area's cultural heritage. Funds were voted annually in the first two Development Plans periods, but because of limited resources and urgent economic requirements, it was deferred. The government is now convinced that the project can not be deferred any longer.

The major objective is to raise the standard of living of the people of Tonga, which means not only an emphasis on in-school education but also on out-of-school education. There is no public library or even a good secondary school library in Tonga. A *public library* therefore assumes an even greater importance than in metropolitan countries as a vital institution for students, civil servants, teachers, laborers, and employees in the private sector as well as for members of the public. It is essential for the development of quality in literacy, for individual and social growth, as well as serving as a center of reference.

The library situation in the government's primary schools is unvarying: they have no libraries. It has been suggested by the Senior Education Officer for Primary Schools that it may be better to start with a teachers' library, for through teachers children will be encouraged to read. Once the teachers' library has been set up and proved to be operating well, a library for the students should then be considered. Regular finance is required for books, both for the teachers and the students. Books donated are hardly ever on the right level, and for anyone starting to read in a second language, it is most important to find reading material at the right level. Therefore, a standard that states the amount of library money for each school should be drawn up.

Books are received currently as gifts both from the Overseas Book Centre (Canada), the British High Commission, and Rotary International (both in New Zealand and Australia). These books have been distributed to secondary schools, although some have been kept by the Department since the Resource Center for Teachers was set up in the middle of 1977. Emphasis on promoting secondary school library centers will continue simultaneously.[15]

Some brief notes on other countries reemphasize problems and delineate special efforts. A low per capita income in Afghanistan, with its predominantly agricultural economic base, has led to an alarmingly high school 'drop-out' rate. A very small percentage of students continue beyond primary levels of education. Under the circumstances, the country has not been able to achieve much in the field of children's books, although there have been some tangible achievements in textbooks and educational planning. A Reading Readiness program has been initiated for the first grades. Besides textbooks, there are a few magazines for the children and Radio Afghanistan broadcasts five-minute storytelling periods every night, besides a bi-weekly educational program and two other such programs per week. Lack of trained personnel for production and printing, shortage of paper, and the shortage of trained artists, calligraphers, modern printing machines, and other necessities have all added to the difficulties.[16]

Iran is quite ahead of most of the developing countries of Asia insofar as printing facilities, paper, etc. are concerned. The Institute for the Intellectual Development of Children and Young Adults has done commendable work ever since its inception in 1965. The standards of production, layout and illustration for its books are comparable with standards anywhere in the world. Being a non-profit-making organization, its books are sold at cost. The Institute has greatly helped in the development of libraries and programs for children, and it also produces filmstrips and films.[17]

One of the greatest achievements of the Republic of Korea has been the establishment of "mini-libraries." A library has been established in each village, and it is expected that the network of these libraries will help increase the demand for books. Lack of authors for children's books has resulted in a greater number of translated books, as compared to original books. Yet, the standard of production in Korea is quite high, and printing cannot be listed as a problem, although the increasing cost of production is an obstacle.[18]

Pakistan is fortunate in having a large number of good writers and illustrators for children's books, but the output of such books has been far from satisfactory. According to a survey conducted in 1975 by the Department of Karachi, only 2,442 children's books were published as of 1972-1973. Printing is not a problem, although Pakistan still has to import some paper, particularly good quality offset paper. The setting up of the National Foundation in Pakistan has been a good step forward, as it published nineteen titles in 1973, with a print order of 6,000 copies for each title.[19] It will be interesting to see how library services to youth develop.

Although 80 percent of Filipinos can be termed literate, most have attended schools only up to the fifth grade, which is not surprising as farming is the main occupation in the Philippines. With more than 87 ethnolinguistic groups speaking their different tongues, the production and sale of books is not a very profitable business. Now, however, Philippine, based on Tagalog (one of the major native languages) has been adopted as a national language. From the academic year 1976-1977, all books for use in schools and colleges will be written by Filipinos themselves.[20] The newly created School Library Association, a part of the

Philippine Library Association, is endeavoring to promote more non-textbook reading at both the primary and secondary levels.

Singapore, with a fairly high literacy rate (72 percent), a good per capita income, excellent communication facilities, and sophisticated printing equipment, apparently does not have any problems, but the growth in production of children's books other than textbooks, has not been satisfactory. Seventy-one percent of the population is Chinese and they form the majority of purchasers; but most Chinese books are imported from Taiwan. The National Library, which also serves as the Public Library for Singapore, has an outstanding department for children's library services, and it also includes a collection of books about Singapore but printed in other countries. The new public library branches located in growing neighborhood community centers are encouraging active programs for both children and young adults; a third branch will be opened in November 1979. Creative writing also is being encouraged at all school levels. Both primary and secondary school library service may be found in the government schools. A coordinator for school library service is located within the Ministry of Education, and a training program is educating a corps of teacher/librarians.

Children constitute half of the population of the developing world. In India alone, 42 percent of the population is below the age of 15, but less than 2 percent of titles other than textbooks published in this country are for this age group.[21] The Children's Book Trust, which came into existence in 1957, has attempted through seminars, displays, and some book publishing to improve the amount and the content of books for youth. Yet, reading for pleasure has not received a great deal of emphasis in the home or school. Mrs. Molina Rao of the National Book Trust recently indicated at a Unesco seminar that there is a scarcity of good material. There is also inadequate incentive to authors to write books for children. A "network of libraries" is the other essential in a country where low family budgets preclude the buying of children's books for pleasure and 70 percent of the population still depends primarily upon oral communication.[22] Government support for a good publication program that will not only produce books in quantity, of quality, but also in the various vernacular languages needed in the many states of India, appears to be the only answer for the tremendous "book hunger" indicated by Indian educators and librarians. Little service that could be described as relevant to the needs of the young adult or adolescent is available in the few public libraries in metropolitan centers.

Current efforts in the Caribbean and Latin America can best be summarized from the report of the Jamaica Library Association's 1971 conference on the "Challenge of Change" in the West Indies. Children's service in the West Indies began to develop after World War II, and the programs in the United States and Scandinavian countries served as examples. Since that time, public library service and school programs have expanded together, as educators and administrators realize the increased urgency of the role education will play in developing nations. The problem of not having a sufficient number of books will continue to plague this part of the world for many years. Bookmobile service to schools has become an important ancillary to the education program at both primary and secondary levels. The following summarizes the conclusions of the conference delegates:

> An arbitrary division into (a) Children's libraries for the age group 4-13, and (b) Young Adult libraries for the age group 14-18, is attempted. The first have been very well established, although in fact they serve youths up to fifteen years of age. To a large extent, they have realized the main objectives of public library service to children, one of the most important in the West Indian context being "to help the child develop to the full his personal ability, and his social understanding."

> While many libraries do not have separate Young Adults rooms the need is recognized and the physical location may either be in the existing children's room or form part of the Adult Library. Whatever the location, careful selection of material and sympathetic guidance for the users are assured. Physical surroundings are also made especially attractive. Response is overwhelming and librarians report great interest in "black literature," Afro-American art, books on self improvement and careers. Extensive use is made of periodical literature. Often the Young Adults exist as an unofficial group bound together by areas of common interest.

A bold plan for the provision of library facilities for Young Adults was carried out by the Institute of Jamaica, the island's foremost cultural centre, founded in 1879 "for the encouragement of Literature, Science and Art". In 1940, the Institute opened two Junior Centres as cultural centres for young people of the Corporate Area, the island's most populous area with 572,653 people. The main building close to the Institute itself is situated in the heart of downtown Kingston; the other occupies the interesting old courthouse at Half-Way-Tree in the uptown area, and is operated part-time. A bookstock of 26,505 serves 8,060 members.

Each Centre therefore concentrated on the establishment of a library to serve young people up to the age of eighteen years. These were the first free libraries in Jamaica, and for many years remained the only public libraries for children on the island. In addition, a number of schools both in the rural and corporate areas were supplied with boxes of books purchased with a grant from the Carnegie Foundation. This service was administered until libraries in primary schools were established by the Jamaica Library Service, beginning in 1952.

Each Centre has the library as its nucleus or focal point around which a number of cultural activities are created. Art, creative dancing and music, sewing, handicrafts, home economics as well as nature study and Spanish are the main activities.

The fact that these islands have no written language of their own could well be a mixed blessing. Total acceptance of English as the official language of the people and the absence of tribal, racial, and language barriers make it easier to provide material with limited budgets. Commonwealth and U.S. book markets are rich. Perhaps because of this rich heritage, very few West Indian authors have felt the need to write for children.[23]

The recent expansion of the Banco del Libro in Caracas, Venezuela, is indication of the recognition now being given by the government to the need to provide books for children in that city and surrounding areas. The "Book Bank," founded as a private non-profit organization in 1960, was designed to promote a more imaginative and fuller utilization of educational materials. The hope was to move beyond quality textbooks, and the main emphasis was on school libraries as the most effective means to "renovate" education. A series of pilot projects to establish elementary school libraries was begun around 1965. These demonstration centers have now stimulated the federal government to establish a national system of school libraries to help students move into adult life backed by their own cultural traditions. The Banco produces new teaching aids, investigates reading habits, and supports an audiovisual center. Public library reading rooms are set up for people residing outside Caracas, and library buses have been in operation since 1971.[24]

In Bolivia, on the other hand, a good, functioning library system does not exist despite the Mettini plan proposed in the early 1970s, which concentrated on school and public library needs. Illiteracy is still the great stumbling block, as well as the fact that many of the people use their own native language rather than Spanish. Only about 25 percent speak Spanish as a first language, and literature in Quechua and Aymara is very sparse. Today, Bolivian public libraries depend upon local authorities or the universities, and the result is poor service in most places. There is inadequate stock, staff, and facilities; and hours of operation are limited. The one exception is the library in the city of Cochabamba, which regularly receives support and contributions and is utilized especially by youth.[25] The problems of Bolivia are those of most underdeveloped nations. National resources are not sufficient, although the plan is there. But local and national authorities must indicate solid fiscal support and interest.

It has been said that the shortest way to acquire universal culture is via the discovery of one's own culture. Despite the efforts of librarians (both school and public) to provide material, facilities, and programs for youth, it is evident that a large percentage of the world's population teen-age or younger is being deprived of opportunities that we in the United States take for granted. The concern is there, but the constant problems—sufficient materials, indigenous authors and publishing firms, government support through ministries of education or culture, solid financial resources, sufficiently trained and adequate staff—

are of such magnitude that one marvels at how much really is being accomplished. The perseverance, creativity, and ingenuity of those persons in other countries and of other cultures should serve as an inspiration to those of us in wealthier, more developed countries where libraries have high visibility and are better supported. The efforts being made by all librarians to share materials from and expand programs within their countries should lead toward that utopia of universal cultural understanding.

NOTES

[1] World Conference of Organizations of the Teaching Profession. *Proceedings of the XXVI Assembly of Delegates*, Lagos, Nigeria, August 3-10, 1977, p. 7.

[2] L. Konyves-Toth, "Youth Library Services in Public Libraries: An International Survey," *International Library Review* 4 (July 1972): 305.

[3] Ibid.

[4] Ibid.

[5] Ibid., p. 309.

[6] Ibid., pp. 310-11.

[7] Notes from IASL Tour, 1975.

[8] Jill McCallum, "Teenagers in the Library," *Australian Library Journal* 23 (1974), p. 252.

[9] "Newsletter," Tokyo Book Center, Asian Cultural Center for Unesco, vol. 11, pp. 6-7.

[10] Francis Otieno Pala, "Children's Literature in Kenya: The National and the International Aspects," *Bookbird* 13 (February 1975): 19.

[11] Dorothy S. Obi, "Children's Libraries and Their Users: Nigeria," (unpublished IFLA paper; September 8, 1978), p. 1.

[12] Kim Sing Wong, "Report of School Library Development in Malaysia," (paper delivered at IFLA/UNESCO Pre-session Seminar for Librarians for Developing Countries, Oslo, Norway; August 4-9, 1975), pp. 3-4.

[13] Ibid.

[14] *IASL Newsletter* [notes from New Zealand] 7 (April 1978): 3-4.

[15] Tuita Tu'ilokamana, "Report from Kingdom of Tonga on School Library Development by the Director of Education," *IASL Newsletter* 7 (April 1978): 4-6.

[16] C. N. Rao, "Books for Children: An Assessment of the Availability of Children's Literature in the Asian Countries," *Bookbird* 15 (January 1977): 19.

[17] Ibid., p. 21.

[18] Ibid., p. 22.

[19] Ibid., p. 23.

[20] Ibid.

[21] Lal Raj Dhillon, "Books for Children" [compiled from newspaper editorials in *Times of India* from the last twenty years; published January 1978].

[22] Molina Rao, "Out of School Books for Children" (unpublished paper delivered at Seminar in Educational Publishing in Developing Countries; February 12-15, 1978).

[23] Amy Robertson, "Libraries for Youth with Special Reference to the Commonwealth Caribbean," *Library, Challenge of Change*, Jamaica Library Association Conference (London: Mansell, 1971), p. 109.

[24] Alvaro Agudo, "Library Service in Venezuela—Activities of the Banco del Libro," *Bookbird* 12, no. 4 (April 1974): 59-60.

[25] L. G. Benkston, "Bolivia: A Plan for the Development of Public and School Libraries," *International Library Review* 10 (January 1978): 71-75.

BIBLIOGRAPHY

Agudo, Alvaro. "Library Service in Venezuela: Activities of the Banco del Libro." *Bookbird* 12 (1974): 59-60.

"Bedlam in Bedford." *Library Association Record* 78 (1976).

Benkston, L. G. "Bolivia: A Plan for the Development of Public and School Libraries." *International Library Review* 10 (January 1978): 71-75.

Dhillon, Lal Raj. "Books for Children" [compiled from newspaper editorials in *Times of India* from the last twenty years as an informal report for Jaswaht Singh, doctoral student, Western Michigan University], January 1978.

Dimang, Jean. "Project for the Co-Production of Children's Books in Africa." *Bookbird* 14 (1976): 127-29.

Dubois, Rauol. "Pedagogical Renovation and Literature for Young People." *Bookbird* 13 (1975): 6-12.

Fayose, P. Osazee. "A Look at Nigerian Children's Literature." *Bookbird* 15 (1977): 2-5.

International Association of School Librarianship. *Annual Conference Proceedings*; Singapore, July 27-30, 1974; Berlin, July 27-29, 1975; Ibadan, Nigeria, July 28-August 2, 1977.

"IASL Newsletter." 7 (April 1978).

Keehan, Anne L. "Coming of Age: Library Services for Children and Young Adults in Western Australia." *Library Journal* 98 (November 1973): 3427-31.

Kolet, Christine. "Working It Out–The School Library, the Chartered Librarian and the Public Library!" *YLG News* [Library Association Youth Libraries Group] 16 (Winter 1972): 4-6.

Konyves-Toth, L. "Youth Library Services in Public Libraries: An International Survey." *International Library Review* 4 (July 1972): 303-311.

McCallum, Jill. "Teenagers in the Library." *The Australian Library Journal* 23 (August 1974): 252-55.

Matsuoka, Kyoko. "Asian Co-Publishing of Books for Children." *Newsletter* [Tokyo Book Centre] 7 (November 1976): 8-9.

Modra, Helen M. "Some Thoughts on Public Library Service to Teenagers." *The Australian Library Journal* 21 (May 1972): 151-56.

"Newsletter." Tokyo Book Centre, Asian Cultural Center for UNESCO. Vol. 11.

Obi, Dorothy S. "Children's Libraries and Their Users: Nigeria." Unpublished paper presented at Children's Libraries Section, IFLA, September 8, 1977.

Pala, Francis Otieno. "Children's Literature in Kenya: The National and the International Aspects." *Bookbird* 13 (February 1975): 17-21.

Patti, Genevieve. "Children's Libraries in France, Part II." *Bookbird* 13 (February 1975): 22-30.

Rao, C. N. "Books for Children: An Assessment of the Availability of Children's Literature in the Asian Countries." *Bookbird* 15 (January 1977): 19-24.

Rao, Molina. "Out of School Books for Children." Unpublished paper delivered at the Seminar in Educational Publishing in Developing Countries, February 12-15, 1978. New Delhi, India: National Book Trust.

Robertson, Amy. "Libraries for Youth with Special Reference to the Commonwealth Caribbean." *Library, Challenge of Change*. Jamaica Library Association Conference. London: Mansell, 1971, pp. 104-114.

"School Libraries in the Arab Countries." *Library World* 60 (January-April 1969).

"School Media Centers: A Response to Change." Melbourne: Australian School Library Association, 1972.

Tu'ilokamana, Tuita. "Report from Kingdom of Tonga on School Library Development by the Director of Education." *IASL Newsletter* 7 (April 1978): 4-6.

Wong, Kim Sing. "Report of School Library Development in Malaysia." Unpublished paper presented at IFLA/UNESCO Pre-session Seminar for Librarians for Developing Countries. Oslo, Norway, August 4-9, 1975.

World Conference of Organizations of the Teaching Profession. *Proceedings of the XXVI Assembly of Delegates, Lagos, Nigeria, August 3-10, 1977.* Morges, Switzerland, 1977.

PART III

YOUNG ADULT LIBRARIANSHIP

INTRODUCTION

Recognizing the unique needs of young adults, many libraries and library systems develop young adult collections or departments that are staffed by young adult specialists who are often aided by a system coordinator responsible for meeting the needs of young adults. Although young adult librarianship is recognized as an area of professional specialization, there is an on-going debate and dialog (mainly between library and information science educators and library practitioners) as to the most appropriate preparation for young adult librarians. Setting aside the question of the merit of on-the-job training and work experience within the established avenues of under-graduate and graduate preparation for library service, Susan Steinfirst, a library educator helping to prepare young adult specialists at the University of North Carolina, summarizes here the range of opinions concerning the form and content of programs to educate the YA specialist.

A survey of the literature reveals that, for almost half a century, the profession has been calling for information, knowledge, and skills in the same basic areas: adolescent psychology, sociology, selection and acquisition of materials, knowledge of reading interests and literature for adolescents, and management skills. More recently, there have been cries for program planning and public relations skills to be included as well. One of the main problems that continues to trouble library educators is the difficulty of making course work in adolescent psychology, sociology, and physiology available through a library science program or through other departments or colleges within a university. There seems to be a need to package individual programs for those who want to specialize in library work with young adults. Yet within a tightly structured one-year master's level program, selection of elective courses in other disciplines presents a problem for the library science student who feels pressured to take a well-rounded program in library and information science.

Some possible solutions to the problem of adequate pre-service preparation include individual interdisciplinary packages, curriculum reform, and providing time in the academic setting for experimental training. The suggestion also is made that library education programs provide continuing education for those working with young people. This is particularly important because library science students often do not anticipate that their positions will include responsibility for young adults, when in fact, those people who work in small libraries and some special libraries such as film libraries are responsible for collecting and programming for all age groups. Many of the issues raised in connection with the education of the young adult specialist are similar to those raised in connection with educating people in any area of specialization. These include questions of undergraduate preparation, length of the master's level program, and the role of continuing education in professional preparation.

Although there are small libraries and special libraries where the only professional on the staff is responsible for all client groups, there are also large library systems that have young adult specialists assigned to each branch library and an overall coordinator of young adult services for the system. Julia Losinski, coordinator of Young Adult Services in Prince George's County Memorial Library System (Hyattsville, Maryland), discusses the role of the coordinator who acts in an advisory capacity in planning and implementation of YA services. Serving as a staff officer, Losinski discusses the interaction between herself and YA specialists. Also, communication between the young adult coordinator and other library system administrators is the basis for a common understanding of the importance of young adult work in meeting the goals and objectives of the library. Losinski thus emphasizes the advisability of developing goals and objectives for YA work within the system, and she further points out that the YA specialist is in a good position to assess the needs of the YA population, which will be used in determining the programming best suited to their needs. Duties of the coordinator focus on staff and materials as well as on programs.

A former library development consultant for Children's and Young Adult Services with the State Library of Ohio, Sarah Long discusses the role of the young adult coordinator at the state level. Identifying young adult services as a special aspect of library work, she suggests that the standards for public libraries imply that some direction and help should be provided by state library agencies. Included in the discussion are suggested activities for a state coordinator or consultant for young adult services and a job description for a state consultant. The apparent lack of interest on the part of state library agencies in serving the young adult is disheartening to many professional librarians, who see a need for improvement in the programs of individual libraries and some of the larger systems. Including young adult services as a part of the responsibility of a state coordinator of children's services is one approach to provision of some type of service, but even in these situations, the young adult remains a second class citizen. Public libraries have traditionally emphasized and often excelled in collecting materials and providing some services for children. Library patrons are often lost during the teen years, however, and state library agencies need to consider the causes of and to help to plan cures for this unfortunate situation.

A major vehicle for communication among librarians who serve youth is the Young Adult Services Division of the American Library Association, a division of the major national organization promoting libraries and library services whose various activities are detailed by Carol Starr, coordinator of Young Adult Services in the Alameda County (California) Library system and a past president of YASD. Long active in the organization, she has had the opportunity to learn about its past and has done much to shape its future. Beginning with some historical perspective, the article emphasizes the way in which the structure of the organization, particularly its working committees, has influenced young adult services and collections through programs presented at ALA annual conferences and through the publications that it has sponsored. The history of the organization shows that it is a dynamic one, anxious to change to meet the changing needs of young people. Particularly for those librarians not able to attend the ALA conferences and programs, the annual publication of the "Best Books for Young Adults" list and other periodically updated bibliographies of good reading, listening, and viewing material for young people are important.

In recent years, the inclusion of more material in *Top of the News* of interest to young adult specialists as well as to those who work with children is helpful. More recently, the liaison work of YASD committees with those who publish and distribute material for the young adult market and with other types of organizations that serve youth is a trend that promises to yield some positive results. This example might be followed on the local level, where librarians who work with young people can go beyond the library to learn about and cooperate with other community agencies involved with youth work. An area of current and continuing concern to all librarians, but particularly to young adult librarians, is that of intellectual freedom and censorship. Many censorship attempts involve materials for young adults, and the national organization has done much to support a free access to all materials for young people.

One of the major publications discussed by Bernard Lukenbill in his survey of research in young adult literature and services is *Media and the Young Adult: A Selected Bibliography, 1950-1972*, a project of the Research Committee of YASD. Categories for inclusion are, briefly: characteristics of youth; information needs and information seeking behavior; materials, media use, and their impact; and strategies for teaching the use of print and nonprint materials by youth. Using the resource file that he keeps to update the bibliography for which he was editor, Lukenbill then describes some additional studies published through 1977 and also points out many sources of information about research dealing with various aspects of adolescents but published outside the literature of librarianship. Among the suggested areas for further research are the information needs of and the delivery systems available to young adults, consideration of library management decisions and their effects on young adult use of libraries, and the role of the young adult specialist from different points of view.

As executive secretary of the Young Adult Services Division of ALA, Evelyn Shaevel is often asked about ways in which librarians and library educators can keep up with information about materials and services for young adults. In the past several years, there has been an increase in interest in young adult library patrons, and locating the best material to read concerning them is becoming more difficult. Her suggestions about items to consult include general library periodicals, specialized library periodicals, and journals in other disciplines concerned with youth. In addition to participation in professional organizations and continuing education activities, monitoring this literature is necessary if the librarian is to be informed about current trends and issues in serving youth in libraries. Included in the article is a list of those periodical publications discussed.

EDUCATION OF THE
YOUNG ADULT LIBRARIAN

Susan Steinfirst

HISTORICAL BACKGROUND

Ideally, this statement on training the YA librarian should have been co-authored by a practitioner and a library educator. From the 1930s on, practitioners have been vocal about and critical of the training received by the fledgling young adult librarian in fifth year graduate programs. The first article by a librarian about YA training to appear in the literature was written by Jean Roos, librarian of the Robert Louis Stevenson Room in the Cleveland Public Library. In this 1930 article, presented originally in Los Angeles at the Young People's Reading Round Table (a forerunner of American Library Association's Young Adult Services Division), Roos commented that specially trained librarians were needed for public library work with young people as well as for school library work, that standards for training YA librarians should be more strenuous for public librarians than for school librarians, and "that previous college work should include survey courses in education, courses in sociology and a study of both child psychology and adolescent psychology."[1] Further, Roos went on,

> at Western Reserve University School of Library Science, the general course in the library school is the basis of the training for young people's workers with specialization in book selection and reference. Further specialization in technical subjects and administration is given for those planning to do high school library work. Field work, class discussions, seminar problems and conference periods are important parts of this training. A detailed study is made of the literature of young people and of their reading interests, working out methods and devices to stimulate and direct those interests. Methods used in group work are discussed and the planning and presenting of book talks to various types of groups are included. A knowledge of children's literature is very helpful in carrying

over the book interests of our juvenile readers and in developing broader reading horizons. Library experience with the early adolescent group is also an asset.[2]

And, Roos went on, if the library "encourages" special training for working with the adolescent, the library may expect

a trained worker to have an understanding of the importance of the problem in working with young people, the importance of carrying over juvenile reading interests into the field of adult interests and of reaching those young people who have not found pleasure in the reading of books. Secondly, the library may expect a trained worker to have an understanding of young people themselves, their psychological makeup, their educational background and their recreational interests. Thirdly, the library may expect a trained worker to have an understanding of the reading interests of this challenging group with all the many really thrilling experiences of opening into entirely new fields of reading. And, lastly, the library may expect a trained worker to have an understanding of the various methods of administrating work with young people with the pros and cons of these varying methods, which should help to solve the problem as it is found in any particular library.[3]

Compare this with an article written by a current, outspoken critic of library training, Mary K. Chelton, who advocated in *School Library Journal* (October 1974) several reforms in the way that library schools were training YA librarians. Specifically, Chelton called for allowing the prospective YA librarian to take "more meaningful electives," and she suggested the following: basic adolescent psychology and physiology (sexuality) courses, courses in public speaking (especially book talks and programming techniques), courses in reading disabilities and the teaching of reading, sociology courses, and courses in graphic communication, including study of film and video.[4]

And compare Roos's suggestions with those of Bruce Daniel, librarian at the Lawncrest Branch of the Free Library of Philadelphia, who called in *School Library Journal* (September 1976) for a "reexamination of the training of YA librarians in library school." Noting the 1976 resolution of the Adult and Young Adult Services Division of the Maryland Library Association that "all library schools should offer a course in adolescent psychology and sociology," Daniels pondered the time crunch and suggested that the course be taught interdepartmentally. As a utopian program, Daniels envisaged a service course, with one-half semester devoted to the psychology and sociology of adolescents and the other half to library services. Resource people—those who work with young people like youth counselors and group workers—would share their practical knowledge. Further, Daniels would like a mini-practicum, not necessarily in the library but with teenagers in some capacity. Aside from this, library school students would learn about book selection, reading disabilities, high interest/low vocabulary materials, program planning, outreach techniques, readers' advisory services, booktalking, and media selection. Practical knowledge could be gained through a "cooperative program . . . established with the local public and school libraries" and allowing involvement of library school students with teenagers as well as with library administrators, teachers, and non-professional staff. Daniels ended his article by mentioning the need for continuing education workshops sponsored by library schools or state library associations, as well as attendance at state and national ALA conferences.[5]

And in a wonderfully insightful article, charmingly titled, "They Didn't Tell Me It Would Be Like This and Other What Do You Do Tales," Karen Krueger (general services consultant for the Illinois Valley Library System, Peoria, Illinois) wrote that YA librarians need: 1) training in management and administration, 2) knowledge of methods of teaching reading, 3) practical experience, and 4) some background in public relations. She also suggested exposure of all public librarians, many of whom will be YA librarians by default, to "special needs of children's and YA services," which would include some study of child and adolescent psychology. Another recommendation included teaching by people who have experience in libraries.[6]

The point to be made is that for over 45 years, the library profession has been requesting basically the same things in the training of YA librarians. They can be categorized as follows: some knowledge of the adolescent as a person (psychology) in a changing world (sociology); book knowledge (selection techniques and tools); knowledge of reading interests (methodology and theory); understanding of administration (management skills); practical experience (a practicum); and programming skills—all with emendations and additions dependent upon when the suggestions were made. For example, in the 1960s, the library schools were asked to add urban studies; today, studies in sexuality.

It was a surprise to me as I reviewed the scarce literature on the subject that library educators have been equally vocal and rigorous in their demands and criticism of the way in which library schools have trained YA librarians throughout the years. In response to Jean Roos's demand in 1930 for "specialization in the training of young people's workers," educator Sarah Bogle, in a 1931 report titled "Trends and Tendencies in Education for Librarianship," called for "a minimum of four years college and one year graduate school in library science."[7]

In 1939, in the five library schools accredited at that time by the Board of Education for Librarianship of the American Library Association (California, Chicago, Columbia, Illinois, and Michigan), 27 different courses were being offered in library work with schools and children, but none were offered in work with young people.[8] And out of 389 graduates from those five institutions, only ten went into children's work.[9]

In 1948, a conference on Education for Librarianship was held at the University of Chicago, at which Ruth Ersted, then state supervisor of School Libraries at the Minnesota State Department of Education, spoke on "Education for Library Service to Children and Youth," and reported that a Committee on Education for Library Work with Children and Young People had been established "to determine objectively what the scope and content of education for these groups of librarians should be."[10] This committee perused the library literature for 1936-1946 and decided that a minimum should be a college education with one year of library school, "with emphasis placed on book knowledge and adolescent psychology."[11]

In 1951, Sara Fenwick supported the need for specialization in her master's thesis written at the University of Chicago ("Education of Librarians Working with Children in Public Schools"), in which she wrote:

> There is evidence assembled in this study to support the hypothesis stated at the beginning of this thesis: that professional training of children's librarians should include education methods, adolescent and child psychology, curricular development, methods of teaching reading, and similar related content; that the evolving social objectives of the public library place a broad community responsibility on the children's librarian which calls for professional education in fields of public relations . . . and that professional education should begin in an undergraduate major.[12]

In 1953, a seminar on the Core of Education for Librarianship was held at the University of Chicago in which a working committee on Training for Library Work with Children and Young People, was constituted, with Margaret Edwards acting as chairperson. Although a full report was never published, a progress report of the committee did appear in the literature; this report stated that "general and professional education of librarianship with children and young people should consist of five years of college education, with the undergraduate program in librarianship being not less than 15 nor more than 18 semester hours," with the fifth year of education containing "either a major or minor in library science depending on the undergraduate program and the vocational plans of the individual." The committee first set out its basic assumptions: 1) that the library is a social and educational agency, and 2) that librarians working with youth accept four large educational objectives: "self-realization, human relationships, economic efficiencies, and civic responsibilities." To meet these stated objectives, librarians need to have the knowledge, skills, attitudes, and appreciation of the following: 1) of people; 2) of books and nonprint materials (including evaluation techniques and tools, selection policies, and wide book knowledge); 3) of guidance and use of materials (programming, book talks, etc.); 4) of basic principles of organization (including acquisition, arranging and indexing, organizing and supervision of staff, compilation of data and preparation of reports); 5) of the library and the community (including community analysis techniques, the relationship of the library to other social agencies, an understanding of recent sociological trends as they affect library service, and "familiarity with current thinking and trends in the field of educational principles and procedures") ; 6) of librarianship as a profession; and, 7) of the relationship of the individual to the profession.[13]

At about the same time, Robert Leigh edited the reports of a seminar on education for librarianship held at Columbia University's School of Library Service in 1954. The Committee on Education of School and Children's Librarians complained chiefly of the "lack of common design or standard for the professional education of librarians serving children and young people in the United States."[14] Articulating a need for joint training of school and public librarians working with children and young people, the committee outlined a specific course of study. On the undergraduate level (to include a half-year of professional training), courses would be given in the following: 1) philosophy and functions of the library, 2) children's literature, 3) adolescent literature, 4) selection and use of library materials (including reference), 5) teaching the use of books and libraries, 6) AV materials, 7) lab work, and 8) cataloging and classification.

The calendar year graduate program would maintain the following sequence: In the first semester, the student would take a perspective course (such as library and society, history of libraries, etc.), an advanced course in book and nonprint materials, school and public library service to adolescents, and electives (curriculum improvement, rural and urban sociology, etc.). In the second semester, the student would take an advanced course in literature for children and adolescents, a basic course in the theory of library administration, research methods, and electives (reading theory, public school administration; etc.). In the summer the student would take a seminar in research problems, more electives (a literature course in the sciences, humanities, social sciences, fine arts, etc.), and a course in advanced information sources.[15]

In 1960, a Committee on Standards for Work with Young Adults in Public Libraries of the Public Library Association Division of ALA, chaired by Jean Roos, prepared a statement called *Young Adult Services in the Public Library* "to stimulate development of work with young adults in public libraries and to meet the increased demand from librarians for information and guidance in this special field."[16] The statement about the training of young adult librarians was sparse. Stating that "the most important single component in library service for young adults is the librarian selected to do this special job," the Committee further said:

> the young adult librarian should have full professional training—five years of formal education beyond secondary schooling including graduation from an accredited library school. Specialized courses in service to this group are an asset. A wide book background, broad interests, and a love of reading are essential. A knowledge of the psychology of the rapidly changing period of adolescent development and a knowledge of literature suited to this age group are also essential.[17]

The only other mention of library school education came in the section titled "In-Service Training," in which the Committee wrote:

increasingly, library schools are offering special courses on materials and services for young adults in the regular curriculum. Fortunately, also, much needed institutes and workshops on service to young adults are increasing in number. Until adequate courses are established to meet the demand for trained adult librarians, however, it will be necessary for public libraries to plan in-service training programs for staff assigned to this field.[18]

Mentioning the possibility of in-service training programs planned by large library systems and library school-sponsored institutes and workshops, the Committee seemed to settle on "regular monthly meetings" as "a source of inspiration, a sharing of common problems, and an impetus for professional growth."[19] Specifically, the meetings would cover such topics as adolescent psychology, surveys of books written for the adolescent and of adult books of interest to the adolescent, principles of book selection for young adults, book promotion, techniques and devices to stimulate reading, book talks and speaking in public, and organization and procedures for work with young adults in the local library.[20]

In 1968, Lucile Hatch wrote an excellent comprehensive article for *Library Trends* ("Training the Young Adult Librarians"). Having outlined the history above and discussed the results of a questionnaire distributed to both librarians and educators, Hatch concluded that:

> to meet the requirements of this new generation of young adult librarians, greatly expanded and much more sophisticated programs must be inaugurated in the accredited schools. Literature courses must be broadened and courses in programming and administration added where they are lacking. Undergirding the whole program must be courses in social problems, community relationships, and the mores and cultural patterns of the young adult.[21]

Specifically, Hatch called for a library science minor of 15-18 semester hours taken at the undergraduate level as a prerequisite to admission to a graduate library school. These undergraduate courses would include an introductory course in the role of libraries in American society, a course on nonprint and book selection principles (which would include censorship problems), reference and bibliography courses, courses in cataloging and classification, and an introductory course in literature for the young adult (fiction and non-fiction). In addition, the student would get in his undergraduate program, "a thorough understanding of the teenager and his needs, problems, and aspirations." In addition to this, electives in adolescent psychology, current social problems, children's literature, and nonprint materials would be taken.[22]

At the graduate level, Hatch foresaw a need for basic courses in the history of libraries, research methods, adult literature (American, English, European), and advanced reference and/or information retrieval courses. In addition, the following specialized courses were recommended: an advanced course in young adult literature, a course in services to young adults, an advanced course in nonprint materials (with emphasis on TV, radio, records, and films), and practical experience. Electives could then "fill out the required course"— courses in the literature of the humanities and/or social sciences, science, and administration of public libraries, as well as courses in other departments— sociology, psychology, education, and public speaking.[23]

No library administrator has approached the subject of library school education for YA librarians-to-be with quite the rigor of Lucile Hatch. Other educators within the past decade, moreover, have spoken to other problems. Marilyn Greenberg at California State University (Los Angeles) wrote that library schools should have a "minimum of two courses for people who have even the remotest intention of working with young adults," one course entirely on materials (print and/or nonprint) and one on "the coordination of y.a. services" (to include administrative functioning, programming, cooperation and relations with other agencies, public relations, personnel, etc.).[24] Mary Kingsbury, in a 1970 *Journal of Education for Librarianship* article, called for library schools to work on the library student's attitudes. Calling for a more exciting product of the library school, people with more malleable attitudes about their patrons, Kingsbury said we should spend less time on the "objects of the selection process which quickly become dated and begin investing time in the selectors themselves."[25]

Together, library educators over the past thirty years have recommended that the student get book knowledge, adolescent psychology and sociology, programming, and a knowledge of the library as a part of society and as a social institution within a community. Most educators also want more or less of what we consider the "basics"—history of libraries, public library service, cataloging and classification, reference, bibliography, book selection techniques, and public library administration.

Methodology differs widely, and many of the writers cited above have called for a strong, basic fifteen-semester-hour training program at the undergraduate level as a prerequisite to library school admission and specialization. The fifth year program is the minimum, and some library schools are considering lengthening their programs to include practica. Most educators mention courses not usually within the competence of library school faculty (psychology, sociology, education courses), but there is little mention of interdepartmental course work in the literature, though there is mention in school catalogs. Almost all educators stress the need for in-service training either in library school workshops or in libraries, but workshops initiated in the library schools themselves are a rarity.

One more addition needed to fill in this historical section and bring us up to 1978 is a survey of what has been offered in courses up to this point. In 1937, as mentioned earlier, in the five accredited library schools, 27 courses were offered in library work with schools and children. By 1950, over half of the accredited library schools offered special courses in literature for young people.[26] In 1968, when Hatch sent her questionnaire out, she had a return of 39 responses from accredited library schools. Of those 39, 31 offered one course in literature for young adults, six schools offered two or more courses, and three schools had no separate courses dealing specifically with young adults. In an analysis of the courses, Hatch found the major emphasis was on book selection principles (24 schools) and discussion of books suitable for young adults (30 schools). Only one school listed "understanding of the adolescent" as a major emphasis, although all but two courses included some discussion of the psychology, needs, and interests of young adults. A majority of the schools stated that adolescent psychology courses were available to them. Despite a dearth of specialized courses, Hatch's respondents "felt their program was adequate for the education of the young adult librarian."[27] In the early 1970s, Mary K. Chelton tabulated information from the catalogs of 47 accredited United States and Canadian library schools and reported that: 1) most schools have a YA materials course; 2) a few offer a YA services course; 3) most do not allow more than six credits to be taken outside the library school, making an interdepartmental program of study impossible; and 4) YA materials courses are required for school librarians but not for public librarians, which results in no exposure of public library administrators to YA materials or services.[28]

This author's review of course offerings listed in the catalogs of the 62 library schools accredited in 1978 in the U.S. and Canada revealed some interesting information about current trends in the education of young adult librarians. Many courses, particularly materials courses, contain more than the title indicates. For example, Emporia (Kansas) State's course "Young Adult Literature," is described as "the young adult in the present social, economic, political and educational setting related to the use of books to supply information and recreational reading needs." This is typical of materials courses, which tend to be geared to considering literature and nonprint materials in terms of the needs and interests of the young adult in a changing world. The amount of emphasis on the psychology or sociology of adolescence is difficult to determine. All except one library school offer at least one materials course, and the trend seems to be continued separation of children's and young adult materials courses. There seem to be fewer separate courses devoted to services, and schools that have courses especially geared to services usually include both children's and young adult public library work.

Very few schools list definite "tracks" in young adult services in the public library as do Chicago and Columbia. Several institutions offer seminars in either or both materials and services for young adults, although about half of these are for both children's and YA library work. Only one institution offers simply a seminar and no other courses for young adult librarians. There are a large number of "reading guidance" or "reading interest" courses. Of the thirteen schools offering these types of courses, most covered both children and young adults, and one included YA interests in a course focusing on the reading interests of adults. Only one school listed a course covering administration of children's and young adults' departments in public libraries, although the administrative aspects of YA work are probably included in other administration courses.

There appears to be a definite trend toward offering one catch-all course, titled, for example, "Resources and Services for Young Adults" (SUNY— Buffalo) or "Libraries, Contemporary Society, and the Adolescent" (Simmons). If one can judge by the descriptions of courses of study in library school catalogs, few schools encourage interdisciplinary study with library science students taking courses in other related departments. Few catalogs listed related courses in other departments or schools, although most alluded to the possibility of taking some courses outside the library school.

In assessing the results of this informal survey of library school offerings, this author's opinion of library education for young adult work is not as negative as was Chelton's (reported in her 1976 article). Most schools offer at least one materials course and a services course covering both children's and young adult services. I was encouraged by a smattering of courses that sound exciting, such as the one offered at Simmons. The many courses in reading guidance and interests, and the availability of seminars on the advanced levels, is also encouraging. I also suspect that an aggressive student who knows what he or she wants, with the help of a well-informed and aggressive advisor, might be able to work out an exciting program interdepartmentally. Although we have no data to confirm this, I suspect that many schools would allow students to take related course work outside library science, but often the student is not sure enough of what is offered elsewhere and what that individual wants to take to benefit from this possibility.

CURRENT TRUTHS AND PROBLEMS

Having glanced backward, let us now confront the present to see where we stand realistically. This can well be done by looking at two everpresent bugaboos of modern times—time and money.

In an article in *Library Journal*, Lillian Gerhardt, editor of *School Library Journal*, reminded us that all young adult and children's services are "now tied to the same economic see-saw of national and regional boom or bust periods."[29] Major urban libraries, more drastically affected in a great economic crisis than others, are no longer "capable of providing reasonable levels of support service in these specialities. . . . We've had ten years of watching a commanding career level in public library services being erased."[30]

It is now practically a cliché to say that library administrators faced with limited budgets see the YA department as the most dispensible unit. Programming goes first, then the librarian, then the book budget. Established library service to young adults is eliminated or diffused into other departments and thereby weakened. Typically, what happens is that the need for young adult service is not diminished. Teenagers still need to get their homework done! Since fewer and fewer libraries are willing to hire a specialist for these young people, a librarian is appointed from the ranks to take charge of the YA section, and thereby becomes a YA librarian by default.[31]

Furthermore, as a result of the money crunch and the diminishing of YA library jobs for specifically trained YA librarians, library schools that are also feeling the money crunch cannot realistically prepare students for non-existent jobs. As JoAnn Rogers put it, "We who prepare librarians to work with young adults have a responsibility to be realistic about the status of YA work."[32] Not only have library administrators and library schools felt the crunch, but the student too has felt it—in job loss. Also, many students are loathe to specialize because they are afraid to narrow their chances for being hired. Hypothetically, if there are five people in an incoming class who are determined to become YA librarians in public libraries, it is certainly not cost-effective to run three courses for them. Much has been written in the library literature about money, or the lack of it, but it is a realistic determinant of library education policy.

The question of time, or what to do with allotted time, is a persistent one in library education. Historically, curriculum philosophy has not changed much in the past forty years. Since the 1930s, it has been considered a truism among library educators that a *core* of required course work is necessary for every professional librarian. The course titles vary just a little, but basically the courses thought to be essential for *all* library school students—no matter what they intend to do after library school—is course work in materials (book and nonbook) evaluation, appreciation, adaption to the needs of the particular user and to the needs of a community, services (including circulation, acquisition, cataloging and classification of materials, and organizational procedures for making materials available, as well as special kinds of services—reference, circulation, readers' advisory, administration (management processes, financing, housing), communication, and usually courses in the library in society, research, and sometimes professionalism. To this core have been added information science and some general knowledge of computers and their applications to librarianship.

In 1954, Lester Asheim, editing the reports of the conference on the Core of Education for Librarianship at the University of Chicago, concluded and defended the core concept by saying that librarians and educators should share the responsibility and that the formal education:

> . . . should be mainly concerned with principles, theory, and general
> overall attitudes rather than with specific techniques—a basic
> philosophy of librarianship, a general idea of professionalism in
> librarianship, a sense of the *why* of practice, and a recognition
> of the wide variety of techniques which are permissible and
> useful. . . . Basic principle rather than specific practice should
> characterize the content of course work in the schools.[33]

These theories were upheld by Robert Leigh, who wrote in 1954 that "the primary instructional objective of the five-year program shall be to develop professional personnel grounded in the fundamental principles and process common to all types of libraries and all phases of library service."[34]

This then is the viewpoint of both librarians and educators that has continued to the present. Leon Carnovsky, in 1964, outlined a core consisting of book selection, arrangement (cataloging and classification), reference work, readers' guidance, library history and setting, administration systems planning, and a course on intellectual freedom. And, like Asheim, he concluded:

> The best any library school can do is to turn out persons capable of *becoming* librarians—librarians of vision and imagination, persons able to adapt their theory and principle; a well-trained person should not have a difficulty in adapting himself to the practice of all but the most specialized kind of library.[35]

Although the trend continued to stress general education, all librarians as well as practitioners insisted on the place of specialized training of children's and YA librarians in the library school curriculum. In 1949, Ralph Munn called "library work with children and young people . . . the most urgently needed specialty" and he went on, "the curricula can easily be modified to provide for it."[36] And Leon Carnovsky, in the 1964 article cited above, wrote that,

> For children's librarians, a background in child psychology is indispensable. . . . Whether or not such a knowledge is gained in a library school is a secondary consideration if, as I believe, it is essential, it must be provided somewhere.[37]

The conflict, then, in library education centers on this quandry: if library education is dedicated to a core that embodies a large amount of learning, how much time is left in a one-year program for a "specialization" in YA work.

SOME SUGGESTIONS

Curriculum Reform

This is a slow process, especially in an academic area that has spent a great portion of its short life formulating and refining the core theory. Furthermore, although there has been some input from students and employers into curriculum change, it is, says Rose Mary Magrill, the faculty itself that "exercises the strongest influence on a library school's curriculum, a faculty whose own competencies limit the curriculum that can be offered."[38]

Although curricular experimentation is hampered also by limited funding, there is an inkling in the literature of a move to reconsider curriculum reform in view of the "need for specialists." In a long 1971 article, "Curricular Change in the Professions," Louis Mayhew cited the following possibilities, which bear mention.

The interdisciplinary approach. This would allow students to take more classes in other departments of the same institution or in other library schools in areas in which the home institution does not have faculty who have "expertise" in a given area. An extension of this, the joint degree program, is one practical way to approach the interdisciplinary route in that two degrees could be received at the same time.

Shortening core courses. Three library schools have condensed their core material into a 12-credit, one-semester, team-taught course. The trend toward shortening the time spent on the core material is evident; says Mayhew,

> Partly because of student demands for greater freedom but more generally because of the realities of specialization even in those professions which traditionally have produced generalists, there is a loosening of specific course requirements and a widespread reaction against a large core curriculum, required of all students.[39]

Lengthening the program to two years. This theory has been bandied about for some ten years as a realistic solution to the time squeeze problem, a solution that will allow, as Magrill puts it, for specialization "that follows sequentially and logically from the general to the specific."[40] The Canadian library schools and one United States school have already extended their programs to two years.

The inclusion of a field experience. The "popularity" of the field experience is cyclical, and it appears to be in vogue right now, perhaps as Mayhew says, "in order to compensate for the mounting academic and theoretical emphasis characterizing professional education during the 1950s and 1960s . . . [and] in an effort to restore the human being as the chief focus of professional concern."[41] Most educators feel that if the practicum is instituted, the one-year program would have to yield to a longer amount of time. Further, educators are rightfully worried about the amount of faculty and administrative time, energy, and money needed to work out meaningful and useful (i.e., not simply clerical) positions for students. The school library practicum is in effect in many library schools (in some instances to fulfill state requirements) and could serve as a model for developing other practica.

Continuing education as a responsibility of the professional school. There is no doubt that the "shelf life" of what is learned in library school in one year is even more limited now than it used to be. Whereas we have had excellent in-service training situations in public libraries and schools for young adult librarians, professional schools must begin to assume responsibility for retraining and upgrading the library skills of their students and other working members of the community. However, there is no funding for this, and, furthermore, junior faculty members who are in the tenure track have to do research, serve on committees, and formulate their own courses, and they simply do not have the time for Saturday workshops. Tenured faculty members may have other commitments and might also be out of touch with the "real world."

Another suggestion for curriculum reform comes from Jesse Shera, who suggested redefining the MLS program to comprise the foundations of librarianship and instituting a new degree (between an MLS and Ph.D) designed specifically to qualify graduates in various specialties.[42] This would mean a basic MLS program with more courses and another program for "specialties." Other suggestions for curriculum revision to deal with the shortages of time for specialization and a *practicum* have been forthcoming, but generally action is slow and we seem to be tinkering more with the old curriculum than instigating mass overhauls of it.

Beyond Curricular Reform

Aside from curriculum reform, which will require the decisions of a whole library school's administration and faculty, library educators and library practitioners must start thinking about the particular problem of training the YA librarian and must take some action both jointly and together. Briefly, library school personnel must consider the following options.

Undergraduate training in library science might become a prerequisite for graduate training. Seen in a review of the literature, there is a great emphasis by educators on an undergraduate major in library training, yet there is little evidence of this in admissions policies. It appears that the requirement for admission is only a liberal arts BA. If we were to become more demanding in our admissions requirements and ask for prerequisite courses in some aspects of librarianship, as educators and librarians have suggested, perhaps graduate courses could begin at advanced levels. This would necessitate establishing criteria for undergraduate courses and, no doubt, this would limit library school applicants. More careful screening of candidates to admission to library school is a responsibility of library schools that perhaps, as Mary Kingsbury has warned us, we have not been stringent enough about.[43] Perhaps this is the time to begin.

Library schools also must take a long, critical look at their course offerings, at the numbers of students who are committed to (or ambivalent about) working with young people, at the availability of faculty in the library school, and at the resources available in other departments in the universities and other library schools in the area. Then the library school must chart possible courses from every possible source and persuade the deans to let students take as many electives as students need to complete training. Perhaps the specialization will necessitate a longer program, with or without a practicum. Perhaps it can be worked out with the dean and other faculty so that students will know that this particular specialization goes beyond the normal library school year. Many school library programs, for example, extend beyond the 36 credit hours, especially if teacher certification is required. Students who are prepared to spend the extra time to specialize might not balk at that extra time if they are forewarned.

Since our numbers are limited, it seems logical that teachers have to do more sharing. Perhaps we even have to re-think the dichotomy of the school library versus public library courses, something that Robert Leigh stressed 25 years ago. Many library schools hire separate staff to teach school library courses and literature courses for children and young adults. There should probably be more integration of these two courses, which, after all, serve the same basic clientele. Moreover, we have to be more open to sharing our ideas within the teaching profession at national and state conferences, in the journals, and by mail. Exchange of syllabi, of reading lists, and of other materials is needed. Sharing resources and ideas is necessary where teaching resources are limited.

We have to begin to realize that many public librarians will become YA librarians by default. We must, therefore, ask those teachers who are in charge of the public library or public services courses to let us share their class time. It is more important than ever that these "appointed" YA librarians get some background about the foibles of adolescence to ward off understandable hostility and ignorance. Some basic knowledge about teen culture—book and nonprint needs—is essential.

We have to begin to plan meaningful practica for YA public librarians-to-be in public libraries, schools, and other community agencies. This means the teacher will have to get out of the building that houses the library school and make contact with librarians, teachers, youth workers, and other social service people in the community.

We have to make the time for coordinating and taking part in continuing education workshops. We must do this no matter how busy we are. We have to make positive contacts with state library personnel to work with them in this endeavor.

And finally, we have to conduct meaningful research to find out what the YA librarian needs to know. We have to determine what the job market really is. Exactly how many are committed to working with young adults when they enter library school? Are all of our library school students afraid to become too specialized and thereby put themselves out of the job market? How much money is needed to add extra faculty for more specialized courses? We need a detailed study of course content. What are we teaching in our courses, no matter what they are titled? What can we share with other teachers on the same faculty? In other departments? In other library schools? It is hoped that research on state and national levels will help us improve what limited resources we have.

The practitioners have to continue to set high ideals for the profession. They must cooperate with library school personnel in supervising practica. They must continue the rigorous in-service training programs along the lines of Margaret Edwards's (Pratt Institute) program and others. They must be willing to fight to keep their departments viable and exciting. And they must demand excellence from the profession itself.

SUMMARY

Together, librarians and library school educators have two main tasks. First, they must set priorities. In view of financial and temporal realities, priorities have to be set jointly by librarians and educators. Interestingly enough, a recent study shows that perhaps educators and librarians are not so far apart in their priorities. Mary Kingsbury conducted research in the spring of 1976 in which she studied the priorities of practitioners and educators "to determine what activities, understanding, and skills are of most importance in the preparation of future young adult librarians."[44] Specifically, the study aimed to determine what practitioners and educators thought should be included in library school programs. Kingsbury questioned 119 coordinators of YA services, 80 practicing librarians, and 113 educators about the activities and skills grouped under four headings: selection of materials, programming and promotion, student understanding, and administration. Kingsbury determined that, although both groups of educators and practitioners agree that more time is needed in the training of YA librarians, they tend to disagree as to how much more time is needed and what should be emphasized. For example, practitioners place a higher priority on the two areas of adolescent problems and programming than do educators, and there is a difference among them as to how much time should be spent discussing the use of paperbacks. Both practitioners and educators agree that practica are necessary, and, surprisingly, educators suggest a greater number of hours than do the librarians. Both groups also agree that library school students should take courses outside of the library school. On the whole, Kingsbury concluded, "educators and practitioners are not very far apart in regard to the priorities reported here; in most cases, in fact, their differences are in the degree of emphasis placed on various topics."[45]

Second, and concomitant with setting mutually agreeable priorities on a national level and seeking support for them from deans of library schools and ALA, librarians and educators have to set national standards for education. As far back as 1954, Robert Leigh remarked that, "in contrast to school librarians who work with adults, and special librarians in most other fields, there is no common standard for the professional education of librarians serving children and young people in the United States."[46] Certainly setting standards would be advantageous for both librarians and educators. Responsibility for formation of such standards should be shared by all educators, librarians, library administrators, coordinators, and should be supported by PLA and YASD.

In 1975, YASD and LED formulated a Library Education Committee on Library Education for Service to Young Adults at the Pre-Service Level, a joint educator/practitioner committee charged with "developing a position paper defining what should be covered in courses dealing with young adults."[47] Although its position paper has been shelved for the moment, the committee can be an excellent springboard for accumulating data to support a national platform of priorities and standards. It is obvious to this writer that the interest in training YA librarians has recently been rekindled in the literature, so this might be an opportune moment at which to begin to implement such a nationally acceptable program.

NOTES

[1] Jean Roos, "Training for Library Service with Young People," *Library Journal* 55 (September 15, 1930): 721.

[2] Ibid., p. 722.

[3] Ibid., p. 723.

[4] Mary K. Chelton, "In the Y.A. Corner," *School Library Journal* 2 (October 1974): 97.

[5] Bruce Daniels, "Education for YA Librarians [In the YA Corner]," *School Library Journal* 23 (September 1976): 41.

[6] Karen Krueger, "They Didn't Tell Me It Would Be Like This and Other What Do You Do Tales," *Illinois Libraries* 58 (December 1976): 788-91.

[7] Sarah Bogle, "Trends & Tendencies in Education for Librarianship," *Library Journal* 56 (December 15, 1931): 1029.

[8] Lucile Hatch, "Training the Young Adult Librarian," *Library Trends* 17 (October 1968): 151.

[9] Ibid.

[10] Ruth Ersted, "Education for Library Service for Youth," in Bernard Berelson, ed., *Education for Librarianship* (Chicago: American Library Association, 1949), p. 104.

[11] Ibid., p. 154.

[12] Sara Fenwick, "Education of Librarians Working with Children," unpublished master's thesis, University of Chicago, 1951, p. 166.

[13] "Training for Library Work with Children and Young People," *School Libraries* 3 (March 1954): 5-8.

[14] Robert D. Leigh. *Major Problems in the Education of Librarians* (New York: Columbia University Press, 1954), p. 67.

[15] Ibid., pp. 81-83.

[16] Public Library Association. *Young Adult Services in the Public Library* (Chicago: American Library Association, 1960), n.p.

[17] Ibid., p. 11.

[18] Ibid., pp. 12-13.

[19] Ibid., p. 13.

[20] Ibid.

[21] Hatch, p. 159.

[22] Ibid., p. 160.

[23] Ibid., pp. 160-63.

[24] Marilyn Greenberg, "Can/Should/Do Library Schools Train Good YA Librarians," *Booklegger Magazine* 3 (Winter 1976): 44-45.

[25] Mary Kingsbury, "Ostriches and Adolescents," *Journal of Education for Librarianship* 11 (Spring 1971): 328.

[26] Hatch, p. 155.

[27] Ibid., 157.

[28] Ibid.

[29] Mary K. Chelton, [no title], *Booklegger Magazine* 3 (Winter 1976): 46.

[30] Lillian N. Gerhardt, "Public Library Services to Children and YAs. An Auto-Interview," *Library Journal* 101 (January 1976): 109.

[31] Ibid., p. 110.

[32] Krueger, p. 789.

[33] JoAnn Rogers, "Preparing YA Librarians—Questions & Answers [in the YA Corner]," *School Library Journal* 23 (April 1977): 51.

[34] Lester Asheim, ed., *Core of Education for Librarianship* (Chicago: American Library Association, 1954), pp. 45-46.

[35] Leigh, pp. 8-9.

[36] Leon Carnovsky, "The Role of the Public Library," in Don R. Swanson, ed., *The Intellectual Foundations of Library Education* (Chicago: University of Chicago Press, 1965), p. 30.

[37] Ralph Munn, "Education for Public Librarianship," in Berelson, p. 124.

[38] Carnovsky, p. 30.

[39] Rose Mary Magrill, "Curriculum," in Mary B. Cassata and Herman L. Totten, eds., *The Administrative Aspects of Education for Librarianship: A Symposium.* (Metuchen, NJ: Scarecrow, 1975), p. 141.

[40] Lewis B. Mayhew, "Curricular Change in the Professions," in Herbert Goldhor, ed., *Education for Librarianship: The Design of the Curriculum* (Urbana, IL: University of Illinois, Graduate School of Librarianship, 1971), p. 51.

[41] Magrill, p. 147.

[42] Mayhew, p. 57.

[43] Jesse Shera, *The Foundations of Education for Librarianship* (New York: Wiley, Becher and Hayes, 1972), p. 373.

[44] Kingsburg, "Ostriches . . . ," p. 329.

45 Mary Kingsbury, "Educating Young Adult Librarians: Priorities of Practitioners and Educators," *Drexel Library Quarterly* 14 (January 1978): 4-18.

46 Ibid.

47 Ibid.

BIBLIOGRAPHY

Asheim, Lester, ed. *Core of Education for Librarianship.* Chicago: American Library Association, 1954.

Bogle, Sarah. "Trends & Tendencies in Education for Librarianship." *Library Journal* 56 (1931): 1029-36.

Carnovsky, Leon. "The Role of the Public Library," in *The Intellectual Foundations of Library Education*, Don R. Swanson, ed. Chicago: University of Chicago Press, 1965, pp. 27-38.

Chelton, Mary K. [untitled article]. *Booklegger Magazine* 3 (1976): 46.

Chelton, Mary K. "In the Y.A. Corner." *School Library Journal* 21 (1974): 97.

Daniels, Bruce. "Education for YA Librarians [in the YA Corner]." *School Library Journal* 23 (1976): 41.

Ersted, Ruth. "Education for Library Service for Youth," in *Education for Librarianship*, Bernard Berelson, ed. Chicago: American Library Association, 1949, pp. 150-64.

Fenwick, Sara. "Education of Librarians Working with Children." Unpublished master's thesus, University of Chicago, 1951.

Gerhardt, Lillian N. "Public Library Services to Children and YAs. An Auto-Interview." *Library Journal* 101 (1976): 109-111.

Greenberg, Marilyn. "Can/Should/Do Library Schools Train Good YA Librarians." *Booklegger Magazine* 3 (1976): 44-46.

Hatch, Lucile. "Training the Young Adult Librarian." *Library Trends* 17 (1968): 150-65.

Kingsbury, Mary. "Educating Young Adult Librarians: Priorities of Practitioners and Educators." *Drexel Library Quarterly* 14 (1978): 4-18.

Kingsbury, Mary. "Ostriches and Adolescents." *Journal of Education for Librarianship* 11 (1971): 325-31.

Krueger, Karen. "They Didn't Tell Me It Would Be Like This and Other What Do You Do Tales." *Illinois Libraries* 58 (1976): 786-91.

Leigh, Robert D. *Major Problems in the Education of Librarians.* New York: Columbia University Press, 1954.

Magrill, Rose Mary. "Curriculum," in *The Administrative Aspects of Education for Librarianship: A Symposium.* Mary B. Cassata and Herman L. Totten, eds. Metuchen, NJ: Scarecrow, 1975, pp. 140-51.

Mayhew, Lewis B. "Curricular Change in the Professions," in *Education for Librarianship: The Design of the Curriculum*, Herbert Goldhor, ed. Urbana, IL: University of Illinois, Graduate School of Library Science, 1971, p. 51.

Munn, Ralph. "Education for Public Librarianship," in *Education for Librarianship*, Bernard Berelson, ed. Chicago: American Library Association, 1949, pp. 117-29.

Public Library Association. *Young Adult Services in the Public Library.* Chicago: American Library Association, 1960.

Rogers, JoAnn. "Preparing YA Librarians—Questions & Answers [in the YA Corner]." *School Library Journal* 23 (1977): 51.

Roos, Jean. "Training for Library Service with Young People." *Library Journal* 55 (1930): 721-23.

Shera, Jesse. *The Foundations of Education for Librarianship.* New York: Wiley, Becher and Hayes, 1972.

"Training for Library Work with Children and Young People." *School Libraries* 3 (1954): 5-8.

THE YOUNG ADULT
SYSTEM COORDINATOR

Julia Losinski

According to Webster's *7th New Collegiate Dictionary*, to coordinate is to "bring into a common action, movement or condition . . . to act together in a smooth concerted way." The role of the coordinator is to accomplish this purpose. However, the definition is deceptively simple for a complex activity about which, unfortunately, little information or direction is available in library literature. The coordinator in the organization of a consolidated library system is described as a staff officer whose function "cuts across several or all departments, sets up intercommunications and gives to all common aims and viewpoints, helps find solutions that all can adopt, and breaks down departmental isolation and self-sufficiency."[1] Staff officers do not give orders or supervise employees in their daily work (other than those in their own office), yet they will need to have some delegated system-wide authority. The coordinator in such a staff position performs in an advisory capacity in planning, recommending, reporting, and communicating on matters relating to young adult services.

The coordinator works closely with administrative staff in discussing policies and procedures that will especially affect service to young adults. For example, the negative as well as the positive aspects of proposed policies on fines or restricted access to library areas and materials should be presented by the coordinator to the administrative staff during the decision-making process. Administrative structures vary, but, if the organization of the library system includes coordinating positions for various age levels, they should be equal in every aspect. That is, position descriptions, salary classification, and authority should be similar for the adult, young adult, and children's services coordinators. The development of a service for young adults is neither less nor more important than any other program that is to serve a segment of the population.

The function of the young adult coordinator is to develop and "bring into common action" the system-wide program of service and activities for young adults. Yet this common action cannot be realized without staff, materials, and a unity of purpose. Part of the coordinator's role is to provide information to persons on both the administrative and staff levels, information that will form the basis of the unity of purpose:

> As work with young adults cuts across many functions and services of the library, it is of paramount importance that there should be complete understanding of the objectives of this service and whole-hearted cooperation of the entire staff in fulfilling them. Both the quality and the amount of service to young adults will depend to a great extent on the organization and integration of the work in the library as a whole. Conviction of the importance of work with young adults by the chief librarian is essential.[2]

Since the young adult program is integrated into the library's total package of services, that coordinator works closely with counterparts in the system by discussing developments as they may touch or involve other services and by communicating information on materials and programs. Parallel communication among all similarly placed librarians in each of the branches should be encouraged to further promote the unity of purpose.

Before any role can be played, whether it be in the theatre, life, or career, a complete understanding of how that role fits into the total picture is necessary. An actor would never attempt to learn a part without knowing the entire script. A complete familiarity with the goals of the library is also necessary before these can be translated into service for young adults. The coordinator must bring to the role a personal conviction and commitment to such service together with standards of professional librarianship. What does "professional librarianship" really mean? What are its perimeters? Are they adjustable? Are there levels of "professional librarianship"? What are the standards the coordinator believes can be attained? The coordinator must often play the role of soul-searcher!

The development of a program for young adults must be based on objectives and goals, both long- and short-range, aimed at a unique target audience as part of the system's total functions. The goals cannot be static; achievement will involve activity and evaluation to formulate new ones. The formulation is a continuous one involving the coordinator and the staff working with young adults. The coordinator should also be involved in the development and revision of statements of the system's function and goals if the young adult program is to be effective and part of the total library program. No one program can exist in a vacuum, and the coordinator must be able to relate the young adult program to the system's program as well as relate it to all parts of the organization and its aims. The role is a simple one, much like conducting an orchestra, many members of which may be playing different melodies at different times and sometimes not always in the same key. It takes a little transposing, baton waving, and certainly a score to keep the players together. Once the objectives and goals for the young adult services program have been set and agreed on by the staff and accepted by the administrative staff, the coordinator must determine the means of implementing and evaluating them. In addition, the coordinator will also need to establish priorities, which will be periodically influenced by the budget.

To be successful, a young adult program must respond to community needs, which will of their nature vary in the geographic localities served by the library's branches. This awareness depends a great deal on the alertness of the young adult staff to community trends and interests and the staff's ability to communicate these to the coordinator, whose role it is to help translate the trends, interests, and needs into service and materials. The coordinator should encourage this staff alertness to needs as a way of improving materials selection and programs on the local level. This is one way for the coordinator to become informed, but it must be augmented by the coordinator's attending and participating in meetings of county or area-wide organizations serving youth. Since the target audience of these organizations usually closely parallels that of the library, such meetings offer an opportunity to share information on activities as well as the concerns of youth as reported by other organizations.

If the 4H or a recreation department is planning a series of programs on food preparation (or crafts, etc.), the library can tie into the sessions by providing a materials display, a place to hold the program, and a booklist that will draw the attention of young adults to the resources of the library. It may also be possible to co-sponsor such programs. The role of the coordinator in working with administrative officers of county-wide organizations becomes that of facilitator. It is not, however, a one-way street but rather an avenue of communication. While the library and its branches become highly visible to groups that had never been aware of its resources, the library can gain information on the concerns and needs of young adults, which then can be reflected in materials and program activities in the branch libraries. Establishing communication either on a formal or informal basis with the director of a hot line youth service bureau and crisis intervention centers can give the coordinator a reading of the young adult pulse. Is drug abuse increasing? Is unemployment a concern among teenagers? Do the questions received at crisis centers indicate a rise in the need for abortion and pregnancy information? Does the library have the information available so that telephone counselors at the centers can recommend either specific titles or a visit to the library for more information?

If the library is used in a referral capacity, the coordinator must be sure that staff attitudes are positive, a characteristic as important as having materials. The coordinator's role as facilitator brings together library staff working with young adults and those in other agencies working with the same age group. All of the youth-oriented agencies of a community are concerned in their own way with providing service and meeting the needs of the young adult. The coordinator must identify and communicate with these agencies in order to help branch staff reach young adults, particularly those who feel that the library is an institution with nothing to offer them.

Since the majority of young adults are in school, it is important for the coordinator to establish good working relationships with the supervisory and administrative staff in the schools, particularly with the staff in the media centers. The coordinator here assumes the role of public relations person or communicator in discussing policies and mutual problems to clear the way for contacts between young adult staff and the staff of the local schools. This multi-faceted cooperative effort can result in mutual support rather than in unnecessary duplication, thereby providing young adults with more responsive programs.

One phase of the responsive program for the library is to ensure that materials that can attract young adults to library resources are available in the *branches* of the library system. In order for branch collections to develop in stimulating reading and attracting young adults, the coordinator plays the dual role of assembler and trainer. Staff working with young adults should have a wide selection of materials from which to choose for the collections in their community branch libraries. The coordinator's responsibility is to assemble a variety of currently published materials and to involve young adult staff in identifying those materials. But assembling materials in the form of review copies is only the first step. While branch collections will and must vary in order to reflect the interests represented in their different communities, the coordinator should establish standards and a policy for materials that will eventually be included in all of the system's collections. Inherent in establishing standards is the formulation of guidelines for the evaluation of materials and the guidance of staff in the use of those guidelines and policy. There are many ways to approach the training, and the coordinator must discover which will be the most effective. Closely connected to training in evaluation is training in selection for individual collections. Staff should also be trained to be able to justify the materials they select for their collections so that questions on materials from members of the community can be satisfactorily handled. The role of the coordinator, in this instance, is to assist the staff in justification of materials and interpretation of the materials selection policy to the public to ensure the young adult's free access to information. The responsibility for materials included in the system's collections must be accompanied by the authority needed to act in this role.

The selection process does not end with a staff member's ordering books and materials for the branch library. There should be no passive placement of an item on the shelf or in the rack, but rather an active promotion of books and other materials by staff through individualized reader's service to young adults. Effective service to satisfy the interests and needs of this age group can only be achieved by staff members who like and understand their public and who have a broad materials background that they can share with enthusiasm. The coordinator must be a reader, a listener to recordings, and a viewer of films if young adult staff are expected to develop their own knowledge and expertise. This development is a continuous process of mutual growth for all involved. The coordinator together with members of the young adult staff should compile basic reading lists as a training tool, especially for new staff working with young adults, and should schedule staff discussions on those books read to explore ways in which they can be used in the library and the community. The same approach should also be used to develop a background in other materials, such as films and recordings.

It should be possible for the coordinator to hold system-wide meetings on a regular basis to assist all staff working with young adults. The most successful meetings will be those that address the needs expressed by the staff. Meeting those needs on the various levels of staff experience represented is probably one of the greatest challenges a coordinator faces. However, if the staff is alert, involved, and interested, the challenge is more than half met. The other half is met by the coordinator's being responsive and resourceful, roles that must be played at all times. The many aspects of staff training that have been mentioned are interdependent and are related to the training provided by branch supervisory personnel. The role of the coordinator in staff training is one of support and assistance, relying on communication with the line staff in developing the types of training to be provided.

The coordinator should be aware of the professional goals of the young adult staff and, in the role of developer, help make it possible for each staff member to realize her or his fullest potential. It is important not only for the person but for the success of the service that the coordinator discover and provide encouragement of an individual's talent. Pushing is for doors, but motivating is for people. As developer, the coordinator must provide opportunities to expand the experience of young adult staff in developing service, realizing that eventually some of the staff may leave to accept positions in other systems on administrative levels. A library system with an active young adult services staff and even with structured promotional advancement opportunities can expect to serve as a training ground for other libraries.

Staff challenged to do their best also challenge the coordinator to perform at the highest level possible. It is important for the coordinator to play the role of listener. It takes a keen eye to know the state of the art, antennae to catch the vibrations of new ideas, and an old-fashioned ear trumpet to hear those things that are not being said. The coordinator often assumes the role of a football coach in developing a team spirit that can solve problems, evolve ideas, and produce results. This teamwork as part of the total library activity can only take place if the staff members feel free to think and to offer criticism to improve service on the basis of mutual trust and confidence. The role of the coordinator is often that of catalyst, to help make things happen for more effective service, but this cannot happen unless the atmosphere is conducive to freedom of exchange. This freedom of exchange is especially important in planning programs to be presented in a branch or a community. After a staff member has been given training in the basic techniques of planning and presentation, the role of the coordinator becomes that of assistant in the development of program ideas.

The success of library service obviously depends to a great extent on the staff appointed to carry out the functions of the library. As a staff person, the coordinator should actively participate in interviewing applicants, working closely with line staff to select the best qualified person for a young adult services position. Prior to the interview, the supervisor and coordinator should discuss the requirements of the vacant position as the basis for applicant selection. Both the supervisor and coordinator will be interested in finding a person who has an interest in the position and potential for development. During the interview, the coordinator should discuss with the supervisor the special qualities and interests needed in working with young adults as part of the total branch service and should assist in determining whether the applicants have them. Once the applicant is chosen and appointed, the coordinator and supervisor should discuss the employee's progress, especially during the time of performance evaluation. In providing the supervisor with observations on the staff member's progress in such areas as training and program presentation, the coordinator becomes of assistance in the measurement of goals.

It has been mentioned that the coordinator serves in a staff capacity, as a back-of-the-scenes support person. This is not a passive role but rather an active one that requires the coordinator to spend time working in the branches, if only to keep in touch with reality. Spending a day, afternoon, or evening doing reader's and reference work keeps the coordinator alert to the state of the collection and service, and it also provides a basis of discussion with the staff. The support needed by staff in presenting programs in the branch or in the community may be moral support, but this often means that the coordinator works in the branch to release the staff member for the activity. The role of support has many implications in offering assistance, ranging from providing information on a book to helping to develop ideas. It requires that the coordinator maintain both a constant awareness and approachability.

The coordinator as advisor relates most often to staff and materials since these are the components of day-to-day service to the public. A developing service and a library system in a growing geographical area will require the on-going planning of new buildings or the expansion of existing structures. The coordinator should be involved in the planning process by providing assistance in studying the community's population and by consulting on the design of the building, which should be related to the community's use. The coordinator should be able to submit ideas on furniture, equipment, decor, and facilities that will attract young adults and yet be appropriate to the total concept of the building. As part of the planning team, the coordinator must be able to see the whole as well as the parts of a building program. The grand opening of a new branch brings its own reward and the realization that each person involved both contributed and learned something in the process.

In considering other roles assumed by the coordinator, that of participator in the library profession emerges over and beyond what is involved in carrying out the function of the position. The coordinator should be a member of regional, state, and national professional organizations, participating in their activities to keep informed and intellectually alive. Ideas gathered at conferences and meetings should be shared with other staff members to stimulate further development. Conversely, information on achievements by library system staff should be contributed with pride to the melting pot of ideas. Because of this need to share, the coordinator's role as disseminator often expands beyond the boundaries of the library system as requests arrive in the mail from librarians interested in establishing or developing a service for young adults.

It would only be honest to admit that the coordinator in playing many roles encounters frustrations imposed by time and other factors, but these are more than outweighed by the satisfaction enjoyed when better service is given, when innovative ideas are generated and implemented, and when reports come in relating success in reaching a goal. Then the role of the coordinator becomes total enjoyment!

NOTES

[1] Joseph L. Wheeler and Herbert Goldhor, *Practical Administration of Public Libraries* (New York: Harper and Row, 1962), p. 172.

[2] American Library Association, Public Library Association, Committee on Standards for Work with Young Adults in Public Libraries, *Young Adult Services in the Public Library* (Chicago: ALA, 1960), p. 1.

BIBLIOGRAPHY

American Library Association. Public Library Association. Committee on Standards for Work with Young Adults in Public Libraries. *Young Adult Services in the Public Library.* Chicago: ALA, 1960.

Wheeler, Joseph L., and Herbert Goldhor. *Practical Administration of Public Libraries.* New York: Harper and Row, 1962.

THE YOUNG ADULT
STATE COORDINATOR

Sarah Ann Long

Chapter one of the *Standards for Library Functions at the State Level* prepared by the American Association of State Libraries opens with a call for state library agencies to lead, participate in, and coordinate the total library planning and development within the state. Standard fourteen states that:

> The state library agency must make provision for consultants sufficient in number to stimulate all libraries to develop their full potential. It is also advisable for qualified consultative service to be provided at the regional level.[1]

And Standard fifteen states:

> State library consultant service should emphasize guidance in special aspects of library service.[2]

It could be reasoned from these standards that areas of library service that are difficult to fashion and maintain, yet that are also essential in providing service to all age groups, should be ones for which consultants are available at the state level. Librarians who have attempted to serve young adults can attest to both the difficulty and the paramount importance of YA services. A casual glance at the record of programs presented by most public libraries reveals many programs for children, some programs for adults, and relatively few programs for young adults. Surely this lack of programs indicates that this area of the population is being poorly served and needs some assistance at the state level. The standards would indicate that state library agencies are responsible for closing gaps such as these by helping local libraries in areas that are important, yet difficult. In addition, when a state-level consultant is assigned to a particular area of library service, that area is recognized by libraries throughout the state as one worthy of promotion and encouragement. This manifestation of official state recognition lends additional status to the particular area of service and further underlines the importance of that area with a cash commitment—a part of the state budget.

A scan of a directory of coordinators of children's and YA services in public library systems (prepared by Pauline Winnick at the U.S. Office of Education) shows that in 1977, five states had a young adult services consultant position budgeted.[3] In all five cases, the position was designated half-time or less. Both New York and New Jersey had full-time young adult consultants briefly in the sixties, and North Carolina had a full-time young adult consultant for eight years, although this position was reduced to half-time in 1977. Throughout the eight-year tenure of the North Carolina YA state coordinator, workshops featuring national personalities, regional meetings, and publications of annotated catalogs of young adult titles were regular occurrences. Another important aspect of this consultant's work consisted of visits to persons working with young adults in libraries. These visits presented an opportunity for the local person to meet the state consultant in order to establish a personal working relationship. The visits gave the consultant a state-wide view of existing YA services and made the consultant a gold mine of workable program ideas and solutions to problems common in the state.

In December 1977, an informal survey was sent to fifteen state library children's consultants in a search for information on state-level young adult positions and activities. Some interesting information and opinions were gathered. One respondent whose job description includes state-wide children's responsibilities reports that her job title also includes young adult services. She felt, though, that she had so little time to work on this latter aspect of librarianship that it should be deleted from her title. She pointed out that including young adult librarianship in her job description is an insult to young adult library supporters in that state. Another children's consultant has been urging her state library administration to include young adult services in her job description. It is her belief that children's services are prospering in her state and that young adult services need more guidance than children's services at this juncture.

Many children's consultants report state-wide young adult activities. In New Jersey, the children's consultant has begun a young adult book reviewing group and hopes that persons attending will become acquainted and exchange program ideas as well. The Arizona State Library Extension Service has funded a regional young adult consultant with Library Services and Construction Act (LSCA) funds as a demonstration project. In Illinois, an LSCA-funded institute is in the planning phase. If funded, it will address itself in part to state-wide young adult services.

In 1974, several young adult librarians asked the Missouri State Library for a full-time young adult consultant. They were told that this was not possible, but the children's consultant agreed to expand her duties to include young adult work. Since then, young adult materials have been added to the Children's/Young Adult Vertical File (a state library project) and the Book Selection Committee has been experimenting with separate review groups for children's and young adult materials. The annotated list that results will be divided: Preschool/ Intermediate/Young Adult. In Missouri, the coordinator of children's and young adult services also serves as the "secretary, etc." for the planning committee of the Young Adult Services Committee of the Missouri Library Association.

Another type of interaction between a state library association and a state library agency brought results in Ohio. In September 1975, the children's consultant at the state library asked persons from across the state who had expressed an interest in young adult librarianship to meet at the state library. That group became the nucleus for the Young Adult Taskforce of the Ohio Library Association. During its first year, the group did a state-wide survey of young adult services,[4] began working on revised standards for young adult service, and presented programs at regional and annual state meetings of the Ohio Library Association. In its second year, the group gave a two-day workshop on young adult services, presented a program at the OLA annual conference, and published *The Whole YA Catalog*.[5] In 1978, the Taskforce published a quarterly and presented programs at several OLA meetings.

The success of the YA Taskforce in Ohio is largely attributable to Barbara Newmark, regional head of Young Adult Services, Mayfield Regional Library (Cuyahoga County Public Library), who has chaired the Taskforce. It is heartening to think that one person can make a difference to an area of librarianship for a whole state, and a similar success story can be found in *Top of the News*, June 1972,[6] in which the work of Faith Hektoen, consultant for Children and Young Adult Services in Connecticut, is detailed.

LSCA monies distributed by state library agencies represent a major source of funds for projects serving young adults, but this is not a new idea. Mary Helen Mahar reported in the *ALA Bulletin* of February 1959 that seven states in a survey of thirty-six state plans for fiscal 1957 specified the strengthening of services to children and/or young people as part of their programs.[7] The LSCA institute currently in the planning stages in Illinois might provide a model for one type of state-initiated activity for the strengthening of YA services. Mahar also predicted that the strengthening would be in both direct and indirect ways. In-service programs for librarians are an example of an indirect method that has a great potential to affect young adults from as many communities as there are localities that participate. Direct strengthening of YA programs with LSCA funds might be done with the purchase of materials and furnishings or film rentals that affect only the young adults in a particular community. With proper planning and publicity, however, such projects could serve as demonstration models for a region or state and might convince libraries to attempt similar programming with local money.

State library associations are also active in the promotion of young adult librarianship. The March-April 1977 issue of *Wisconsin Library Bulletin* is devoted to services for young adults. This reporting represents a great amount of activity and provides a picture of a thriving area of librarianship.[8]

An area neglected by both state agencies and professional associations is the development of quantifiable reporting mechanisms for evaluating state-wide services. Without this information, which can be compared with benchmarks or standards of service, it is impossible to plan, to evaluate, or to note progress. In Ohio, the 1976 Young Adult Taskforce Survey found that 80 percent of the respondents representing 74 out of 250 library systems had no budget or personnel for young adult services. However, 41 percent provided space for a YA collection. Even these figures, when gathered on a regular basis, provide points of comparison for later years and help to determine direction for planning. Armed with the information that almost all libraries provided paperback collections and that only 41 percent provided records, media, and equipment, it would be possible to determine that the need for state-wide conferences and workshops emphasizing media was greater than for workshops devoted to consideration of paperbacks.[9]

It is regrettable that no evidence supported by hard statistical data proves the efficacy of having state-level young adult consultants. Although there is an exceptionally active and well established program state-wide in North Carolina, for example, how can it be proven that the youth of North Carolina have been better served than they would have been had this state young adult position not existed? Also, how can what exists in North Carolina libraries be compared to what exists in the libraries in the other states? Perhaps when full-time YA state consultants are employed, part of their role will be to establish criteria and guidelines for services that can be translated into quantifiable categories so that the impact of services can be made known.

Because few examples are available to use as guidelines, the following models have been prepared: a job description for a YA state consultant (page 177), and a chart outlining first-year goals, objectives, and activities for the consultant (page 178). They can perhaps serve as a point of departure for the development of descriptions for positions that will, of course, be designed to meet the respective needs of the libraries in different states.

Footnotes for this essay appear on page 179.

JOB DESCRIPTION

The State Library
Library Development Consultant—Services to Young Adults
Salary—competitive

POSITION: Develops and administers statewide program for improvement of public library services to young adults (ages 13 to 18). In this capacity, consults with librarians, young adult specialists, professional groups, and others to develop resources, plans, and service programs on a statewide, regional, or local basis; visits libraries to consult with administrators and specialists; inspects and evaluates library service programs against standards; makes reports and recommendations to specialists, administrators, the state librarian, and others concerned with programs; analyzes and makes recommendations upon applications from libraries, library schools, and other institutions for federal assistance in programs related to young adult services; prepares newsletter and other publications for dissemination in the field.

QUALIFICATIONS: Knowledge of basic library principles, procedures, technology, goals, and philosophy of service as related to young adult services. Have leadership and administrative and analytical ability. Able to exercise tact and judgment in dealing with people. Able to plan and initiate programs and activities. Able to speak to groups. Masters degree from ALA-accredited library school and five years professional experience, or equivalent, including appropriate experience in young adult services; supervision of library service program or library consultant work.

■ ■ ■

YOUNG ADULT CONSULTANT–STATE LIBRARY

Fiscal Year (FY) Objectives

GOAL

I. To assist persons serving young adults in libraries in planning and evaluating quality library programs for all young adults.

OBJECTIVES

A. To offer continuing education activities for young adult workers in public libraries in the community served by the library.

B. To become acquainted with the present state of young adult services and to expand communications between persons serving young adults in libraries and the state library's young adult consultant.

C. To continue personal education as a librarian and as a young adult consultant.

ACTIVITIES

A1. To publish six issues of a newsletter containing ideas for young adult library service, a review of current professional reading, tested program ideas, and a problem/solution page.

A2. To organize a review network for young adult titles now received at the state library, utilizing the talents of reviewers around the state.

A3. To publish the output of the review network as a supplement to the six-issues-per-year newsletter.

A4. To encourage persons serving young adults in state libraries to participate in workshops and courses by:
a) giving details of upcoming events in the newsletter;
b) citing the availability of the state library's calendar of continuing education;
c) encouraging membership in state library associations and ALA/YASD.

A5. To hold a series of workshops (four) on library service to young adults, utilizing the experience of an institution's librarians. These workshops will be planned in concert with each institution's consultant and help in state correctional institutions.

A6. To plan the contents of kits to serve as a borrowable workshop in a box on filmmaking, music and recordings, videotaping, and community analysis. These will be completed and begin circulating in the following FY from the state library.

A7. To research sources of funds for young adult programs, including Library Services and Construction Act monies. The results of this research will be published in an issue of the newsletter, with a meeting announced for those interested in pursuing these grants.

A8. To aid at least one LSCA project and one other outside-funded project to implementation in the present FY.

B1. To make 100 consultant visits to libraries to encourage service to young adults. These visits will be made to libraries answering letters offering the services of the state library's young adult consultant.

B2. To hold two meetings per year of the young adult coordinators in cities over 250,000 population, and, where positions exist, the regional young adult coordinators of multi-county cooperative groups. The chairperson of the young adult round table of the state library association will also be invited. This group will serve as an ad hoc advisory council and planning committee for state-wide young adult services.

B3. To encourage persons serving young adults to visit the state library by having an open house at which titles that have appeared on the year's review sheet will be on display, along with topical displays of an aspect of young adult library service and a continuous film showing of YASD-noted "best films."

C1. To maintain active membership and attend conferences of the state library association, the state school library association, and the Young Adult Services Division of the American Library Association.

C2. To read professional magazines and books.

C3. To take full advantage of all continuing education opportunities offered by the state library.

NOTES

[1] Standards Revision Committee of the American Association of State Libraries, *Standards for Library Functions at the State Level*, rev. ed. (Chicago: American Library Association, 1970), p. 6.

[2] Ibid.

[3] Pauline Winnick, *1977 Directory of Coordinators of Children's Services and of Young Adult Services in Public Library Systems Serving at Least 100,000 People* (Chicago: American Library Association, 1978).

[4] Barbara Newmark, "Survey of Young Adult Services," *Ohio Library Association Bulletin* 46-47 (1976): 23-24.

[5] Barbara Newmark, ed., *Whole YA Catalog* (Cleveland: Cuyahoga County [Ohio] Public Library, 1977).

[6] Joan Bogatz and others, "Beyond Complacency: Connecticut YA Librarians Expand Their Minds and Services," *Top of the News* 28 (1972): 370-73.

[7] Mary Helen Mahar, "Implications of the Library Services Act to Children and Young People," *ALA Bulletin* 53 (1959): 118-22.

[8] Elizabeth Burr, "How-to-Do-It in YA Services," *Wisconsin Library Bulletin* 66 (1970): 136-37.

[9] Newmark, "Survey of Young Adult Services," 23-24.

BIBLIOGRAPHY

Bogatz, Joan, and others. "Beyond Complacency: Connecticut YA Librarians Expand Their Minds and Services." *Top of the News* 28 (1972): 370-73.

Burr, Elizabeth. "How-to-Do-It in YA Services." *Wisconsin Library Bulletin* 66 (1970): 136-37.

Mahar, Mary Helen. "Implications of the Library Services Act to Children and Young People." *ALA Bulletin* 53 (1959): 118-22.

Newmark, Barbara. "Survey of Young Adult Services." *Ohio Library Association Bulletin* 46-47 (1976): 23-24.

Newmark, Barbara, ed. *Whole YA Catalog.* Cleveland: Cuyahoga County [Ohio] Public Library, 1977.

Standards Revision Committee of the American Association of State Libraries. *Standards for Library Functions at the State Level.* Rev. ed. Chicago: American Library Association, 1970.

Winnick, Pauline. *1977 Directory of Coordinators of Children's Services and of Young Adult Services in Public Library Systems Serving at Least 100,000 People.* Chicago: American Library Association, 1978.

THE YOUNG ADULT SERVICES DIVISION:
Yesterday, Today, and Tomorrow

Carol Starr

The Young Adult Services Division (YASD) of the American Library Association is many things to many people. To some, it is the national organization that turns out booklists and *Top of the News*; to others, a place to turn for help with specific work problems; and to still others, an opportunity to meet and work with other librarians who share their interests. Over the years, YASD has done all of these things, and more. The organization has produced booklists, guidelines, displays, and exhibits; sponsored conference programs and preconference workshops; worked with other associations and ALA divisions; plus continued to co-sponsor, with the Association for Library Service to Children, the journal, *Top of the News*.

Besides its tangible products available for sale or free distribution, the Young Adult Services Division has provided a focal point for young adult librarianship across the country and has inserted into the overall ALA organization a measure of idealism, enthusiasm, and energy. It provides a formal link between our young adult public and the goals of modern library and information science, based on understanding and commitment to YA service.

ORGANIZATIONAL STRUCTURE

As of 1977, the Division comprised 1,760 personal members and 2,060 organizational members. It has a full-time executive secretary, plus stenographic help at ALA headquarters; an elected president; a 9-member board of directors; 24 committees; and 3 liaison appointees. It also has a constitution and by-laws, an *Organizational Manual* for officers and board, and a *Handbook for Committees*. A roster of current officers and committee members, a checklist of publications available from YASD, and a short paper on how to become involved in YASD are available free from the office.

The current structure was established in June 1957, after a massive reorganization effort within ALA made substantive organizational changes, including splitting the Association of Young People's Librarians (established in 1941) into the Children's Services Division and the Young Adult Services Division. While the two divisions were thus separated, they continued to share the services of the same executive secretary. The first major organizational problem facing both the Young Adult Services Division and the Children's Services Division was a move by the ALA Executive Board to absorb *Top of the News* into the *ALA Bulletin* in 1958. A special committee was set up to study the matter and subsequently suggested to the YASD Board that the advantages were greatly outweighed by the disadvantages. Those disadvantages included no guarantee of pages, loss of identification with membership, and lack of insurance of regular helpful articles and lists for YASD members. The advantages included a potentially larger audience, the increased likelihood of reaching administrators, and separation from Children's Services. *Top of the News* remained on its own.

The second major organizational hassle that the Young Adult Services Division faced was a confrontation with the American Association of School Librarians (AASL), which successfully argued with the ALA Executive Board to win the right to evaluate and select materials and interpret the use of such materials solely designated for school use (1961). This resulted in our current function statement:

> The Young Adult Services Division is interested in the improvement and extension of services to young people in all types of libraries. YASD has specific responsibility for the evaluation and selection of books and nonbook materials and the interpretation and use of materials for young adults, except when such materials are designated for only one type of library.

Some committees of the Association of Young People's Librarians (AYPL) were transferred, in 1957, to other divisions—YA Standards went to the Public Library Association; YA Membership became a subcommittee of the ALA Membership Committee; the Audio-Visual Committee became a subcommittee of the ALA Audio-Visual Committee; the Publicity Committee was assigned to the ALA Public Relations unit in the Library Administration Division; and work of the Activities Committee was transferred to the Library Education Division.

Another intensely introspective study on the part of ALA came in 1969, and each division was instructed by the Committee on Organization to re-examine their goals, overall efforts, activities, and possible conflicting responsibilities within the existing organizational structure. YASD set up a special committee to organize the self-study, and an elaborate and wide-reaching study was proposed. It was to include a membership survey, response from committee chairpersons and the board, and a summary by the past president. Unfortunately, the results were poor. There were only 32 responses from the membership, the forms from the committee chairpersons that were received showed little evidence of critical thinking, and the board members too often had nothing to evaluate. Nevertheless, the study resulted in dismissing at least three committees and recommended establishing an Organization Committee. While the YASD function statement remained the same, the following list of priorities was passed by the YASD Board in January 1971:

1. planning and development of programs of study and research for this type of activity for the total profession;

2. stimulation of the development of librarians working with young adults;

3. planning of special services and programs for young adults;

4. representation, interpretation and promotion of mutual cooperation with youth-serving agencies in furthering activities for the welfare of young people, and furtherance of the interests of the teenager and young adult with publishers;

5. synthesis of the activities of all units within ALA that have a bearing on work with young adults;

6. continuous study and review of activities within the scope of the YASD.

A 1976 study by then president-elect Mary Kay Chelton fit these priorities into overall ALA priorities and clearly outlined the lack of YASD work in such important areas as intellectual freedom, legislation, and continuing education. A joint exploratory committee with the Reference and Adult Services Division of ALA was set up in 1972 to see if there was a need for more formal associations or projects between the two boards. A joint board meeting was held at the ALA Midwinter meeting in 1974, and thereafter the two boards have exchanged liaison members. This board liaison did not work out well, and after the 1976 ALA Annual Conference, the liaison was discontinued.

YASD STAFF AND WORKERS

Mildred Batchelder was the first executive secretary (1957-1965); Ruth Tarbox was executive secretary from 1966 to October 1973; and she was followed by Mary Jane Anderson (December 1973 to September 1975). In 1975, the parent organization established a new dues structure, which amounted to restructuring the Association, based on budgeting and financial support. No longer were members of ALA given membership in two free divisions, with the Committee on Program Evaluation and Support passing judgment on divisional activities by passing out funds. Instead, each ALA member had to pay an extra fee for every division joined. The effect of this was to give divisions control of their own affairs. The immediate specific effect on YASD was a 60 percent drop in membership; however, as the lowest-funded division in ALA, the additional money ($3.00 per member before 1975; $15.00 per member thereafter) allowed the division to continue and, indeed, prosper. In September 1975, the division hired its first executive secretary, Evelyn Shaevel, whose time was exclusively devoted to YA matters. Unfortunately, her job was four-fifths time until November 1977, when income permitted paying a full-time salary.

The division meets twice annually at ALA Annual and Midwinter Conferences, during which time the YASD Board of Directors discusses policy and program activities, decides on future directions, and reviews the current work of the committees. All board meetings are open to observers unless they are discussing a private matter as it affects a specific individual or institution. The committees also meet at these two conferences, solidifying work that has of necessity gone on between conferences by mail and individual effort. The summer conference also includes the programs prepared by the current president, plus any committee programs, open hearings, or general discussions organized by a group within YASD. That is the formal part of YASD, as reflected through the ALA printed program. The excitement of informal discussions and exchanges between new and old friends as YA librarians interact with each other and share their insights, hopes, problems, and ideas is the lure that keeps us all coming back again and again.

YASD COMMITTEES

Housekeeping or standing committees include Activities (to suggest new projects), By-laws, Nominating, Organization (to provide function statements, membership limitations and needed criteria for selection), Program and Budget, and Membership Promotion.

Ad hoc committees are the Division's attempts to meet identified and emerging needs of the specialty. Before establishing a permanent committee, the ad hoc committee first works with the problem at hand, perhaps preparing a project and defining a continuing need; or preparing some product/project as a final answer; or dithering around and dying from inertia. Currently, the division has ad hoc committees for an affiliates regional structure liaison, the rewriting of goals and objectives, a personal crisis information task force, and sexism in adolescent materials.

MEDIA AND MATERIALS

Historically, the most active committee has been the Book Selection Committee. This committee started preparing annual lists of "Best Books for Young Adults" in 1952, although the name has not always been the same, having evolved over the years from "Significant Books" and "Interesting Books." In 1954, the list was first reprinted, from *Top of the News* and *Booklist*, for membership promotion. The next year, it was decided that reprinting the list was valuable, and it has been reprinted, sold, and distributed ever since then. In 1956, the list was formally presented orally to the ALA Council; after that, the Council cut it from the agenda, having more important and substantive agenda items.

In addition, the early Book Selection Committee prepared lists of new adult books for young adults, which appeared regularly in *Top of the News*. In 1959, the *NEA Journal* requested a booklist of outstanding fiction for the college-bound high school student. "Outstanding Fiction" was the first such list. The next year, NEA asked for a similar list on biography. After preparing the biography list, YASD went on to produce two more—theatre and nonfiction. A similar list on poetry was never completed. These four outstanding lists, along with a "Now Scene" list done in 1971, have been revised individually several times. A YASD committee in 1975 took on the task of revising and updating all five at once, and currently YASD is receiving royalties from ALA on all of these items.

The Book Selection Committee was split into two groups in 1965, one committee charged with preparing an annual list of best books and the other committee with covering everything else. It was at this time that the Best Books Committee started meeting at Midwinter Conference to discuss which books to put on this list. Prior to that, all work had been done by mail, with the chairperson compiling the final votes. These meetings were closed as were most ALA meetings until a membership resolution in Dallas ALA (1971) forced YASD into compliance with the recent general open-meeting policy established by ALA. Now the committee has an elaborate schedule for reviewing books, asking for input from anyone interested, gathering teenage reaction to potential candidates for the list, and soliciting teen-produced art for the cover design. The biannual discussions are lively, revealing, stimulating, and thought-provoking—so much so that this seems to be the one committee on which every YASD member wants to serve. Currently, the committee has fifteen members, with the YA editor of *Booklist* as an ex officio member.

Meanwhile, the "everything else" committee, currently called Media Selection and Usage, was busy preparing special subject lists and an "added entries" section for *Top of the News*, until that journal stopped publishing YA book reviews. The AV Committee, which had produced "Film Profiles for Youth" (1972) and a "Supplement" (1973), was combined with this committee in 1974. This enlarged committee compiled two mediagraphic essays—one on "Loving Choices" and one on "Science Fiction and Fantasy," both published in *Top of the News*. The committee proposed and drew up guidelines, and selected the first annual "Selected Films for Young Adults 1975," a list to complement the annual "Best Books" list. Also, the committee gathered together flyers, brochures, and descriptions of successful, on-going YA services programs around the country into a collection called "Living Library Patterns." This collection travels around the country, by request. In 1977, the name of this circulating file was changed to Young Adult Program Ideas. At Midwinter 1978, it was weeded and reorganized, and it continues to be available on loan from the YASD Office.

All of this, however, was getting to be too big a job for the Media Selection and Usage Committee. Film previewing for the "Selected Films" list was consuming all the meeting time at Midwinter, and other projects were thus falling by the wayside. Hence, in 1977, the Selected Films for Young Adults Committee was formed as a separate group. They have continued working solely on selecting quality films, refining their selection procedures, paralleling "Best Books" procedures for input and teenage reaction. They developed a specific list of quality criteria for judging films at the 1978 Midwinter meeting. Other early media and materials committee projects included a Peace Corps Subcommittee of the ALA International Relations Committee, which worked hard for several years in the early 1960s with a paperback locker library list, programs, and exhibit booths.

One of the most popular early projects of a special committee was the Dial-a-Book Project at the New York World's Fair in 1964. These were tapes of minute book reviews selected and prepared for young people that Fair attendees could dial and listen to at the ALA booth. It proved very successful and led to a project to compile one-minute booktalks. This, however, was never completed.

Two other highly successful booklists prepared by YASD were *Richer by Asia* (prepared and distributed with funds from the Asia Foundation) and *African Encounter*. Both of these publications are now out of print. A similar booklist on Latin America was never completed. "Adult Paperbacks for Young Adults" was compiled as a buying guide for school book fairs, sponsored by various local and regional jaycees in 1962. This list was later updated and called "Mod Mod." *Book Bait* (by Elinor Walker) was done by AYPL before 1957; the second edition appeared in 1969.

The Magazine Committee moved to YASD from AASL in 1957, continued to evaluate new magazines for young adults, and reviews were published in *Top of the News*. In 1970, the Magazine Committee changed from reviewing individual magazines to reviewing a subject field. The committee was disbanded in 1974, when the YASD Board decided that the committee essentially was duplicating information available in the "New Periodicals" section of *Library Journal* and *Periodicals for School Libraries* currently under revision from the American Association of School Librarians. The Television Committee was established in the mid-1960s and started producing booklists on request, often within 24-hours' notice, for NBC's *Teacher's Guide to Television*. Because of the nature of their work, this committee's membership is based in New York City. YASD reprinted in 1967-1968 a booklist originally published by the Free Library of Philadelphia called "Happenings" and distributed and sold some 400,000 copies in conjunction with National Library Week.

Four times, YASD has established committees to develop the concept of a YA book award. Each time, the committee has gotten bogged down in criteria and standards plus method of selection, and no award has ever been developed. The latest effort (1974-1976) resulted in the idea of having a Top Pop poster with teenagers voting on the last three years' worth of publications. Some of the more compelling details concerning financing the project and responsibility for designing such a poster are as yet unresolved. The project promises to be abandoned, as were the first three attempts.

TRAINING AND CONTINUING
EDUCATION PROJECTS

In 1960, the Public Library Association's Standards Committee appointed a subcommittee that produced *Young Adult Services in Public Libraries*. As a division, YASD is not responsible for the development of standards. In an effort to outline the basics of the young adult specialty, however, an ad hoc committee was appointed in 1976 to follow up on the paper presented by PLA's YA Sub-Task Force of the Goals, Guidelines and Standards Committee in 1975. This paper was reworked, reworded, expanded, and approved by the YASD Board. It is currently available from ALA Publishing for $2.50. Called "Directions for Library Service to Young Adults," it is a basic philosophic and descriptive statement of young adult service. Another important statement of philosophy and "how-to" is *Look, Listen, Explain: Developing Community Library Services for Young Adults*, a booklet developed by the Outreach Committee, which evolved from the Working with Disadvantaged Youth Committee that produced the New York conference, "Two Blocks Apart." This publication describes how to become effectively involved in your local young adult community and is also available from ALA Publishing for $2.00. A special ad hoc Survival Kit Committee worked in 1974-1976 to develop a list of helpful resources for establishing, promoting, and maintaining Young Adult Services at the local level. This kit is available from the YASD Office for $2.00.

The Research Committee began working in the early 1970s on a compilation of research on adolescence, hoping to provide brief abstracts of materials for the practitioner from both the library and associated fields of knowledge. Although they limited their scope to materials published between 1950 and 1972, the enormity of the task overwhelmed them, and it was not until 1977 that the project was completed and finally published by ALA. It is called *Media and the Young Adult: A Selected Bibliography, 1950 to 1972*.

Other current committee work includes high-interest/low-literacy level materials evaluation, library education for service to young adults at the pre-service level, and a selection aids bibliography revision project.

CONFERENCE AND PRECONFERENCE PROGRAMS

One of the most important ways in which YASD shares its concerns and abilities is through conference and preconference programs. These are the responsibility of the current president and are usually a reflection of that person's concerns within the profession. The first preconference sponsored by YASD was called "Two Blocks Apart," presented in 1965 in New York. It was a result of the Disadvantaged Committee's work and focused on ways to reach and understand young adults from disadvantaged backgrounds. A publication, *Non-Book Materials for Have-Not Youth*, resulted from this, and was revised in 1970 into *Making the Most of Media*.

The 1967 preconference in San Francisco was "Intellectual Freedom and the Teenager" and was co-sponsored with the ALA Intellectual Freedom Committee. As a result of this exciting, philosophical discussion meeting, the word "age" was added to the Library Bill of Rights as a descriptor by which librarians should *not* discriminate. In other words, the rights of minors to access to the libraries' storehouse is affirmed by the Association and thus stands as an important philosophical principle of ethical librarians. It was a vital policy statement for YASD.

The Dallas preconference (1972), called "The Young Adult in the Media World," focused on AV equipment and materials and ways to integrate these with more traditional, print-oriented young adult services. A pamphlet, "Mixed-Means Programming with Young Adults," was produced from the YASD Office in conjunction with this preconference.

The fourth preconference was presented in 1975 in San Francisco, and was called "Book You." It analyzed and discussed the past fifteen years of "Best Books for Young Adults" lists to come up with a new retrospective list of old and new titles, called "Still Alive in '75." The fifth preconference was presented in 1978 in Chicago, and was called "Dispelling the High-Low Blues," focusing on evaluation, selection, and use of materials with young people who have a low reading level and lack the motivation to read.

Conference programs have ranged from using films in YA programming, intellectual freedom issues, serving special youth groups like the disadvantaged, young adult feedback on the effectiveness of libraries and librarians as an information and growth resource, adolescent problems, sexism, the YA librarian as youth counselor, paperback use, and self-images of both librarians and clientele. Luncheon speakers have included Nat Hentoff, June Jordan, Studs Terkel, Dale Carlson, M. E. Kerr, Sol Gordon, and Anne McCaffrey.

The journal, *Top of the News*, was established in 1942 as a communications channel and informative news source for members of the Association of Young Peoples' Librarians. Since the two divisions, Children's and Young Adult Librarians, split, they have continued to publish it under joint sponsorship. The editor is selected by the respective boards for a two-year term and serves the Division gratis. The editor is responsible for editorial policy decisions, while the two executive secretaries serve as business managers. The journal is published four times a year and is sent to every member as part of their subscription dues. Non-members may pay $15.00 to receive the journal, a practice established in 1974. *Top of the News* is indexed in *Library Literature, Library and Information Science Abstract, Current Index to Journals in Education*, and *Book Review Index*. It has a press run of 10,000. There is a joint *Top of the News* Advisory Committee that gives the editor advice, suggestions, membership feedback, and general direction.

LIAISON WORK

Several committees are responsible for the division's liaison work, including those on Audio-Visual Producers and Distributors, National Organizations Serving the Young Adult, and Publishers. While the former two are quite new, the latter has been in existence for a long time. The Publishers Liaison Committee sponsored a luncheon at the 1964 St. Louis Annual Conference that got a dialog going between YA librarians and publishers. During the early 1970s, the Committee provided speakers for various regional and state associations meetings on YAs and publishing. Most recently, they presented the Paper Power Panel program at the Detroit 1977 Annual Conference. The Audio-Visual Producers and Distributors liaison work has been to put together an awareness packet of hard- and soft-ware production company catalogs that a librarian can receive upon inquiry. They are also maintaining a current mailing list of interested librarians for future catalog distribution.

The National Organizations Serving the Young Adult Committee has established some formal contacts between YASD and three other national organizations: Planned Parenthood, Girl Scouts, and National Youth Alternatives Project. YASD has agreed to help revise a Planned Parenthood publication, *A Guide to Sexuality Handbooks*, also working with the Society for Adolescent Medicine, a group with connections to the American Medical Association. Other groups the committee is working with include the National Council of Teachers of English and their Adolescent Literature Assembly, the International Reading Association, and the American Pediatricians Association.

Not all liaison work evolves into some tangible product; yet, even so, it is no less viable or important. For example, YASD sent delegates to both the 1960 and 1971 White House Conference on Youth. The opportunity to help develop national youth policies and concerns ultimately reflects on libraries and their young adult constituencies, and thus is seen as an important and appropriate communications link for the division to uphold.

CURRENT CONCERNS

A growing and continuing concern of YASD has been in the area of youth rights and intellectual freedom. An official observer from YASD was appointed to the Freedom to Read Foundation starting in 1974. The division appointed an Intellectual Freedom Committee in 1976; one of their members is liaison now to the Freedom to Read Foundation and the YASD/IFC's chair is liaison to an overall ALA/IFC joint committee. The division has given background information on the youth rights issue to the ALA attorney concerning the Long Island Trees case, for which ALA filed an amicus curiae brief. At the 1978 Midwinter meeting, the YASD/IFC and board sat down and worked out a basic policy statement on intellectual freedom as a reflection of the division's concern and commitment. The 1979 Dallas conference will concern itself with youth rights.

Legislation is another recent area of concern for YASD. A committee has been established, liaison with the ALA Legislation Assembly being built into this committee, too. Plans involving training for effective lobbying and network development are in progress. Other current concerns of the division are services to Spanish-speaking youth, continuing education, and a specific age-level definition.

While YASD does not have all the answers to all the questions, it does provide a forum for points of view, and it works always for future growth. The Division is a most dynamic, challenging, and dedicated group of people, committed to improving the library world for both our young adult patrons and ourselves.

BIBLIOGRAPHY*

Books

Committee on Outreach Programs for Young Adults. Young Adult Services Division. *Look, Listen, Explain: Developing Community Library Services for Young Adults.* Chicago: American Library Association, 1975.

Research Committee. Young Adult Services Division. *Media and the Young Adult.* Chicago: American Library Association, 1977.

Services Statement Development Committee. Young Adult Services Division. *Directions for Library Service to Young Adults.* Chicago: American Library Association, 1978.

Walker, Elinor, comp. *Book Bait: Detailed Notes on Adult Books Popular with Young People.* 2nd ed. Chicago: American Library Association, 1969.

Pamphlets

"Happenings." c.1968.

"Making the Most of Media." c.1971.

"Mixed-Means Programming for Young Adults." c.1972.

"Outstanding Biographies for the College Bound." c.1976.

"Outstanding Books on the Now Scene for the College Bound." c.1976.

"Outstanding Fiction for the College Bound." c.1976.

"Outstanding Non-Fiction for the College Bound." c.1976.

"Outstanding Theater for the College Bound." c.1976.

"Selected Films for Young Adults 1977." c.1977.

"Selected Films for Young Adults 1978." c.1978.

"Still Alive: The Best of the Best 1960-1974." c.1976.

*Includes only publications currently available from the American Library Association.

RESEARCH IN YOUNG ADULT
LITERATURE AND SERVICES

W. Bernard Lukenbill

The complaint has often been voiced that the study of adolescent litera-ture and its allied fields of information and library services to youth suffer from a lack of scholarly literature, criticism, and theory unique unto themselves. To some extent such comments are justified. Nevertheless, these fields are currently in states of growth and expansion. For example, since 1970 numerous disserta-tions on adolescent literature and materials have been written; new organiza-tions concerned with furthering adolescent literature and research, such as the Assembly on Literature for Adolescents (ALAN) of the National Council of Teachers of English, have been formed; textbooks in the area of adolescent liter-ature and services have been published; and new monographs concerned with adolescent literature and services have appeared.

Along with this new vitality has come a demand for more and better research upon which to build and improve the existing body of scholarship, criticism, and theory. It is my intention to discuss here the importance of theory in furthering the growth of young adult literature and library and informa-tion services for youth, and to note some theoretical directions which seem open to researchers having interest in this area. While doing this, I hope also to direct attention to the often heard complaint from practitioners that basic research which stresses theory, generalizations, and principles fails to help them in meet-ing the demands for solutions to practical problems faced in the work-a-day world. By briefly discussing *Action Research* and *Operations Research*, I hope to emphasize the potentials of these techniques for helping to solve practical and immediate problems faced by librarians and to describe briefly their attri-butes for aiding decision-making processes. Attention will also be given to a brief listing of standard research methods and to a discussion of significant studies and research trends of general interest which have surfaced recently.

THE NATURE OF RESEARCH

Before beginning this discussion, two definitions should be given concerning research. First, *basic* or *fundamental* research is a rigorous and structured type of analysis which is seen as a means of generating theories, broad generalizations, and principles. In a classical sense, basic research has little concern for the application of its findings to actual problems. Much of the research in the behavioral sciences is basic research in that it is concerned with theory development. *Applied* research, on the other hand, is also a rigorous and structured research analysis, but its purpose is to improve a product or process or to test a theoretical concept in a real problem situation.[1] Most research in library science tends to be applied research.

Two Major Research Traditions. Although often conflictive in approach, two major research traditions have contributed significantly to the growing body of research literature related to young adult interests. One of these approaches, the historical research method, claims a long and respected genealogy. Essentially, the historical research method is dedicated to the discovery of truth about a past event through the examination of objects available for study in the present.[2] Extending the historical approach further, we can see how its methods and approaches are applicable to literary criticism and other aspects of adolescent literature and services. This research method calls for true and complete accounts of events based on accuracy, order, logic, honesty, and self-awareness as a safeguard against biased interpretation and imagination.[3] Nevertheless, the real strengths of the historical method lie not so much in the building of a body of facts, as in the interpretation and synthesis of data and its logical application to continuing problems or phenomena.[4] In its quest for truth, the historical method requires verification, or separating the false from the true, and the rigorous examination of documents and other sources which might give evidence as to patterns, sources, biases, and conceptual systems which emerge from the data.[5] Literary scholars using the historical approach are charged with approaching their sources and topics with objectivity, guided by a central, unanswered question or even by an hypothesis. Yet, from the point of view of the scientist, the historical method is speculative and rational rather than susceptible to consensual agreement. Scientists claim that this method can never ensure the high level of accuracy in drawing conclusions as can the scientific method.[6] Nevertheless, numerous research studies using the historical approach in adolescent literature and services can be given as examples of its usefulness.[7]

Although the importance of the historical method and its contributions to research in adolescent literature and services must be recognized and appreciated, this discussion will emphasize the scientific method because it seems to offer the best approach for building a body of facts suitable for the growth of a theoretical foundation for the field. Lawrence Wrightsman of George Peabody College for Teachers describes the essential elements of the scientific method as these:

1) the scientific method is based on determinism; i.e., the assertion that events are determined by the principles of cause and effect, rather than by chance or accident;

2) the scientific approach employs the empirical approach in the pursuit of knowledge by observation and experiment through active, systematic gathering of data. This approach is in contrast to the historical method, which permits the formation of opinions and conclusions on what is considered rational, although sometimes speculative grounds;

3) the scientific method uses operational definitions. These definitions are based on exact specifications of measurable operations that permit communication between researchers and allow for repeated observation and measurement of these same operations by others;

4) the scientific method is objective and is receptive to and/or permits consensual argument. This method greatly enhances the researcher's ability to make objective deductions and verifications.[8] Although the scientific method does limit the researcher to problems that can be observed and measured objectively, the careful application of the approach insures accuracy in drawing conclusions.

Facts and Theories in Fundamental Research. The scientific method is cyclical in nature.[9] It starts with facts, progresses through theories and predictions, and ends with new facts which function to end that cycle and begin another. A fact in the scientific method is an observation that has been made repeatedly and consistently by different observers. In other words, facts are observations upon which there can be wide agreement.[10] A theory, on the other hand, is a system of ideas containing some abstract concepts, some rules about the interrelation of these concepts and ways of linking these concepts to observed and known facts.[11]

If we are to successfully formulate theories about young adult literature and library and information services, first we must begin with an inventory of fundamental facts based on a consensus of different observers. From there we should establish essential abstract ideas, concepts, and linkage points which lead back to the observers' facts. Herein lies the problem. Do facts relating to YA literature and library and informational services really exist that are supportable through consensual agreement based on observation and/or research? In some areas, they do. For example, reading, viewing, and listening interests and library-use data have a long research history; and these studies do indeed contribute facts and data which are generally accepted.[12, 13] Also, we are beginning to collect data on the information needs and the information-seeking habits of young adults in relation to such topics as sex, drugs, and career information.

In the area of literature, numerous studies have built a base of facts which seem to say that the broad body of literature written for young adults has traditionally reflected the common values of white middle-class society. On the other hand, we have little in the way of data to build facts about interpersonal concepts of young adult librarians and their clients or the role perspectives of young adult librarians in their work settings.

It is only when facts have been determined that it is possible to build a body of theory and concepts capable of permitting the drawing of interconnecting links between the observed facts and theoretical concepts. To build theory using the scientific method requires three steps. The first step is *induction*, or starting from the observed facts and building a theory that is consistent with those facts. The second step is that of logical *deduction*. That is, based on the theory developed in the inductive process, one infers additional consequences of that theory. Such consequences are stated in abstract terms as predictions of what would happen under certain conditions. Because a theory must be verified or not verified, the third, natural step following the formulation of consequences or predictions based on deductive reasoning is *verification* through further research. The theory should be capable of producing hypotheses which can be tested through research and which will produce new observations which can help either to support or to refute the predictions made during the deduction stage. Often, verified observations based on a hypothesis are at odds with the theory's predictions; and this, in turn, requires a modification of the theory and introduces a new cycle of induction, deduction, and verification. The chart that follows on page 196 may help to explain the process using reading examples. It should be remembered that theories are essentially a way of uniting assorted facts and observations for problem solving. Stated more poetically, "theory is the net [people weave] to catch the world of observation—to explain, predict, and influence it."[14]

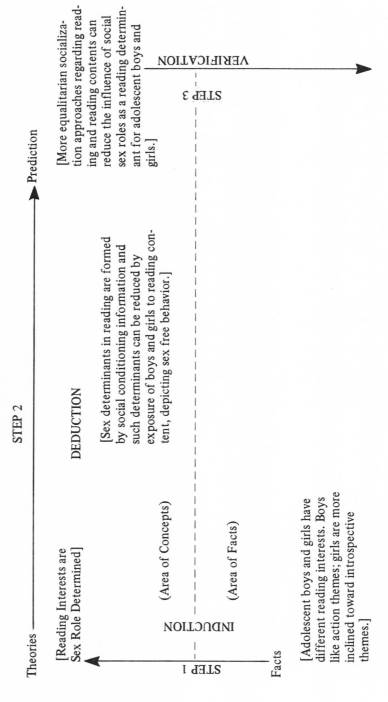

"STEPS OF THE SCIENTIFIC METHOD"
By Lawrence S. Wrightsman

Theories

STEP 2

Prediction

[Reading Interests are Sex Role Determined]

DEDUCTION

[Sex determinants in reading are formed by social conditioning information and such determinants can be reduced by exposure of boys and girls to reading content, depicting sex free behavior.]

(Area of Concepts)

INDUCTION

STEP 1

(Area of Facts)

Facts

[Adolescent boys and girls have different reading interests. Boys like action themes; girls are more inclined toward introspective themes.]

VERIFICATION

STEP 3

[More equalitarian socialization approaches regarding reading and reading contents can reduce the influence of social sex roles as a reading determinant for adolescent boys and girls.]

Source: Alan C. Purves and Richard Beach. *Literature and the Reader: Research, Reading Interests and the Teaching of Literature* (Urbana-Champaign, National Council of Teachers of English), pp. 93-95. Used by permission.

APPLYING SOCIAL AND LITERARY THEORIES
TO YOUNG ADULT WORK

It seems appropriate now to consider some theories developed in other disciplines which may have application for basic research in young adult library literature and information service. The following theories seem especially relevant: behaviorism (stimulus-response and reinforcement), Gestalt and cognitive theory, field theory, role theory, and socio-literary theories.

Behaviorism. Behaviorism operates under the assumption that people can be molded into almost any behavior patterns desired through appropriate reinforcements. B. F. Skinner is undoubtedly the best-known spokesperson of behaviorism. His influence on teaching methods and learning has contributed greatly to the development of much research related to media and behavior and to the development of educational technology, including programmed learning, instructional media, and some aspects of the learning resources center movement.[15] The behavior reinforcement approach may have contributed to assumptions about the need for planning for participant rewards and reinforcements in youth programs in libraries. For example, "come to the library, see what we have" and be instantly rewarded by participating in a rock concert, a dance, or a craft fair.

In relation to adolescent literature, media, and behaviorism, the work of Albert Bandura, psychologist at Stanford University, has great implications for librarians.[16, 17] Bandura maintains that children learn behavior through imitation of adult behavior in their world as well as from observing adult behavior in the media. The acquisition of this adult behavior requires very little rehearsal on the part of the child; reinforcement for such behavior comes to the child vicariously. In other words, children adopt behavior they see rewarded in life and in the media; and they internalize the rewards which they have observed the adults receiving as a consequence of these same behaviors. Much of the theory of recent years supporting media-effect research seems to have been influenced directly or indirectly by Bandura's theory; and a great deal of professional library rhetoric regarding the influence of books and reading on adolescent behavior reflects, perhaps unknowingly, Bandura's assertions.

Gestalt and Cognitive Theory. The basic assumption of Gestalt theory is that "the whole is greater than the sum of the parts." In contrast to behaviorism, the Gestaltists hold that behavior is purposeful, integrated, and goal directed. Behavior is not compartmentalized into small units based on specific stimulus-response cues and associations linked to the mind's peripheral processes, which involve mostly the actions of body receptors and muscle.[18] To the Gestaltists, one's perceptions, sensations, and responses are interrelated, and the brain acts as a central instrument in the organization and interpretation in a goal-directed way of data coming to the body. According to the educator Jerome Brunner, structure is essential to the individual who is engaged in this goal seeking. Structure acts as a beginning point, a means of providing fundamental guidelines and information which will be needed by individuals in their intuitive probing and discovery of elements necessary for meeting their goals and satisfying the need for closure.[19]

Because this theory places so much emphasis on structure, intuitive searching, and the discovery of related information, its implications for young adult library work seem paramount. According to Gestaltists, if individuals are to learn and bring order to their lives, they are likely to do it through exploring, organizing, and interpreting their world. Structure, yet the freedom to discover and the availability of information in various formats, is essential to this process. This theory seems to have contributed greatly to the conceptual base of the recently published bibliography of research studies, *Media and the Young Adult: A Selected Bibliography, 1950-1972*.[20] The introduction to this bibliography asserts that young adults have a desire for information capable of satisfying their needs in response to the demands of their environment. More will be said about this bibliography later.

Field Theory. Field theory as developed by Kurt Lewin has much in common with Gestalt theory. It basically holds that human behavior is a function of the person and the environment.[21] In other words, an individual's internal qualities—heredity, abilities, personality, state of health, etc.—and the person's current social environment—interactions with others, satisfaction of goals, community attitudes, and so on—all play a part in defining and determining that individual's personality and behavior. "Tension system," a basic tenet in field theory, dictates that unresolved tasks which an individual may face create and extend such stressful personal environments.[22] Lewin asserted that when tasks have been completed or resolved, the tension system disappears. Again, like cognitive theory, this concept has application for the place of information and library services because in meeting the needs generated by conflicts within an individual's social environment, information helps to dissipate the tension system growing out of those needs. The current activities of various committees and groups of the Young Adult Services Division of the American Library Association, reflecting the role of librarians in personal crisis intervention, in counseling, and in delivering "life-coping" information, illustrate the applicability of this theory to library practice and research and usher in a new area open for exploratory research.

Role Theory. Role theory has been popular as a line of inquiry in library research for some time. Several studies examining the role concepts of school librarians, media specialists, reference librarians, and administrators exist.[23] Essentially role theory helps to conceptualize the study of the interpersonal behavior of participants in social interactions. It does this not from an individual's perspective, but it explains social behavior in terms of roles, role expectations, role skills, behavior norms, role conflicts, and the influence of reference groups on members of a given social order.[24] Little in the way of research into young adult-oriented library and information roles exists; yet we need only look at present-day young adult activities in libraries and schools, as well as the activites and rhetoric coming from YASD, ALAN, and other organizations, to see that varying role concepts and behaviors are very much a part of the current scene. Once again, here is an area open for exploratory research.

Socio-literary Theories. Concerning the relationship of literature and society, it is generally agreed that most socio-literary theories imply three elements: 1) literature reflects society in terms of depicting significant social norms, values, culture, class struggle, and even documented social "facts"; 2) that literature shapes society by influencing social and cultural developments; and 3) that literature controls society by stabilizing and strengthening basic social and cultural norms.[25] As Milton Albrecht, educator and sociologist, states, the reflective and even the influence theories move the writer from a purely individualistic and artistic setting into a more active role as a social agent and turn literature away from solely aesthetic principles and artistic individualism towards cultural relativism and determinism.[26] In other words, the writer can determine the direction of society by reflecting or exposing its current reality. Research in the area of adolescent literature for the past few decades has undoubtedly been influenced by these theories. Numerous studies have attempted to document the reflection of social norms and values in novels for the adolescent reader. Authors of adolescent novels are often viewed by scholars as well as practitioners as capable of either changing or perpetuating the social order.[27]

The social control theory says that literature maintains and stabilizes society. It promotes broad understanding of social ideals and beliefs, confirming and strengthening cultural norms, attitudes, and convictions.[28] Usually this theory is applied to the strengthening of what is seen as basic social values and order, as in the family. Literature, according to this theory, instructs, justifies, and morally supports members of society in conforming to the established social structure and value system. For many years children's and adolescent literature were seen as this type of instrument, and some researchers have asserted that they still serve this function.[29] On the other hand, there are limitations and weaknesses in this theory which are revealed when one examines literature in a complex social order.

Albrecht contends that the social control theory is limited in a complex and open society because all groups cannot identify common values, that individuals and groups tend to accept literature which reflects their own values. In fact, literature within a society can be expected to expose differences; to increase antagonism, inter-group conflict, and social disunity; and according to Marxian theory in a capitalistic country, to maintain the entrenched middle-class power structure.[30] It can be asserted that by maintaining certain value systems, such as traditional adult-power-centered family concepts, literature acts as a control device and may actually serve as a reactionary force in retarding needed social change.[31] Again, research and commentary in adolescent literature have undoubtedly been influenced by this theory. Research has shown that much adolescent fiction reflects middle class values. Nevertheless, simultaneously, new and different values have appeared within society, and these are also reflected within the literature written for adolescents. Even within this small area, proponents of each type of adolescent literature have called for the eradication of the other type of literature favored by their opponents.[32] Perhaps research using this theoretical concept is needed to document the conflicts within the field of adolescent literature and to record what appears to be a phenomenon reflecting growing intergroup antagonism, conflict, and disunity based on broad social beliefs expressed through literature intended for a young and easily influenced audience. In fact, some aspects of this conflict process within society have been investigated in a study by Jerry S. Watson, in which he determined the acceptance or non-acceptance by parents, teachers, and librarians of social values expressed in adolescent literature.[33] In our concern for the conflicts about adolescent literature as a controlling method, we should not forget that a literature which reflects the multi-dimensional values of many groups offers individual readers a wide range of behaviorial alternatives which they may either accept or reject;[34] and we should note that research has sometimes been conducted on the question of how adolescents use literature to make behavior choices.[35]

The concept of social control is extremely important to young adult librarians because, historically, it is the basis on which censorship efforts by the state, church, and other elements within the community have been initiated. Traditionally, these efforts have been designed to control political, moral, and religious thought. Children have often been the prime target of such concern because of the assumption that they are passive and particularly susceptible to the influence of literature in various media—especially books, movies, radio, or television. Such concern for the disruptive effects of literature on youth behavior seems particularly evident during periods of rapid social and cultural change,[36] as we are now experiencing. The effects of television on behavior and its influence on the shaping of society have become burning issues. A great deal of research has been conducted on this question with tentative answers (and more questions) only beginning to emerge.[37]

Under the rubric of the same theory, librarians and teachers have customarily held that books and other media with the "right" message have a beneficial moral effect on youth. It also would appear that this theory has many supporters among authorities in young adult literature and service, as witnessed by the struggle to see that all sorts of "appropriate" positions on issues ranging from racism and sexism to homosexual lifestyles are incorporated into adolescent literature.[38] Research purporting to document the appearance of socially destructive, as well as socially constructive, messages in media for adolescents seem to abound. Research as to the validity of this theoretical assumption is needed. Albrecht himself expresses caution as to the ultimate power of literature or art to shape society, contending that most moral principles and ideals in literature are based on principles of brotherhood, humanity, and religion, and are difficult to formulate for scientific testing.[39] He does acknowledge, nevertheless, that further research is needed to determine whether literature has indeed superseded religion in the guidance of human conduct in this rational world.[40]

Research, Practical Problems and Decision Making. Often library practitioners complain that basic research is too theoretical, remote, and unfulfilling in terms of meeting practical needs of their everyday work environments. Not only is much of this research theoretical, but often it is also inaccessible to practitioners, being hidden in esoteric journals and expensive data systems. When it is available, such research is often difficult to understand in terms of concepts and terminologies. Even the findings, although important, cannot always be applied immediately to a specific library problem. Nevertheless, the practitioner is continually faced with immediate problems which call for action, decisions, and solutions. Such decisions and solutions call for data gathered and analyzed systematically and scientifically. Two research methods have been developed in recent decades which provide much promise for practitioners who wish to research immediate here-and-now library problems.

The first of these, *Action Research*, originated in the late 1930s, and it is designed to involve both research specialists and practitioners in the study and application of research to the solving of immediate and specific problems within a given setting.[41] Its major focus lies in immediate and practical application and not in the development of theory. Its emphasis is on solving a specific problem in a specific local situation through scientific and analytical approaches. Its by-product is practitioner growth through the development of objectivity, refining of research process skills, analytical thinking, better working relationship skills, and a heightening of professionalism. It is cooperative in that practitioners and research experts work together in deciding what to study and how to study it.[42] Hilda Taba and Elizabeth Noel outline five steps in the Action Research process: 1) problem identification; 2) problem analysis; 3) formulating hypotheses; 4) experimentation and action; 5) evaluation.[43] Although each of these steps is important and requires a great deal of skill, space does not permit a full discussion here. Taba and Noel's pamphlet *Action Research: A Case Study*, discusses Action Research in relation to educational problems and offers a good overview for librarians in terms of techniques and problems. Many helpful examples are provided for clear understanding of its application.[44]

Another research technique which has been developed to solve practical problems in organizations, including libraries, is *Operations Research* (OR). Briefly defined,

> OR is the application of scientific methods, techniques and tools to problems involving the operations of a system so as to provide those in control of the system with optimum solutions to the problems.[45]

According to its proponents, OR offers a rational, scientific, and quantitative approach to decision-making. Operations Research looks at all aspects of the problem, it notes possible and probable outcomes of alternative decisions, and it arrives at measurements of effectiveness for assessing those various alternatives.[46] It has been employed in libraries to analyze library policies regarding collection development, serial acquisitions, loan and circulation policies, and duplication policies. Young adult librarians who are interested in Operations Research and need instruction in it are referred to the book by Charles Churchman and his associates, *Introduction to Operations Research* (New York: Wiley, 1957), as well as to the article by Hindle, Buckland, and Brophy (see note 46).

A Review of Young Adult Research. In 1969 the Research Committee of the Young Adult Services Division of the American Library Association became concerned about the lack of good research on subjects of immediate concern to both library scholars and practitioners interested in adolescents. The committee realized that an inventory of research studies was overdue; but to accomplish this, a theoretical framework was needed which would not only guide the collecting and inventory of these studies into a meaningful data system, but one which would also serve as a stimulus for further research in the fields of adolescent literature, information, and library services. A bibliographic project was conceived and a supporting conceptual framework was developed to guide the project. This framework has been reported in the literature.[47] The essential elements of this concept are given below:

> . . . Young adults have a *need* for information and library services. This need is formed and influenced by at least two important variables—the attitudes of young adults toward themselves and their environment, and the expressed and unexpressed problems of young adults which are created by a multiplicity of environmental influences and factors and which require information and library services for a better, more satisfying solution of these problems. . . .

> Another important conceptual consideration was the belief that *access* to informational and library services is indistinguishably related to the informational needs of youth. Important factors that influence accessibility include, for example, characteristics relating to the use of information, media, and library facilities. Other important considerations of accessibility to information and library services are organizational factors, such as policy and management decisions, which either positively or negatively influence access to materials, programs, services, and information.[48]

These eight broad categories were identified as the basic framework for the bibliography: 1) *general characteristics of youth* (educational and familial environments, socio-economic-cultural conditions and conditioning—including the mass media—and physiological and psychological developments); 2) *information needs* (including needs generated by school assignments, family relationships, personal growth and development; e.g., sex, religion, drugs, recreation, fantasy, escape, exploration); 3) *institutional services* (library services provided youth by school, public, college, and university libraries; information services outside of libraries—counseling, information and referral services, alternative or counter-culture services—and internal library management and organizational problems); 4) *contents of materials and media* (content characteristics of books, periodicals, television, cinema, and other audiovisual materials); 5) *information-seeking behavior* (informational needs and approaches of youth, including use of libraries and other formal and informal information services); 6) *media use* (television watching, reading, and listening habits); 7) *impact of media* (effects of reading, listening to, and viewing of media on behavior); and 8) *teaching strategies for media and literature use and appreciation* (includes the teaching of literature and the effective use of media in teaching situations).[49]

Because *Media and the Young Adult: A Selected Bibliography, 1950-1972* represents the most comprehensive survey of research relating to young adult literature and libraries and informational services undertaken to date, the remaining part of this essay will be concerned with reviewing some of the significant research trends which emerged from the *Media and the Young Adult* survey and suggesting further avenues for research. Although the coverage for the published bibliography ended with 1972, the Research Committee of the YASD maintained an up-to-date resource file of studies published through 1977 and, for this essay, this file was used to augment data in the published document.

Sexuality, Sex Role Identity, and Sex Information. Numerous sexuality and sex role identity studies have appeared in recent years. These studies usually encompass a wide range of activities, including dating behavior, pre-marital cohabitation practices and other forms of pre-marital sexual conduct, courtship, and social sex role perceptions. The influence of pornography on young adult behavior and attitudes is also included in this general category. The interest which librarians and teachers have in this area is multi-faceted. Such research is helpful in supplying information for building more accurate profiles about this client group in terms of indicating the information and social needs which are likely to be expressed by young adults. Another contribution which this type of research offers to young adult authorities is supplying a conceptual framework to help with the objective analysis of sex information and sex role messages appearing in media for young adults.

Numerous studies also have appeared which report on the types of sex information needed by young adults, the level and accuracy of sex information needed, and the informational sources available for supplying sex information to adolescents. Such journals as the *American Journal of Orthopsychiatry, Youth and Society, Journal of Youth and Society, Archives of Sexual Behavior, Adolescent, Sex Roles: A Journal of Research, Journal of School Health, Family Coordinator*, and *SIECUS Report* publish research of this nature. Most studies usually report that adolescents hold an inaccurate view of sex based on their information; they acquire most of their information from peers rather than print sources; and they affirm that sex-related information is desperately needed by young adults to help them make better decisions regarding sexuality. Such studies again contribute conceptually to the objective evaluation of sex-related media for youth and add to our understanding of requirements for more effective sex information delivery systems.

Drugs, Alcohol, and Other Health Considerations. Research on drug use among young adults abounds, and this area is being overtaken quickly by research on alcohol use and abuse by adolescents. Much that applies to sex and sex information in terms of usefulness and application to the young adult specialist applies to this topic. These data can help in building more accurate client profiles for assessing user needs; they can also aid in the evaluation of materials and in developing information-delivery systems. Some of the more specialized sources for these studies include *Journal of School Health, Community Mental Health Journal, Alcohol*, and the *Journal of Studies on Alcohol.*

Interests. Paramount to effective work with young adults is an understanding of adolescent interests, and studies of this type continue to show that the sex of the individual plays a large part in determining those interests. Some studies also have attempted to document interest changes in youth from generation to generation or from decade to decade, while other research has looked at how accurately adults working with youth judge adolescent interests and activities. *The Talents of American Youth* by John C. Flanagan and others (Boston: Houghton Mifflin, 1962), also known as "Project Talent," scientifically surveyed a wide range of American youth during 1960, and this study is perhaps the most significant body of data collected to date on young adult interests.

Career Interests and Career Information Seeking Behavior. Closely related to general interests are career needs and ways to ascertain information related to career decisions. Research on this topic has usually centered on the social, economic, familial, and school influences which contribute to career choices and decisions. Another interesting approach taken in many of these studies has been to determine the feasibility for success of career choices made by adolescents in terms of educational and social backgrounds. Many studies assert that young adults lack sufficient and adequate career information for making realistic career choices and that rarely do adolescents consider the library as a valid alternative in seeking career information. Even more disturbing is the fact that rarely do research designs for studies of this type, which are usually conducted outside the library profession, consider the library as an available information system. Such publications as *Personnel and Guidance Journal, Vocational Guidance Quarterly, School Counselor, Journal of Vocational Behavior*, and the *Journal of Counseling Psychology*, as well as academic dissertations, are fundamental sources for these career information studies.

Institutional Services. This is a broad topic, embracing both services and management policies in libraries, as well as non-library systems. Management problems and policies are fundamental to the delivery of information and recreational services to young adults, because it is through management decisions that information access is established. As the compilers of *Media and the Young Adult* commented,

> Management policies [can] influence the availability of abortion materials to minors, the availability of sex materials in school and public libraries, and accessibility of audiovisual equipment and materials to students in schools.[50]

The question of management policies and information accessibility extends not only to services within public and school libraries, but also to information services outside of traditional librarianship, such as community action programs, counseling and referral services, and alternative or counter-culture institutions.

For the past few decades, research in the area of school and post-secondary library and media services and management has been growing. When these studies are supplemented by the numerous studies which have been produced in the broad area of educational technology, it is evident that a large body of institutional-related research does indeed exist. It is also apparent that research into alternative information sources for youth, such as crisis centers and hotlines, is beginning to emerge. Often this is in the form of case studies or descriptive evaluations of programs, sometimes lacking in rigorous research designs. Nevertheless, this group of studies should be carefully monitored by young adults' library specialists. Except for a limited number of state- and city-wide surveys and user studies, it is evident that relatively little research has been conducted in the area of young adult services in public libraries.

Probably the most significant recent studies are the 1974 historical study by Miriam Braverman of young adult services in the New York Public Library, Cleveland Public Library, and Enoch Pratt Free Library,[51] and the young adult user studies of Baltimore, Chicago, and Indiana in the 1960s.[52] Little or nothing in the way of research has been produced on young adult librarians' role perceptions; on library management policies and the resultant effects of these policies on the development of young adult services; on alternative young adult programming policies; on pre- and in-service training needs and methodologies; on information needs of clients; or on information-seeking behavior in terms of library information delivery systems.

Individuals who wish to keep abreast of research development in these areas will find *Adolescent, Journal of Orthopsychiatry, Journal of Community Psychology*, and *Youth Alternatives* particularly useful. Remember, too, that *Resources in Education, Psychological Abstracts, Dissertations Abstracts International*, and library-oriented journals such as *Top of the News* and *School Media Quarterly* occasionally abstract, review, and/or publish such studies.

Content Characteristics of Media. Research in the content characteristics of media is by far the most prevalent in terms of studies produced and the most diversified in relation to concepts, approaches, and methodologies used. Various disciplines ranging from mass communications, education, psychology, sociology, and librarianship to history and English have contributed to the field. Pressing social issues such as racism, sexism, ageism, services to the handicapped, and interpersonal relationships undoubtedly have contributed greatly to this outpouring of studies, and they involve all types of media (radio, television, books, periodicals, films, etc.). Methodologies ranging from rigorous, scientifically-based content analyses and objective historical studies to interdisciplinary, subjective literary commentaries have contributed to this array of materials. Journals outside of librarianship which should be consulted for this type of material include *Journal of Broadcasting; Reading Research Quarterly; Journal of Communication; English Journal; College English; ALAN Newsletter; Phaedrus: A Newsletter of Children's Literature Research*; and *Children's Literature: The Great Excluded*.

Impact of Media. Because important social and moral issues arise in every generation, the ability of media to influence the behavior of young adults has always been of great concern to researchers, as well as to the general public. Today's concerns about media's influence revolve around media to which youth are primarily exposed, namely television, radio, and books. Although recognizing that effect studies often suffer from design difficulties and biases, librarians and teachers will not only want to keep abreast of research relating especially to the effects of television and books on behavior, but they will need to be aware of research on censorship and its effects on the accessibility of information to youth. New directions for research would seem to be warranted in terms of assessing how censorship affects information accessibility to youth in relation to the civil rights of minors.

Use of Media. Questions relating to how young adults use media of all types represent one of the more popular areas of research interests to both specialists and laypeople alike. The research literature of this topic is rather broad, including not only investigations into the use of mass media by youth, but also including specifically the uses of television and such other mass media as newspapers, magazines (including school presses), popular music, and radio. Other areas of research have involved the influence of parents on adolescent media use, differences in media use among social classes, media and creativity, and preferences of media use according to sex. Significant sources again include academic dissertations, the *Journal of Broadcasting, Journal of Communication, Journalism Quarterly*, and others cited elsewhere in this discussion.

Reading Interests and Behavior. Always of fundamental interest to young adult workers, reading interest studies abound! Some of these are based on objective, rigorous research designs, while others are poorly formulated, administered, analyzed, and written. Topics in this area include general reading interests, interests according to sex, interests according to racial and cultural groups, leisure reading habits, regional reading interests, and personality and family influences on reading. The reading interests and skills of the culturally different have received considerable attention in recent years. Educational journals are especially useful in supplying this type of information, including the *Journal of Reading, English Journal, Reading Teacher* and the *Journal of Educational Research*.

Teaching Strategies for Media and Literature Use and Appreciation. Questions as to how to use and integrate media better into the teaching situation have produced a large body of research. Much of this takes the form of academic dissertations, which rarely make their way into print. Nevertheless, the scope of this research is vast and is increasing rapidly. Included in this eclectic array of studies are those on the teaching of literature by forms (poetry, novels, short stories, mythology, etc.) and the use of non-book media (films, television, etc.). Also included here are investigations into the psychological and personal processes involved in teaching the subtleties of acquiring literary knowledge and appreciation. Research about educational technology and the teaching of subject matter also adds greatly to this body of research. Most of the educational journals previously cited may be profitably consulted for this type of material.

Assessment of Research Needs and Methodologies. Although suggestions for research in young adult literature, library services, and informational needs have been stated and implied throughout this discussion, I will attempt to further synthesize these suggestions. It appears that additional research is needed in connection with a variety of problems associated with determining the informational needs of adolescents and information delivery systems serving youth. In conjunction with this, researchers may want to investigate the basic psychological aspects of information needs and information-seeking behavior as conceptualized in psychological studies. Perhaps these studies need to be correlated with and placed within the conceptual framework of library-related research and thought. More specifically, scholars will want to consider the influence of youth consumer needs and behavior in relation to library information delivery systems. Health and social considerations such as drugs, sex, alcohol, etc. will need to be investigated continually with the goal of refining our understanding of the influences of these considerations on youth behavior and of determining the effectiveness of information systems designed to serve youth. Career needs and resultant information needs are also aspects of the information matrix of youth that need to be considered.

In line with determining information needs, it seems that some basic research is also needed into methodologies and approaches for determining the effectiveness of information delivery systems designed to support the informational needs of the young adult and to respond to adolescents in a psychologically supportive way. From an affective point of view, do young adult library specialists have the necessary "helping relationship" or counselor skills to meet, understand, and respond to the emotional needs of their client group?

Because social phenomena are never static, continuing research is needed to monitor the general interests of adolescents, as well as media interests and media use by adolescents, including their reading, viewing and listening interests. Continued assessment of media content is also required in terms of social issues, which are interpreted through media. Sex role messages, ageism, racism, questions of morality, as well as the accuracy of non-fictional material will always require objective research.

Studies of library management decisions and their effects on information and service accessibility for adolescents seem warranted. How damaging or beneficial have those library management decisions made in recent years been on this specific client group? This question has special implications for meeting the needs of the early adolescent, who has been traditionally neglected by most social service agencies.[53]

Research into the role perceptions of young adult library specialists should not only include their attitudes about clients, but should also encompass their feelings about their role functions and relationships in their work and social environments. In conjunction with role profile, it appears, too, that research is called for in documenting attitudes about newly emerging role patterns in young adult services. For example, should young adult library services include the provision of "life-coping" information, crisis interventions, and counseling? If so, what is needed in the way of interpersonal and "helping relationship" skills and training on the part of young adult librarians?

In addition, research is suggested to help define the relationship of library-based to non-library-based information delivery systems for youth. What relationships can be drawn or developed among libraries and hotlines, crisis centers, and information and referral centers? How well do alternative information services provide information when compared with library information options? Before research is conducted into these newly formulated concepts of services, research is greatly needed in determining the current state of young adult library services and programming practices. This seems especially important in relation to adverse management decisions regarding services to adolescents and the financial limitations of the last decade.

Researchers must continue to search for the answers to the question, "can media messages influence the behavior of adolescents?" Not only is continued research required, but efforts to find new methodologies capable of correctly assessing media effects is necessary as well. Other needs include research into the effects of censorship on youth-oriented materials and information. How have censorship efforts impeded the flow of information to youth and how has this violated their civil rights?

The various approaches taken by media critics to analyze adolescent literature and media require investigation. This seems especially important in consideration of the current focus being placed on media in determining social goals and ideologies.

Strategies for teaching literature and media use and appreciation are a proverbial need. Closely related to this is the need to determine how information seeking skills are being taught and integrated into the modern school curriculum. The influences on media selection and collection development of such new educational trends as values clarification, behavior modification, moral education, and humanistic education also should be determined. Information and data on the learning and educational needs, practices, and methodologies of the library young adult specialists both at the pre- and in-service levels are required. Current practices, as well as forecast based on supportable data about teaching and learning alternatives, are demanded as well.

Forecasts should not be limited only to education, but should also be extended to the consideration of future developments in media formats, contents, and informational delivery systems; and the future educational and recreational needs of youth should also be considered in these studies.

Finally, analytical historical and biographical studies should also be conducted. Without an accurately and analytically developed history, a field of study can never project a stable presence or contemplate a productive future. A great many research methodologies are available to researchers working within this area. Because numerous research guides are available, details of research methodologies will not be discussed at length here, except to note that such procedures embrace a wide array of approaches, including experimental and survey research, the field study, intensive interviewing, aggregate data analysis, content analysis, evaluation research, and other forms of observational study. Longitudinal studies are especially needed to determine long-term characteristics of information-seeking behavior and media effects.

Conclusion. It seems apparent from this discussion that the whole area of young adult literature and library and informational services is in a critical stage of development and in great need of good research data. Traditional concepts are changing, and new directions are emerging. Research is needed to guide not only scholars in the development of a sound body of facts, literature, criticism, and theory, but also to help the practitioner plan for and deliver vital social, personal, and educational services for youth today.

NOTES

[1] John W. Best, *Research in Education*, 2nd ed. (Englewood Cliffs, NJ: Prentice-Hall, 1970), pp. 11-12.

[2] Herbert Goldhor, *An Introduction to Scientific Research in Librarianship* (Urbana: University of Illinois, Graduate School of Library Science, 1972), p. 100.

[3] Jacques Barzun and Henry F. Graff, *The Modern Researcher* (New York: Harcourt Brace, 1957), pp. 57-60.

[4] Goldhor, p. 100.

[5] Barzun, pp. 154-75.

[6] Lawrence S. Wrightsman, *Social Psychology in the Seventies: Brief Edition* (Monterey, CA: Brooks/Cole Publishing Co., 1973).

[7] See listings in W. Bernard Lukenbill, *A Working Bibliography of American Doctoral Dissertations in Children's and Adolescents' Literature, 1930-1971.* (Occasional paper no. 103. Urbana: University of Illinois, Graduate School of Library Science, 1972; and "Selected Dissertations and Periodical Literature," *Phaedrus: An International Journal of Children's Literature* 1- (1973).

[8] Wrightsman, p. 35.

[9] Ibid., p. 33.

[10] Ibid.

[11] Ibid.

[12] Alan C. Purves and Richard Beach, *Literature and the Reader: Research in Response to Literature, Reading Interests and the Teaching of Literature* (Urbana, IL: National Council of Teachers of English, 1972).

[13] Jean Spealman Kujoth, comp., *Reading Interests of Children and Young Adults.* Metuchen, NJ: Scarecrow, 1970.

[14] Morton Deutsch and Robert M. Krauss, *Theories in Social Psychology* (New York: Basic Books, Inc., 1965), p. vii.

[15] Charlene D. Kirschner, et al., *Doctoral Research in Educational Media, 1969-1972* (Stanford, CA: Stanford University, ERIC Clearinghouse on Information Resources, Stanford Center for Research and Development in Teaching, School of Education, 1975).

[16] Albert Bandura, *Aggression: A Social Learning Analysis* (Englewood Cliffs, NJ: Prentice Hall, 1973).

[17] Albert Bandura, *Principles of Behavior Modification* (New York: Holt, 1969).

[18] Wrightsman, p. 13.

[19] Jerome S. Bruner, *The Process of Education* (New York: Vantage Books, 1960).

[20] American Library Association, Research Committee, Young Adult Services Division, *Media and the Young Adult: A Selected Bibliography, 1950-1972* (Chicago: ALA, 1977) [hereafter cited as *Media and the Young Adult*].

[21] Wrightsman, p. 16.

[22] Ibid., p. 17.

[23] Lowell Ellis Olson, "Teachers' Principles and Librarians' Perceptions of the School Librarian's Role," Ph.D. dissertation, University of Minnesota, 1966 [consult also *Dissertations Relating to Library Science* (Ann Arbor, MI: University Microfilms International, n.d.)].

[24] Wrightsman, p. 23.

[25] Milton C. Albrecht, "The Relationship of Literature and Society," *American Journal of Sociology* 59 (March 1954): 425-26, 431-32.

[26] Ibid., p. 431.

[27] Sheila Egoff, "Precepts and Pleasure: Changing Emphases in the Writing and Criticism of Children's Literature," in *Only Connect: Readings on Children's Literature*, Sheila Egoff, G. T. Stubbs, and L. F. Ashley, eds. (Toronto: Oxford University Press, 1969), pp. 419-33, 433-46.

[28] Albrecht, p. 425.

[29] Egoff, pp. 433-46.

[30] Albrecht, p. 432.

[31] Ibid.

[32] Sheila Schwartz, "Using Adolescent Fiction That Deals with Current Problems and Lifestyles to Explore Contemporary Values," paper presented at the 4th Annual Meeting of the English Teachers on Creative Survival (Rutherford, NJ: January 1976), pp. 34, 17; and Mary Corde Lorang, *Burning Ice: The Moral and Emotional Effects of Reading* (New York: Scribner's, 1968).

[33] Jerry J. Watson, "A Study of Adults' Reactions to Contemporary Junior Novels Reflecting Adolescents' Interest in Reading about Aspects of Peer and Non-Peer Relationships," Ph.D. dissertation, Michigan State University, 1974.

[34] Albrecht, p. 433.

[35] Mary Beth Wode Culp, "A Study of the Influence of Literature on the Behavior of Adolescents," Ph.D. dissertation, The Florida State University, 1975.

[36] Albrecht, p. 434.

[37] George A. Comstock, *Television and Human Behavior: A Guide to the Pertinent Scientific Literature* (Santa Monica, CA: Rand Corporation, 1975).

[38] "Areas and Issues—Children and Books" in Zena Sutherland and May Hill Arbuthnot, *Children and Books*, 5th ed. (Glenview, IL: Scott, Foresman, 1977), pp. 580-627; *Issues in Children's Book Selection: A School Library Journal/Library Journal Anthology* (New York: R. R. Bowker, 1973).

[39] Albrecht, p. 435.

[40] Ibid., p. 436.

[41] Best, p. 12.

[42] Ibid., p. 13.

[43] Hilda Taba and Elizabeth Noel, *Action Research: A Case Study* (Washington: Association for Supervision and Curriculum Development, 1957), p. 2.

[44] Ibid., pp. 12-27.

[45] A. Graham MacKenzie and Michael K. Buckland, "Operational Research," in Peter Brophy, Michael K. Buckland, and Anthony Hindle, eds., *Reader in Operations Research for Libraries* (Englewood, CO: Information Handling Services, 1976), p. 349 [quoting C. W. Churchman and others]; *Introduction to Operations Research* (Santa Barbara, CA: Wiley/Hamilton, 1957.)

[46] Anthony Hindle, et al., "The Techniques of Operations Research: A Tutorial," in Peter Brophy, Michael K. Buckland, and Anthony Hindle, eds., *Reader in Operations Research for Libraries* (Englewood, CO: Information Handling Services, 1976), p. 27.

[47] YASD Research Committee, "Media and the Young Adult: 1950-1972," *Top of the News* 33 (Spring 1977): 258-67.

[48] *Media and the Young Adult*, p. ix. Quoted by permission.

[49] Ibid., pp. x-xi.

[50] Ibid., p. x.

[51] Miriam Ruth Braverman, "Public Library and the Young Adult: The Development of the Service and Its Philosophy in the New York Public Library, Cleveland Public and the Enoch Pratt Free Library," D.L.S. dissertation, Columbia University, 1974. Also published as *Youth, Society and the Public Library* (Chicago: American Library Association, 1978).

[52] Philip S. Wilder, *Library Usage by Students and Young Adults* (Bloomington: Indiana University, Graduate Library School, 1970); Lowell A. Martin, *Library Response to Urban Change: A Study of the Chicago Public Library* (Chicago: American Library Association, 1969); Lowell A. Martin, *Students and the Pratt Library: Challenge and Opportunity* (Deiches Fund Studies of Public Library Service no. 1. Baltimore, MD: Enoch Pratt Free Library, 1963).

[53] Joan Lipsitz, *Growing Up Forgotten: A Review of Research and Programs Concerning Early Adolescence* (Lexington, MA: Lexington Books, 1977).

BIBLIOGRAPHY

Albrecht, Milton C. "The Relationship of Literature and Society." *American Journal of Sociology* 59 (1954): 425-26, 431-32.

American Library Association. Research Committee. Young Adult Services Division. *Media and the Young Adult: A Selected Bibliography, 1950-1972.* Chicago: ALA, 1977.

"Areas and Issues—Children and Books." In *Children and Books*, 5th ed. Lena Sutherland and May Hill Arbuthnot, eds. Glenview, IL: Scott, Foresman, 1977. pp. 580-627.

Bandura, Albert. *Aggression: A Social Learning Analysis.* Englewood Cliffs, NJ: Prentice-Hall, 1973.

Bandura, Albert. *Principles of Behavior Modification.* New York: Holt, 1969.

Barzun, Jacques, and Henry F. Graff. *The Modern Researcher.* New York: Harcourt Brace, 1957.

Best, John W. *Research in Education*, 2nd ed. Englewood Cliffs, NJ: Prentice-Hall, 1970.

Braverman, Miriam Ruth. *Youth, Society and the Public Library.* Chicago: American Library Association, 1978.

Bruner, Jerome S. *The Process of Education.* New York: Vantage Books, 1960.

Comstock, George A. *Television and Human Behavior: A Guide to the Pertinent Scientific Literature.* Santa Monica, CA: Rand Corporation, 1975.

Culp, Mary Beth Wode. "A Study of the Influence of Literature on the Behavior of Adolescents." Ph.D. dissertation, The Florida State University, 1975.

Deutsch, Morton, and Robert M. Krauss. *Theories in Social Psychology.* New York: Basic Books, Inc., 1965.

Egoff, Sheila. "Precepts and Pleasure: Changing Emphases in the Writing and Criticism of Children's Literature." In *Only Connect: Readings on Children's Literature.* Sheila Egoff, G. T. Stubbs, and L. F. Ashley, eds. Toronto: Oxford University Press, 1969. pp. 419-46.

Goldhor, Herbert. *An Introduction to Scientific Research in Librarianship.* Urbana: University of Illinois, Graduate School of Library Science, 1972.

Hindle, Anthony, et al. "The Techniques of Operations Research: A Tutorial." In *Reader in Operations Research for Libraries.* Peter Brophy, Michael K. Buckland, and Anthony Hindle, eds. Englewood, CO: Information Handling Services, 1976. p. 27.

Issues in Children's Book Selection. A School Library Journal/Library Journal Anthology. New York: R. R. Bowker, 1973.

Kirschner, Charlene D., et al. *Doctoral Research in Educational Media, 1969-1972.* Stanford, CA: Stanford University. ERIC Clearinghouse on Information Resources. Stanford Center for Research and Development in Teaching. School of Education, 1975.

Kujoth, Jean Spealman, comp. *Reading Interests of Children and Young Adults.* Metuchen, NJ: Scarecrow, 1970.

Lipsitz, Joan. *Growing Up Forgotten: A Review of Research and Programs Concerning Early Adolescence.* Lexington, MA: Lexington Books, 1977.

Lorang, Mary Corde. *Burning Ice: The Moral and Emotional Effects of Reading.* New York: Scribner's, 1968.

Lukenbill, W. Bernard. *A Working Bibliography of American Doctoral Dissertations in Children's and Adolescents' Literature, 1930-1971.* Occasional Paper No. 103. Urbana: University of Illinois. The Graduate School of Library Science, 1972.

MacKenzie, A. Graham, and Michael K. Buckland. "Operational Research." In *Reader in Operations Research for Libraries.* Peter Brophy, Michael K. Buckland, and Anthony Hindle, eds. Englewood, CO: Information Handling Services, 1976. p. 349.

Martin, Lowell A. *Library Response to Urban Change: A Study of the Chicago Public Library.* Chicago: American Library Association, 1969.

Martin, Lowell A. *Students and the Pratt Library: Challenge and Opportunity.* Deiches Fund Studies of Public Library Service no. 1. Baltimore, MD: Enoch Pratt Free Library, 1963.

Olson, Lowell Ellis. "Teachers' Principles and Librarians' Perceptions of the School Librarian's Role." Ph.D. dissertation, University of Minnesota, 1966.

Purves, Alan C., and Richard Beach. *Literature and the Reader: Research in Response to Literature, Reading Interests and the Teaching of Literature.* Urbana, IL: National Council of Teachers of English, 1972.

Schwartz, Sheila. "Using Adolescent Fiction That Deals with Current Problems and Lifestyles to Explore Contemporary Values." Paper presented at the 4th Annual Meeting of the English Teachers on Creative Survival, January 1976 (Rutherford, New Jersey).

Sutherland, Zena, and May Hill Arbuthnot. *Children and Books*, 5th ed. Glenview, IL: Scott Foresman, 1977.

Taba, Hilda, and Elizabeth Noel. *Action Research: A Case Study.* Washington: Association for Supervision and Curriculum Development, 1957.

Watson, Jerry J. "A Study of Adults' Reactions to Contemporary Junior Novels Reflecting Adolescents' Interest in Reading about Aspects of Peer and Non-Peer Relationships." Ph.D. dissertation, Michigan State University, 1974.

Wilder, Philip S. *Library Usage by Students and Young Adults.* Bloomington: Indiana University. Graduate Library School, 1970.

Wrightsman, Lawrence S. *Social Psychology in the Seventies: Brief Edition.* Monterey, CA: Brooks/Cole Publishing Co., 1973.

YASD Research Committee. "Media and the Young Adult: 1950-1972." *Top of the News* 33 (1977): 258-67.

PROFESSIONAL AWARENESS:
Keeping Up with the News

Evelyn Shaevel

Although it may often seem like an overwhelming task, keeping up with the current trends and issues in the library world and other closely related groups is a primary professional responsibility for all librarians. This is particularly true for the young adult librarian, who is often isolated from the mainstream of the library world because of 1) the "clients" (the YAs) being served, and 2) the attitude of the rest of the profession toward both the young adults and professionals designated to serve them. We often must face two basic problems when attempting to simultaneously keep up with the news and work in a real library: time and the availability of the material. There never seems to be enough time to spend on "professional" reading after working all day. But keeping up with the news—which is a way of providing ourselves with a vital, on-going self-education program through reading professional material both library and library-related—must not be considered an optional activity. It would be best to schedule a time for professional reading on a regular basis, which might be daily or weekly; otherwise, the best laid plans of mice, men, and women. . . .

The problem of limited availability of material may occur because the library or system in which the young adult librarian works has limited funds for such material or because the material itself might be hard to find. If this is the case, the material that we are able to read must be carefully selected to provide the widest possible range. And a little creativity in procuring the material is always in order. Exchanging items with the English or social studies teacher or offering the local Planned Parenthood or legal aid group a place to house some of their materials might be tried. We must do whatever is necessary to see that we regularly read as much professional material as possible. What follows is a discussion of material including journals, periodicals, and newsletters recommended for regular reading by young adult librarians in order for them to keep up with the news in the library profession and other related areas. Each young adult librarian will have suggestions for additions to or deletions from this list. Choice depends on individual interests, the community, and the young adults being served.

Because professional reading is done for various reasons, the material to be read may be categorized in several ways, depending on the purpose for reading as well as the content. The categories into which professional YA reading may be placed are: general library periodicals, specialized library periodicals, and special-interest or professional journals not aimed primarily at librarians. Sources for reviews of material of YA interest are not included here because they have been covered in other articles and bibliographies.

GENERAL LIBRARY PERIODICALS

Most lists of professional materials of a general nature start with *American Libraries, Library Journal,* and *Wilson Library Bulletin.* Articles in these publications may range from reports on violence in libraries ("Sex and Violence in the Library," *American Libraries,* October 1977) to a discussion of homosexuality in young adult books ("Can Young Gays Find Happiness in YA Books?," *Wilson Library Bulletin,* March 1976). In each of these journals are regular features that would be of interest to young adult librarians. In *American Libraries,* a regular feature of "The Source" called "Young People" contains notes on recent or forthcoming programs, conferences, and publications of interest to youth librarians. *Library Journal*'s "Checklist" page lists sources for free or inexpensive material (e.g., pamphlets, posters, bibliographies), and the "Magazines" column by Bill Katz is one of the few sources for reviews of magazines. A column called "For the Young Adult" in *Wilson Library Bulletin* reviews about one-half dozen items—fiction and non-fiction, books and pamphlets—each month.

Many states have publications that provide good material of a general professional nature, which may be applied to young adult services. Articles or entire issues of these state publications are devoted to young adult services. For example, New York's *Bookmark* (Winter 1978), the *Ohio Library Association Bulletin* (July 1976) and *Wisconsin Library Bulletin* (March/April 1977) have recently devoted entire issues to young adult services.

Materials categorized as "alternative" or "underground" library press publications help to broaden our professional perspective and are often good sources for interesting articles, with non-traditional program and service ideas as well as bibliographies. Several suggested for regular reading are *Booklegger* (which in early 1978 began publishing again after over a year of inactivity) and *The U*N*A*B*A*S*H*E*D Librarian,* subtitled "How I Run My Library Good Newsletter." *Emergency Librarian,* a Canadian feminist library publication, often contains articles relating to adult services besides its regular "Books for Liberated Kids" column, and it has regularly devoted entire issues to "kids" or "young people." Although not written specifically for YA librarians, these publications and many others have applicability to the varied interests and the work of YA librarians as well as to most others in the profession. And as is evident from titles cited, at times articles or entire issues are devoted to YA services.

SPECIALIZED LIBRARY PERIODICALS

The library publications aimed at special interests or activity groups within the profession are not to be overlooked by the young adult librarian. Obviously, for the professional needs and purposes of librarians working with young adults, the most important of these specialized publications are those specifically published for the YA librarian. At present, though, there is a very small world of young adult library periodicals. Just two periodicals on the national level are published for only the young adult librarian. Both were started by librarians concerned with young adult services who felt that the specialized needs and professional interests of young adult librarians were not being adequately met in other library periodicals.

In 1973, Carol Starr began the *Young Adult Alternative Newsletter* (YAAN), which serves as clearing house for ideas and information for young adult librarians. Reports on programs, activities, and professional concerns of YA librarians from around the country are gathered together in YAAN. For over five years, it has been the only publication on the national level that attempted to address the professional problems and concerns of YA librarians. In the spring of 1978, the second periodical devoted exclusively to YA interests in the broadest sense appeared on the scene. *Voice of Youth Advocates*, published and edited by Dorothy Broderick and Mary K. Chelton, presents reports of conferences (including ALA and YASD), workshops, and articles covering topics of concern to young adult librarians (e.g., "Runaway Children and Social Network Intervention" or "Defending Free Speech"–VOYA, April 1978), as well as reviews of material in areas of interest to young adults (e.g., science fiction, mysteries, general adult books, rock music, and film). As stated in VOYA's first editorial, the

> primary goal . . . is to demonstrate that library service to young
> adults in schools, public libraries and institutions has a valid
> theoretical basis [and that] through VOYA we hope to give [YA
> librarians] ideas and skills that will enable [them] to create a service
> network of adults: parents, librarians, and allied professionals, which
> will work toward increased life options for young adults.

Three other periodicals, two of which are published by divisions of the American Library Association, devote much of their space to the concerns of librarians working with young adults.

School Library Journal, with a circulation of almost 40,000, has the largest audience of any library publication even though (or because) it is "for children's, young adult, and school librarians," the youth services divisions of librarianship. Besides the lengthy book review sections, including "Books for Young Adults," regular features are "In the YA Corner," the "Checklist," and news reports.

Each issue has interesting and timely articles, often on pertinent topics for the young adult librarian, as well as editor Lillian Gerhardt's often provocative editorials, which target issues of concern to youth librarianship.

Top of the News (TON), a quarterly journal of ALA's Young Adult Services Division and the Association for Library Services to Children, is aimed at librarians working with young people from pre-school through high school. In the past, many young adult librarians felt that TON was a publication for children's librarians that rarely addressed the problems and interests of the young adult library world. Recently, though, there has been a change in editorial direction with the introduction of theme issues (Fall 1977, "The Paperback Explosion"; Winter 1978, "Sex and Youth: A Symposium"; and Spring 1978, "Some 'Isms' Revisited"), which have identified areas of concern shared by both YA and children's librarians. Other features of TON that regularly contain items of interest to YA librarians are "Added Entries," a section devoted to reviews of professional material, and "The Top," a section containing a potpourri of news from the two divisions (ALSC and YASD), announcements of publications and events of interest to youth librarians, as well as references to "recent reading too good to miss!"

School Media Quarterly (SMQ), the journal of ALA's American Association of School Librarians (AASL), has a more scholarly tone than TON and is directed at professionals on all levels working in schools.

In order to keep up with the news and events in special interest areas of the profession that are also related and important to YA librarians, several items are of particular value. *Newsletter on Intellectual Freedom* provides an on-going record of instances where censorship has taken place. Whether it is a book, a movie, or a speaker that has been "censored," or whether the censoring took place in a library, school, or anywhere in a community, the *Newsletter* will report what has happened. Information presented here is especially important because so many of the cases involve young adults. *Library PR News* takes over where *Tips from Clip* (which ceased publication in December 1977) left off in providing "effective, practical ideas and techniques to save you time, effort and money in maintaining and expanding your library public information program." Two other professional periodicals of importance are *Drexel Library Quarterly* and *Library Trends*, both of which devote each issue to a special theme or subject—often of special interest to YA librarians (Young Adult Services, Information and Referral).

SPECIAL INTEREST JOURNALS

Although not aimed at librarians, several magazines, newsletters, and journals published by special interest or professional groups (such as educators and media professionals) almost always contain articles, special features, or reviews pertinent to the work and professional interests of YA librarians. Besides being the general source for the latest news and current trends in the publishing industry, *Publishers Weekly* is a valuable, useful source of information as to what titles are *going* to be published, which have been sold to television and the movies, who will be doing a paperback reprint, and what authors will be appearing on television or radio to promote their books.

The professional journals for English and social studies teachers contain articles in areas of great concern to the young adult school world and thus to the young adult librarian. *English Journal*, the National Council of Teachers of English (NCTE) secondary level publication, often has articles that discuss adolescent literature ("Hollywood and American Literature," January 1977; "How to Encourage the Unwilling Reader of Fiction," February 1977), censorship, films, and the relationship of all of these to the student. Regular features include reviews of professional readings as well as notes on sources of free or inexpensive materials. The *ALAN Newsletter*, published by the Adolescent Literature Assembly of NCTE (ALAN), is another source of interesting discussion and reviews of the literature for young adults. *Language Arts*, the elementary level NCTE publication, although not regularly as useful, often contains good articles on "junior novels" and the reading interests, patterns and problems of the junior high age-level student.

Social Education, often overlooked by librarians, is another source for discussions of materials and subjects of interest to young adults, their social studies teachers, and librarians who serve them all. Social issues such as death and dying, censorship, welfare, and the Holocaust are covered in articles and bibliographies.

Media and Methods emphasizes non-print material, although print is regularly included, and it is used by educators, including both school and public librarians. Annual issues are devoted to paperbacks and a 16mm film resource guide. Regular reviews of print and non-print media and articles relating to their use (easily transferable to library situations) should not be missed by YA librarians.

Several disparate publications touch on the interests of young adults as well as on the important issues and concerns of librarians serving them. *Children's Rights Report*, a publication of the American Civil Liberties Union, delves into a different area of the rights of youth in each issue. Among recent topics discussed were curfews; students and censorship; conflict of rights among children, parents, and the state; and juvenile crime.

A fine publication concerning adolescent development is the *Center Quarterly Focus*, published by the Center for Youth Development and Research, University of Minnesota, which states as its purpose, "to communicate significant current thinking and research on issues and problems concerning youth." Youth is defined as that state in the lifecycle that begins in adolescence and continues until adulthood—essentially the period between childhood and economic independence. Among topics presented in recent issues, most of which have obvious relevance to young adult librarians, were "Adolescent and Parent" and "Adolescent Girls," a two-year study done by Gisela Konopka, director of the Center, who has done much important study and research in the area of adolescent development.

Getting It Together, the newsletter from the Youth and Student Affairs section of Planned Parenthood Federation of America, keeps readers abreast of current concerns regarding sexual health services for youth and includes legal developments, innovative programs, new publications, seminars, conferences, and materials reviews.

Published by the Sex Information and Education Council of the United States and edited by Dr. Mary Calderone, the *SIECUS Report* contains articles on sex education (e.g., "Sex in Children's Fiction: Freedom to Frighten?," May 1977; or "Childhood Sexuality: The Last of the Great Taboos," March 1977), and also reviews journals, books, and films. It is one of the best sources for sex education information and materials for *all* librarians, and should be a top priority item.

In conclusion, although at times it may be difficult and there will be inevitable obstacles to overcome, every professional librarian should make a regularly scheduled effort to keep up with the news found in the literature described. If librarians want to consider themselves professional youth workers and professional librarians, being informed of current news and trends in services for youth in libraries and in other settings is essential.

BIBLIOGRAPHY

ALAN Newsletter. Semi-annual. $5/year. Adolescent Literature Assembly of NCTE; c/o Mary Sucher, 1776 Brookview Rd., Baltimore, MD 21222.

American Libraries. Monthly. Included with ALA membership; subscriptions available to institutions $20/year. ALA; 50 E. Huron St., Chicago, IL 60611.

Booklegger. $4/issue. Celeste West; 555 29th St., San Francisco, CA 94131.

Bookmark. Quarterly. $1.50/year. New York State Library; Gift and Exchange Section; Albany, NY 12234.

Center Quarterly Focus. Quarterly. Center for Youth Development and Research; University of Minnesota; 48 McNeal Hall—1985 Buford Ave., St. Paul, MN 55108.

Children's Rights Report. 10 issues yearly. $15/year. ACLU Foundation; 22 East 40th St., New York, NY 10016.

Drexel Library Quarterly. Quarterly. $12/year. Drexel University; Philadelphia, PA 19104.

Emergency Librarian. Bi-monthly. $9/year. S. Chede; 46 Gormley Ave., Toronto, Ontario, Canada M4V 1Z1.

English Journal. Monthly (September-May). $20/year. NCTE; 1111 Kenyon Rd., Urbana, IL 61801.

Getting It Together. Bi-monthly. $4/year. Youth and Student Affairs; Planned Parenthood Federation; 810 7th Ave., New York, NY 10019.

Language Arts. 8 issues a year. $20/year. NCTE; 1111 Kenyon Rd., Urbana, IL 61801.

Library Journal. 22 issues/year. $19/year. R. R. Bowker, Subscription Dept.; P.O. Box 67, Whitinsville, MA 01588.

Library PR News. Bi-monthly. $15/year. Library Educational Institute; P.O. Box 867, Bloomfield, NJ 00703.

Library Trends. Quarterly. $15/year. Subscription Dept., University of Illinois Press, Urbana, IL 61801.

Media and Methods. 9 issues/year. $9/year. North American Publishing Company; 401 North Broad St., Philadelphia, PA 19108.

Newsletter on Intellectual Freedom. Bi-monthly. $8/year. ALA; 50 E. Huron St., Chicago, IL 60611.

Ohio Library Association Bulletin. Quarterly. Free to members. Subscription information: OLA Executive Offices; c/o Executive Director, Room 409, 40 S. Third St., Columbus, OH 43215.

Publishers Weekly. Weekly. $30/year. R. R. Bowker Co., Subscription Dept.; P.O. Box 67, Whitinsville, MA 01588.

School Library Journal. Monthly (September-May). $17/year. R. R. Bowker Co., Subscription Dept.; P.O. Box 67, Whitinsville, MA 01588.

School Media Quarterly. Quarterly. $15/year. ALA; 50 E. Huron St., Chicago, IL 60611.

SIECUS Report. Bi-monthly. $10/year. Human Services Press; 72 5th Ave., New York, NY 10011.

Social Education. 7 times a year. $25/year. National Council for the Social Studies; Suite 400, 2030 M Street, N.W., Washington, DC 20036.

Top of the News. Quarterly. Included with ALA/YASD membership; subscriptions $15/year. ALA; 50 E. Huron St., Chicago, IL 60611.

Unabashed Librarian. Quarterly. $10/year. GPO Box 2631; New York, NY 10001.

Voice of Youth Advocates. Bi-monthly. $10/year. Dorothy M. Broderick; 10 Landing Lane, Apt. 6M, New Brunswick, NJ 08901.

Wilson Library Bulletin. Monthly (September-June). $14/year. H. W. Wilson Co.; 950 University Ave., Bronx, NY 10452.

Wisconsin Library Bulletin. Bi-monthly. $5/year. Division for Library Services; Department of Public Instruction; 126 Langdon St., Madison, WI 53702.

Young Adult Alternative Newsletter. 5 issues yearly. $4/year. Carol Starr; 37167 Mission Blvd., Fremont, CA 94536.

LIBRARIES AND YOUNG ADULTS:
A Selected Bibliography

LIBRARIES AND YOUNG ADULTS:
A Selected Bibliography

Media

Carlsen, G. Robert. *Books and the Teenage Reader: A Guide for Teachers, Librarians, and Parents.* Rev. ed. New York: Harper, 1972.

Carter, Yvonne, et al. *Aids to Media Selection for Students and Teachers.* Washington: U.S. Government Printing Office, 1976.

Fader, Daniel N. *The New Hooked on Books.* New York: Putnam, 1977.

Freilberger, Rema. *The New York Times Report on Teenage Reading Tastes and Habits.* New York: New York Times Company, 1974.

Gillespie, John T. *Paperback Books for Young People: An Annotated Guide to Publishers and Distributors.* 2nd ed. Chicago: American Library Association, 1977.

Hart, Thomas L., Mary Alice Hunt, and Blanche Woolls. *Multi-Media Indexes, Lists and Review Sources: A Bibliographic Guide.* New York: Marcel Dekker, Inc., 1975.

Kujoth, Jean Spealman, ed. *Reading Interests of Children and Young Adults.* Metuchen, NJ: Scarecrow, 1970.

Meade, Richard A., and Robert C. Small, eds. *Literature for Adolescents: Selection and Use.* Columbus, OH: Merrill, 1976.

Palmer, Julia Reed. *Read for Your Life: Two Successful Efforts to Help People Read and an Annotated List of Books That Made Them Want To.* Metuchen, NJ: Scarecrow, 1974.

Perkins, Flossie L. *Book and Non-Book Media: Annotated Guide to Selection Aids for Educational Materials.* Urbana, IL: National Council of Teachers of English, 1972.

Rufsvold, Margaret I., and Carolyn Guss. *Guides to Educational Media.* 3rd ed. Chicago: American Library Association, 1971.

Sive, Mary Robinson. *Educators' Guide to Media Lists*. Littleton, CO: Libraries Unlimited, 1975.

Sive, Mary Robinson. *Selecting Instructional Media*. Littleton, CO: Libraries Unlimited, 1978.

Thomison, Dennis. *Readings about Adolescent Literature*. Metuchen, NJ: Scarecrow, 1970.

Wynar, Christine L. *Guide to Reference Books for School Media Centers*. Littleton, CO: Libraries Unlimited, 1973.

Wynar, Christine L. *1974-75 Supplement, Guide to Reference Books for School Media Centers*. Littleton, CO: Libraries Unlimited, 1976.

Services

American Library Association. Services Statement Development Committee. Young Adult Services Division. *Directions for Library Service to Young Adults*. Chicago: ALA, 1978.

American Library Association. Young Adult Services Division. *Look, Listen, Explain: Developing Community Library Services for Young Adults*. Chicago: ALA, 1975.

Baker, D. Philip. *School and Public Library Media Programs for Children and Young Adults*. Syracuse, NY: Gaylord Professional Publications, 1977.

Chelton, Mary K. "YA Programming Roundup." *Top of the News* 32 (November 1975): 43-50.

Cohn, Emma, and Brita Olsson. *Library Service to Young Adults*. Copenhagen: International Federation of Library Associations, 1968.

Fenwick, Sara Innis. "Library Service to Children and Young People." *Library Trends* 25 (July 1976): 329-60.

Forsman, Carolyn. "Crisis Information Services to Youth." *Library Journal* 15 (March 1972): 1127-34.

Haycock, Ken. *The School Media Centre and the Public Library: Combination or Co-operation*. Toronto: Ontario Library Association, 1974.

Idea Sourcebook for Young Adult Programs. Prelim. ed. Boston: Boston Public Library, 1973.

Kandel, Denise B., and Gerald S. Lesser. *Youth in Two Worlds: United States and Denmark.* San Francisco: Jossey-Bass, 1972.

Manthorne, Jane. "Provisions and Programs for Disadvantaged Young People." *Library Trends* 20 (October 1971): 416-31.

Minudri, Regina M. "What's a YAP? The Federal Young Adult Library Services Project." *Top of the News* 26 (November 1969): 62-68.

Minudri, Regina M., and Reed C. Coates. "Two Years After: Reflections from YAP." *Library Journal* 98 (March 1973): 967-71.

Moon, Eric E. "High John: Report on a Unique Experiment in Maryland . . . " *Library Journal* 93 (January 1968): 147-55.

McGinniss, Dorothy A. *Libraries and Youth: Cooperation to Give Service to Children and Young People.* Syracuse, NY: Syracuse University Press, 1968.

Robotham, John S., and Lydia LaFleur. *Library Programs: How to Select, Plan, and Produce Them.* Metuchen, NJ: Scarecrow, 1976.

Student Use of Libraries: An Inquiry into the Needs of Students, Libraries, and the Educational Process. Chicago: American Library Association, 1964.

Turock, B., and K. Jackson. "Program Planning for Young Adults: A Response to Young Adult Needs." *Top of the News* 31 (January 1975): 182-84.

Young Adult Librarianship

Chelton, Mary K. "Booktalking: You Can Do It." *School Library Journal* 22 (April 1976): 39-43.

Hope, Anne. "Bob Smith, Young Adult Librarian—Advocate for Youth." *American Libraries* 7 (June 1976): 348-49.

Lukenbill, W. Bernard. *A Working Bibliography of American Doctoral Dissertations in Children's and Adolescents' Literature, 1930-1971.* Urbana-Champaign: University of Illinois, Graduate School of Library Science, 1972. (Occasional Paper, No. 103).

Madden, M. J. "YASD Tapes: Service Talks, Book Talks, Discussions." *Top of the News* 25 (June 1969): 408-413.

Minudri, Regina M. "How to Win Friends and Influence Administrators." *School Library Journal* 22 (January 1976): 33.

Minudri, Regina M. "Reference Interviews and the Young Adult." *School Library Journal* 30 (June 1974): 415-19.

Osborn, Anne V. "It's Not Enough to Love Books, Ya Gotta Love People Too." *School Library Journal* 98 (March 15, 1973): 78-82.

Shapiro, Lillian L. "Librarians and Young Adults: Equals or Enemies?" *School Library Journal* 19 (May 15, 1973): 40-43.

Starr, Carol. "Youthomania: The Care and Treatment of Discipline in the Public Library." *Wisconsin Library Bulletin* 68 (January 1972): 37-38.

General Titles

Ballard, Jan, and Christine Kirby. *The Care and Feeding of Young Adults.* Orlando, FL: Orlando Public Library, 1974.

Barnes, Melvyn P., and Sheila Ray. *Youth Library Work.* Hamden, CT: Linnet, 1976.

Blos, Peter. *The Young Adolescent.* New York: The Free Press, 1970.

Braverman, Miriam R. *Youth, Society, and the Public Library.* Chicago: American Library Association, 1978.

Burke, John Gordon, and Gerald R. Shields. *Children's Library Service: School or Public.* Metuchen, NJ: Scarecrow Press, 1974.

Buxton, Claude E. *Adolescents in School.* New Haven, CT: Yale University Press, 1973.

Center for Youth Development and Research. *Youth Encounters a Changing World.* Minneapolis: University of Minnesota, Center for Youth Development & Research, August 1972.

Coleman, J. A. *Youth: Transition to Adulthood.* Report of the Panel on Youth of the President's Science Advisory Committee. Washington: U.S. Government Printing Office, 1973.

Edwards, Margaret A. *The Fair Garden and the Swarm of Beasts: The Library and the Young Adult.* New York: Hawthorn, 1974.

Edwards, Margaret A. "The Urban Library and the Adolescent." *Library Quarterly* 38 (January 1968): 70-77.

Ellis, Alec. *Library Services for Young People in England and Wales, 1830-1970.* Oxford: Pergamon Press, 1971.

Erikson, Erik. *Identity, Youth and Crisis.* New York: W. W. Norton, 1968.

Friedenberg, Edgar Z. *The Vanishing Adolescent.* New York: Dell Pub. Co., 1959.

Gallatin, Judith E. *Adolescence and Individuality: A Conceptual Approach to Adolescent Psychology.* New York: Harper and Row, 1975.

Goethals, George W., and Dennis S. Klos. *Experiencing Youth: First-Person Accounts.* 2nd ed. Boston: Little Brown, 1976.

Harris, Barbara. *Expanding Services to Young Disadvantaged Adults.* Morehead, KY: Morehead State University, Appalachian Adult Education Center, 1974. [ED 108 649].

Kett, Joseph E. *Rites of Passage: Adolescence in America, 1790 to the Present.* New York: Basic Books, 1977.

Liesener, James W., and Margaret E. Chisholm. "Youth as a Special Client Group." *Advances in Librarianship* 3 (1972): 15-27.

Lipsitz, Joan, ed. *Growing Up Forgotten.* Lexington, MA: D. C. Heath, 1977.

Lubans, John, ed. *Educating the Library User.* New York: R. R. Bowker, 1974.

Lukenbill, W. Bernard, ed. *Media and the Young Adult: A Selected Bibliography, 1950-1972.* Chicago: American Library Association, 1977.

Marshall, Margaret R. *Libraries and Literature for Teenagers.* London: Andre Deutsch, 1975.

McClosky, Mildred, with Peter Kleinbard. *Youth into Adult.* New York: The National Commission on Resources for Youth, 1974.

Mead, Margaret. *Culture and Commitment: A Study of the Generation Gap.* Garden City, NY: Natural History Press, 1970.

Moriarty, Alice, and Paul W. Toussieng. *Adolescent Coping.* New York: Grune and Stratton, 1976.

Muuss, Rolf E., ed. *Adolescent Behavior and Society: A Book of Readings.* New York: Random House, 1971.

Muuss, Rolf E. *Theories of Adolescence.* 3rd ed. New York: Random House, 1975.

New York Library Association. Children's and Young Adult Services Section. *Criteria and Guidelines in Planning for Young Adult Services in Public Library Building Programs: With Implications for Existing Services and Structures.* Albany, NY: New York Library Association, 1966.

Offer, Daniel. *The Psychological World of the Teen-ager.* New York: Basic Books, 1969.

Public Library Association. Committee on Standards for Work with Young Adults in Public Libraries. *Young Adult Services in the Public Library.* Chicago: American Library Association, 1960.

Rogers, Dorothy. *Psychology of Adolescence.* 3rd ed. Englewood Cliffs, NJ: Prentice-Hall, 1977.

Sebald, Hans. *Adolescence: A Sociological Analysis.* 2nd ed. New York: Appleton-Century-Crofts, 1977.

Shapiro, Lillian L. *Serving Youth: Communication and Commitment in the High School Library.* New York: R. R. Bowker, 1975.

Social Research Group. *Toward Interagency Coordination: FY 75 Federal Research and Development Activities Pertaining to Adolescence: Third Annual Report.* Washington: The George Washington University, December 1975.

Sorensen, Robert C. *Adolescent Sexuality in Contemporary America: Personal Values and Sexual Behavior, Ages Thirteen to Nineteen.* New York: World Pub., 1973.

U.S. Department of Health, Education and Welfare. Office of Education. *The Education of Adolescents: The Final Report and Recommendations of the National Panel on High School and Adolescent Education.* Washington: Superintendent of Documents; U.S. Government Printing Office, 1976.

"Young Adult Services in the Public Library." *Library Trends* 17 (October 1968): entire issue.

"Young Adults: A Profile." *Ohio Library Association Bulletin* (July 1976): entire issue.

LIST OF CONTRIBUTORS

Dorothy Briley
Editor-in-Chief
Lathrop, Lee & Shipard
New York, NY

Linda M. Evers
Belpre, OH

Rosemarie E. Falanga
Pyramid
Walnut Creek, CA

Marilyn W. Greenberg
Library Services Credential Program
California State University at L.A.
Los Angeles, CA

Carolyn G. Hammond
Danville, KY

Katherine M. Kish
Guidance Associates
New York, NY

Sarah Ann Long
Coordinator
Children's & Young Adult's Services
Public Library of Columbus & Franklin
 County
Columbus, OH

Julia Losinski
Young Adult Services
Prince George's County Memorial
 Library System
Hyattsville, MD

Jean E. Lowrie
School of Librarianship
Western Michigan University
Kalamazoo, MI

W. Bernard Lukenbill
Graduate School of Library Science
University of Texas
Austin, Texas

Eleanor K. Pourron
YA Services
Arlington County Public Library
Arlington, VA

Evelyn Shaevel
American Library Association
Chicago, IL

Carol Starr
Fremont, CA

Susan Steinfirst
School of Library Science
University of North Carolina
Chapel Hill, NC

Peggy A. Sullivan
Assistant Commissioner for Extension
 Services
Chicago Public Library
Chicago, IL

Mary L. Woodworth
Library School
University of Wisconsin at Madison
Madison, WI

AUTHOR/TITLE/SUBJECT INDEX